Searching for a Distant God

Searching for a Distant God

The Legacy of Maimonides

Kenneth Seeskin

New York   Oxford
Oxford University Press
2000

Oxford University Press

Oxford   New York

Athens   Auckland   Bangkok   Begotá   Buenos Aires   Calcutta
CapeTown   Chennai   Dar es Salaam   Delhi   Florence   Hong Kong   Istanbul
Karachi   Kuala Lumpur   Madrid   Melbourne   Mexico City   Mumbai
Nairobi   Paris   São Paulo   Singapore   Taipei   Tokyo   Toronto   Warsaw

and associated companies in

Berlin   Ibadan

Copyright © 2000 by Kenneth Seeskin

Published by Oxford University Press, Inc.
198 Madison Avenue, New York, New York 10016

Oxford is a registered trademark of Oxford University Press

Library of Congress Cataloging-in-Publication Data
Seeskin, Kenneth, 1947–
Searching for a distant God : the legacy of Maimonides / Kenneth Seeskin.
p.   cm.
Includes bibliographical references and index.
ISBN 0-19-512846-X
1. Maimonides, Moses, 1135–1204—Contributions in the doctrine of God.
2. God (Judaism)—History of doctrines.   3. Philosophy, Jewish.   I. Title.
BM610.S38   1999
296.3'11'092—dc21   98-37882

1 3 5 7 9 8 6 4 2
Printed in the United States of America
on acid-free paper

To the memory of
Steven S. Schwarzschild

Preface

Odd though it may seem, this book did not begin as an extended discussion of Maimonides; it began as an extended discussion of monotheism. That Maimonides would be a central figure I had no doubt. But I soon learned that it is difficult to say anything about one part of Maimonides' philosophy without saying something about the whole. His view of monotheism is connected to his view of human knowledge, which is connected to his view of language, which is connected to his view of prophecy, and so on. Before long I realized that the more ground I covered, the more I was committed to covering. The result is a book-length conversation with a historical figure whose thought has an uncanny ability to renew itself.

I would like to thank Menachem Kellner and Josef Stern for line-to-line comments on an earlier version of this manuscript. Others who provided valuable insights or helpful encouragement include Cristina D'Ancona Costa, Joseph Edelheit, Muhammad Eissa, Daniel Frank, Lenn Goodman, Julie P. Gordon, John McCumber, David Novak, and Aaron Seeskin. As always I am indebted to the Academy for Jewish Philosophy for providing a stimulating environment in which to share ideas. All talmudic references are to the Babylonian Talmud. As for transliteration, I have tried to balance consistency with familiarity, hoping to satisfy both specialized and general audiences.

A portion of chapter 5 first appeared as "Holiness as a Moral Ideal" in *The Journal of Jewish Thought and Philosophy* 5 (1996): 191–203; a portion of chapter 1 and the appendix as "Maimonides' Conception of Philosophy" in David Novak, ed., *Leo Strauss and Judaism*, Lanham, MD.: Rowman and Littlefield, 1996, p. 8.

Contents

Abbreviations   xi

One. The Urge to Philosophize   3

Two. The Challenge of Monotheism   23

Three. Speaking of and to God   43

Four. The Problem of Creation   66

Five. Imitatio Dei   91

Six. Monotheism and Freedom   124

Seven. Popular Religion and a Personal God   142

Appendix: Esotericism and the Limits of Knowledge:
A Critique of Strauss   177

Notes   189

Bibliography   229

General Index   243

Index of Principal Sources   249

Abbreviations

BBO   Saadia Gaon, *The Book of Beliefs and Opinions*

C   Hermann Cohen, "Charakteristik der Ethik Maimunis," *Jüdische Schriften*, vol. 3

CPR   Immanuel Kant, *Critique of Pure Reason*

CPrR   Immanuel Kant, *Critique of Practical Reason*

DF   Emmanuel Levinas, *Difficult Freedom*

DH   Baḥya ibn Pakudah, *Duties of the Heart*

EN   Plotinus, *The Enneads*

FMM   Immanuel Kant, *Foundations of the Metaphysics of Morals*

GP   Maimonides, *The Guide of the Perplexed*

HJP   *History of Jewish Philosophy*, edited by D. Frank and O. Leaman

LPR   G. W. F. Hegel, *Lectures on the Philosophy of Religion*

M   *Maimonides: A Collection of Critical Essays*, edited by Joseph A. Buijs

MM   *Moses Maimonides and His Time*, edited by Eric L. Ormbsy

MP   *Maimonides and Philosophy*, edited by S. Pines and Y. Yovel

MT   Maimonides, *Mishneh Torah*

PJ   Julius Guttmann, *The Philosophy of Judaism*

PM   *Perspectives on Maimonides*, edited by Joel Kraemer

RR   Hermann Cohen, *Religion of Reason out of the Sources of Judaism*

RWL   Immanuel Kant, *Religion within the Limits of Reason Alone*

SCG   Thomas Aquinas, *Summa Contra Gentiles*
SR   Franz Rosenzweig, *The Star of Redemption*
ST   Thomas Aquinas, *Summa Theologiae*
TMM   *The Thought of Moses Maimonides*, edited by I. Robinson et al.
WL   Gersonides, *The Wars of the Lord*

Searching for a Distant God

1

The Urge to Philosophize

"The Jewish People," as Julius Guttmann argues on the first page of his monumental study, "did not begin to philosophize because of an irresistible urge to do so. They received philosophy from outside sources, and the history of Jewish philosophy is a history of successive absorptions of foreign ideas which were then transformed and adapted according to specific Jewish points of view."[1]

This is undoubtedly true if we take it to mean that the greats of Jewish philosophy did not learn the subject at their mothers' or fathers' knees but by reading Greek, Christian, and Islamic sources. But is Guttmann right in a deeper sense? Was the primary impetus for doing philosophy a desire to show how Judaism would respond to external challenges? To put the question another way, were the great medieval thinkers happy with Judaism as they saw it and willing to do philosophy only as an extracurricular activity?

The answer is that in many cases they were profoundly *unhappy* with Judaism or with the attitudes of many of their fellow Jews. Saadia opens *The Book of Beliefs and Opinions* by saying that when he considers the beliefs of many of his contemporaries, his heart grieves for the human race and his soul is stirred on account of his own people, many of whom are "sunk in seas of doubt and overwhelmed by waves of confusion."[2] Along the same lines, Maimonides (*GP* 1.59, p. 141) castigates "poets and preachers" whose utterances contain such rubbish and such perverse imaginings as to cause laughter in some

contexts and tears when one considers that the utterances are applied
to God.

The problem is not trivial. Judaism typically justifies itself by
claiming that it introduced the world to a radically new conception
of God. We are told that when Abraham left his father's house, he did
so not just to live in a new land but to leave behind idol worship and
everything connected with it. Thus the second commandment maintains that the issue is not worshipping the wrong image but making
or serving any image at all:

> Thou shalt have no other gods before Me. Thou shalt not make unto
> thee a graven image, nor any manner of likeness, of any thing that is in
> heaven above, or that is in the earth beneath, or that is in the water
> under the earth; thou shalt not bow down to them or serve them; for I
> the Lord thy God am a jealous God.

According to one tradition, the prohibition of idolatry is equal in
weight to the whole Torah, so the person who violates it disavows the
Torah in its entirety while the person who accepts it upholds the
Torah in its entirety.[3] According to another, anyone who rejects idolatry is accorded a Jew.[4] In fact, the sin of idolatry is so severe that a
Jew is supposed to chose martyrdom rather than succumb to it. In
short, idolatry is the sin of sins.

But one does not have to look very far through the sacred literature to see that Jewish tradition is full of the most grievous anthropomorphism. While Deuteronomy 4:12 reminds the people that they
saw no form at Sinai and only heard a voice, there is a long tradition
of prophets, rabbis, and mystics who claimed to see God, often in the
form of an elderly man, to touch God, or to have sexual relations
with God.[5] As far as the Bible is concerned, the burden of proof is really on those who think God cannot be seen. Though rabbinic passages that contain anthropomorphic descriptions of God typically
add the qualification *kivyakhol* (as it were), there is still the question
of why a religion that goes to such lengths to prevent idolatry also
devotes a sizable chunk of its liturgy to making God seem human
and concrete.

Faced with this problem, the medieval philosophers argued that
philosophy is indispensable because without it vast portions of the
sacred literature would be false and thus not sacred at all. Maimonides went further, arguing that Judaism had always been philosophical and that Moses and the patriarchs mastered philosophy before the
Greeks. According to this conception, the goal of Jewish philosophy
is not to respond to external criticism as much as to restore a tradi-

tion of learning that was lost centuries earlier when Israel suffered from political oppression. As Isadore Twersky put it, "Maimonides clearly felt—and the general milieu nurtured this—that Judaism had strayed, had depreciated its intellectual content, and had short-changed itself philosophically."[6]

Did Maimonides really believe that Moses and the patriarchs were philosophers, or was he introducing a legal fiction designed to legitimate a subject about which many of his fellow Jews were skeptical? From a historical perspective, there is no question that Maimonides and his contemporaries learned philosophy by reading Al-farabi, Avicenna, and their ilk. Be that as it may, I think Maimonides did believe that philosophy is indigenous to Judaism and that his use of philosophic argument to interpret the sacred literature was perfectly in keeping with tradition.

There is no question that Judaism mandates study of the Torah. How can we study it, Maimonides asks, without understanding the principles upon which it is based? Even if a person were to think and talk about God all the time, if that person's idea of divinity is nothing but a fantasy image, in Maimonides' opinion, he is not really thinking or talking about God at all.[7] If he is not thinking or talking about God, he cannot fulfill the commandments. Not surprisingly, Maimonides went on record as saying that a minimal amount of philosophic understanding is a sacred obligation binding on all Jews.[8] Achieve it and you have a place in the world to come no matter what other sins you may have committed; violate it and you are excluded from Israel and have no place in the world to come. In the *Mishneh Torah* (1, Basic Principles of the Torah, 1.6) he writes:

> To acknowledge this truth [that God alone is real and nothing else resembles God] is an affirmative precept, as it is said, "I am the Lord your God" (Exodus 20:2; Deuteronomy 5:6). And whoever permits the thought to enter his mind that there is another deity besides this God, violates a prohibition—as it is said, "You shall have no other gods before Me" (Ex. 20:3; Deut. 5:7)—and denies the essence of religion—this doctrine being the great principle on which everything depends.

If Maimonides is right, philosophy is not just a response to external challenges, not, as one might say, an acquired taste. In his hands, it is a way to bring people back to the true teaching of their faith, and in that respect the urge to philosophize is irresistible.

It should be emphasized that Maimonides does not speak for all of Jewish tradition and that both the *Guide* and the first book of the *Mishneh Torah* were banned and burned during his lifetime.[9] The controversy concerned the issue raised by Pascal 500 years later: the conflict between "the God of the philosophers" and "the God of Abraham, Isaac, and Jacob." The former is supposed to be distant and abstract, the latter personal and accessible. As Guttmann wrote, "The God of Philosophy, whether in the Neoplatonic version of the highest unity or in the Aristotelian version of the highest thought, is radically different from that of the personal, willing, and ethical god of the monotheistic religions."[10] But again we must ask whether Guttmann's generalization is true.

I want to argue with Emmanuel Levinas, and more recently Lenn Goodman, that in the terms in which it is usually discussed, the choice between the God of philosophy and the God of religion amounts to a false dichotomy. In other words, I want to show that philosophy is an integral part of Jewish self-understanding and that trying to approach God as we imagine the patriarchs doing is bogus. But rather than reinvent the wheel, I will discuss these issues by taking Maimonides as a central figure. The choice of Maimonides is obvious for several reasons. He is a watershed figure in Jewish history and played a critical role in the transition of philosophy from East to West. Not so obvious but equally important is that unlike many philosophers, he was not content to discuss God in the abstract while letting others deal with practical problems like prayer, repentance, and Sabbath observance. In short, Maimonides offers us a Judaism in which the commitment to monotheism takes precedence over and encompasses everything else. Whether his view of the religion can stand up to the rising tide of criticism it has generated remains to be seen.

God in Human Form

Like many great ideas, monotheism did not emerge all at once, and even when it did emerge, it created a host of problems. At one point, monotheism was associated with the struggle for national sovereignty, the development of a priestly cult, and a patriarchal view of society. In the Middle Ages it was associated with a geocentric view of the universe. Even from a philosophic perspective, there is a real question about what monotheism commits us to: belief in one God, belief in an immaterial God, or belief in a metaphysically transcendent God? Finally there is the question of how a theory *about* God is related to worship undertaken *on behalf* of God. Throughout this book I will argue that monotheism is a controversial doctrine difficult for any religion to embody in its pure form.

I say that monotheism is difficult for *any* religion to embody because Jews often feel superior to Christians on the grounds that Judaism is not saddled with doctrines like the trinity or incarnation. But if I am right, there is little reason for Jews to be smug. Overall Judaism is a mixed bag of insights, rituals, and institutions, some of which appear to uphold monotheism, some of which do not. We saw that the second commandment prohibits service to false gods or the making of "any manner of likeness" of the true one; but it does not tell us why likenesses of God are objectionable. Is the problem that people will pay more attention to the likeness than they will to the original? That they will think the likeness infuses them with supernatural powers? Or that attempting to capture God's likeness in plastic form is misguided from the start? And what about mental images? The philosophic tradition took the commandment to prohibit any representation of God, physical *or* mental, but the biblical text is silent about the latter.

Nor does the second commandment say anything about whether it is possible to see God directly and dispense with images altogether. Even if we emphasize Deuteronomy 4:12, there is still the question *why* God cannot be seen. Is the point that God is immaterial and cannot be seen by anyone or that dire consequences will follow if one does? On the basis of Exodus 29 and 33, where such consequences are mentioned, it would seem to be the latter. And if God cannot be seen "face to face," there is still the question of what to say about dreams and visions of God. Finally there is the question of what the sin of idolatry amounts to: betrayal of God in the most general sense, adoption of pagan customs, moral license, or rejection of metaphysical doctrines like divine unity and incorporeality? According to Moshe Halbertal and Avishai Margalit, it has been all of the above depending on the time and place in which the question was raised.[11] So however evil idolatry may be, it is by no means clear that the people who claimed to see God were guilty of it. Why, then, should we deny the legitimacy of their experience? Why should we say that seeing God or imagining God is as bad as making a graven image?

There are a number of ways to answer this question, but the most obvious is to point out that most of those who claimed to see God in the form of a man were themselves men. As Xenophanes once remarked, the Thracians depict God with red hair and blue eyes, the Ethiopians with dark hair and a short nose, and if horses could depict God, it would be with a long mane, four legs, and a tail. Unless we make room for philosophic critique, there is a real chance that religion will become an institutionalized form of narcissism. According to Judith Plaskow: "If anything moderates God's maleness or allows for its obfuscation, it is not so much the existence of female images as the influence of Jewish philosophy."[12]

The culprit is not only the belief that God looks like us but the idea that God can be described in the same terms that apply to us, that all we have to do to reach God is elevate our discourse by shifting from comparatives to superlatives. Again from Plaskow: "While Jews are used to thinking of idols as pillars and stones, verbal idols can be every bit as powerful as sculpted ones—indeed more powerful for being less visible."[13] This sentiment is remarkably close to the view of Maimonides, who argues (*GP* 1.57, p. 132) that customary words are "the greatest among causes leading unto error."

The problem is particularly acute in Hebrew, where every noun has a gender and contributes to the problem of anthropomorphism. To refer to God as "He" and address God as father, king, or lord of hosts is to encourage people to think of God as a man on a throne. To the degree that these associations take hold in people's minds, we are in danger of thinking that men are more like God than women. To be sure, people often insist that religious language cannot be taken literally and therefore the use of male nouns is a linguistic convention that we have to put up with. After all, God has no gender. But Rita Gross is right to point out that many of the people who claim that male nouns cannot be taken literally protest when feminists say the same thing about female nouns.[14] If *King* implies sovereignty rather than gender, why is *Queen* any different? Why would it not also be appropriate to use feminine nouns and preface them with "as it were"?

To put the matter another way, suppose Hebrew grammar not only separated male and female nouns but made a further distinction among males. Suppose that there was one category of words for youthful, athletic men with handsome features and a full head of hair and another category for all the rest. Suppose in addition that God was described mainly with terms from the first category and that people objected to the use of terms from the second. Even if all men were given an equal share in the liturgy, does anyone seriously think that the majority of men would be happy with this situation? Would it help to point out that describing God with terms from the first category was just a linguistic convention and that all descriptions were prefaced with "as it were"? Or rather would large numbers of men feel alienated? In answering this question, we should keep in mind that the terms we use to describe God are not value neutral. To worship a God with well-defined characteristics is to imply that anyone who does not share them is deficient.

From a philosophic perspective, descriptions implying male or female gender are on an equal footing: Whatever can be said for or against one set can be said for or against the other. But after warning us about the dangers of masculine terms, feminists like Gross and Plaskow go on to argue that some degree of anthropomorphism is inevitable. In the words of Gross:[15]

> Theistic religions, including Judaism, have always had to make peace with anthropomorphism, which necessarily includes making peace with genderized language about deity. Unless Jewish theology *and practice* take a 180-degree turn from the metaphor of relationship with a personal deity to the metaphor of a nonpersonal Ultimate, to which one could scarcely *daven* [pray] and which would be unlikely to give *mitzvot* [commandments], they too will have to continue to utilize anthropomorphisms, all of which are always problematic and inaccurate nonliteral manners of speaking.

The usual remedy is to introduce a set of female characterizations that will counterbalance the traditional masculine ones. Like traditionalists, both Gross and Plaskow want their language to contain the usual escape clause: "as it were."

But if everything that can be said for masculine terms can be said for feminine, it is also true that everything that can be said against the former can be said against the latter. If, as Gross argues, male God-language tells us nothing about the reality of God, then while female alternatives would break what has been a near monopoly, they would still not give us what we are searching for. On the contrary, anthropomorphic language of any type directs attention to us rather than to God and reinforces—nay glorifies—cultural stereotypes that may be inaccurate to begin with. To describe God as a father, mother, friend, or lover is to project our experience of these roles into heaven, to domesticate God. "Theologians," as Louis Jacobs once remarked, "frequently speak as if they had just had lunch with the Deity."[16] But even domestication understates the seriousness of the problem. In the words of Levinas, to make God fit our categories is to do violence by trying to force what is other than us into the mold of the same.[17]

It is often said that a God who can be depicted as a parent, friend, or lover is accessible to people in a way that an abstract God is not. But with accessibility comes a price: Can a God described in human terms *also* elicit awe? Will a person who looks upon God as a friend be moved to repent in silence as Job did when he heard God's voice, or is it more likely that such a person will come to see God as one friend among many, a person in some sense of the term but one whose distinguishing characteristics are that He/She responds to our needs and views the world from our perspective? If some people are going to say "God/He," then by all means others have a right to say "God/She." The question is whether we are locked into either expression or both together, whether we should think in terms of gender or in terms of names like *Ehyeh-Asher-Ehyeh* (I am who I am) that are deliberately ambiguous. The thrust of Maimonides' argument is that any characterization of God is suspect no matter what connotations it has. If he is right, we do not have to make peace with anthropomorphism in order to pray and observe the commandments; on the contrary, we are obliged to oppose it.

One point feminists and traditionalists seem to agree on is use of the qualification "as it were." But we must be careful not to pack too much into such an abbreviated formula. Unless we explain why our language cannot be taken literally and what, if anything, lies beyond the use of anthropomorphic terms, "as it were" will have no more impact than a parent telling a hungry child not to eat cookies before dinner. In short, the formula is empty without philosophic critique to back it up.

To be sure, the philosophic tradition is not beyond criticism either. Maimonides was not above pointing out where philosophers failed to resolve questions or to consider powerful alternatives to their theories. And the philosophic tradition, too, produced excesses, the most obvious of which was a male-dominated form of intellectualism. According to Maimonides' "Parable of the Palace," closeness to God is a function of intellectual apprehension, with philosophers in the inner court, people who accept true doctrines on traditional authority further away, and people with no interest in truth further away still.[18] In several passages Maimonides associates women with matter and men with form and goes on to characterize matter as filthy, distracting, and disloyal, in short, a married harlot.[19] Though he allows for the possibility of good matter at *GP* 3.8, p. 433, this turns out to be matter that is neither dominating nor corrupting. Since God has no material component at all, and we must overcome the pull of matter to contemplate God, the parable could be taken to imply that men are better suited to intellectual perfection than women. It is true that he makes an exception for Miriam (*GP* 3.51, pp. 627–28); still his remarks cannot help but offend modern sensibilities. So our question becomes not whether it is possible to defend every idea Maimonides had, but whether it is possible to defend the conception of religion to which his arguments point.

Strauss and the Jerusalem/Athens Controversy

The mention of Maimonides and the philosophic critique of religion calls to mind Leo Strauss. Strauss, of course, is very unsympathetic to the project on which I am embarked. For him philosophy is not something Jewish thinkers invented or tried to absorb but an activity whose very nature makes it incompatible with Judaism in anything like its traditional form. "Jews of the philosophic competence of Halevi and Maimonides," he tells us, "took it for granted that being a Jew and being a philosopher are mutually exclusive."[20] And: "He [Maimonides] obviously assumes that the philosophers form a group distinguished from the adherents of the law and that both groups are mutually exclusive."[21]

According to Strauss, philosophy is committed to free inquiry and must bring everything to the bar of reason; by contrast religion asks for obedience to God and faithfulness to a tradition. Just as there can be no room for revelation in a philosophic argument, there is no way in which religion can accommodate the relentless questioning of a Socrates. As one of Strauss's disciples put it, the philosopher doubts what she can and believes what she must, while the believer believes what she can and doubts what she must.[22] On the possibility of overcoming the dichotomy between a life of obedient love and a life of free inquiry, Strauss assures us: "In every attempt at harmonization, in every synthesis however impressive, one of the two opposed elements is sacrificed, more or less subtly but in any event surely, to the other."[23] The opposition between philosophy and theology creates a dynamic tension that, in Strauss's opinion, is "the secret of the vitality of the West."[24]

Whatever one thinks of this view, there is no question that Strauss did much to change the way people read Maimonides and by implication the way they understand Jewish philosophy.[25] In particular, he called attention to the fact that the *Guide of the Perplexed* is not a treatise like Thomas Aquinas' *Summa Theologiae* but a book with a literary structure of its own: a letter written to a disciple named Joseph, an observant Jew unsure whether to follow his intellect and renounce the Law or hold fast to the Law and renounce the intellect. At the start, the problems that beset Joseph have to do with the anthropomorphism of the Bible. But if the *Guide* is a letter written to a specific person who asked how to read the sacred literature, it is also a book intended for a wider audience. As Maimonides says, "I have composed for you and for others like you, however few they are." For Strauss the problem is how to balance the obedient love demanded by religion with the free thought characteristic of philosophy. His answer is that they cannot be balanced, so a person has to pick one or the other.

The first thing to see in trying to assess Strauss's argument is that it is useless to talk about philosophy and religion in the abstract. Obviously there are people for whom the incompatibility between philosophy and religion is ultimate. But the fact that the *Guide* is not just a Jewish version of the *Summa Theologiae* should give us pause. How did Maimonides understand philosophy and where did he think it should begin? To answer the latter question, it does not begin with a statement of principles but with an intellectual conflict. In this respect, his introduction to the *Guide* is in keeping with Aristotle's claim that philosophy begins in wonder.[26] In fact, Aristotle, the man Maimonides refers to as "chief among the philosophers," goes on to say that wonder (*thaumadzein*) is another name for puzzlement (*aporein*), a state in which the pathway to understanding is blocked. Puzzlement, in turn, makes one confess ignorance and become a philosopher or lover of wisdom. Like religion, then, philosophy is motivated by love.

Unfortunately the history of philosophy reveals that the love of wisdom is not always fulfilled, because great thinkers do not agree on first principles or how they should be studied. According to Aristotle, people then encounter a second level of puzzlement when they realize that it is possible to advance arguments on opposite sides of important questions.[27] In metaphorical terms, reason finds itself tied in knots. So whether we are talking about the twelfth century or the twentieth, it is wrong to think that "Athens" or "philosophy" stands for a single subject with a single body of results. More often than not, it stands for a set of problems about which reasonable people disagree. For Aristotle philosophy is an attempt to untie these knots and point the mind in the right direction. It is here, then, that the urge to philosophize first asserts itself. To untie knots is to allow reason to work and human nature to perfect itself.

An immediate consequence of the lack of consensus among intelligent people is that first philosophy cannot be demonstrative. Since its premises are in doubt, it cannot always move in a linear fashion from premise to conclusion. Its function is rather to scrutinize difficulties and resolve conflicts. Aristotle's general name for this type of reasoning is *dialectic*. In the *Topics* he lists three uses for dialectical argument, the last of which pertains to philosophy:[28]

The ability to see puzzles on both sides of a subject will make us see more easily the truth and error in the points that arise. It is also useful in regard to the principles employed in the individual sciences. For it is impossible to discuss them on the basis of the principles proper to the particular science because the principles are prior to everything else. That is why we must deal with generally accepted opinions [*endoxa*]. This task belongs properly and most appropriately to dialectic; for dialectic is a process of scrutinizing opinions and holds the path to the principles of all investigations.

Aristotle does not say that every problem should be resolved in a dialectical fashion. If primary premises are already in place, it would be foolish to begin an investigation by turning to generally accepted opinions. Again in the *Topics*, he claims that dialectical problems involve situations where (1) people hold no opinion either way, (2) the mass of people hold an opinion contrary to the philosophers, (3) the philosophers hold an opinion contrary to the masses, (4) members of each group hold opinions contrary to other members, (5) arguments conflict with one another, or (6) the subject matter is so vast that it is difficult to give any arguments at all, for example, the eternity of the world.[29]

The hallmark of dialectical reasoning is that the puzzle be genuine and the arguments on both sides of the issue such that reasonable people either can or do hold them.[30] The assumption is that if we examine the arguments in a systematic way, subjecting each side to criticism and revising our opinion as we go along, we can untie the knots in which reason has become ensnared. The issue has nothing to do with trying to satisfy two sets of audiences; it is rather the conviction that the claims of great thinkers cannot be completely mistaken, so they are likely to have some bearing on the resolution of the problem.[31]

We can therefore appreciate Joseph Owens' remark that while Aristotle is often viewed as the prince of dogmatists and the patron of deductive reasoning, this interpretation is highly misleading.[32] The deductive methods discussed in the *Posterior Analytics* provide an idealized conception of a finished science; yet surely Aristotle is the last person to argue that a method appropriate to one area of knowledge is appropriate to all. In the *Metaphysics* he begins by reviewing the history of the problems he wants to discuss, considers alternative accounts of important ideas, allows himself the liberty to return to the beginning of a problem and make a fresh start, and even raises the question of whether metaphysics is possible. *Metaphysics*, of course, is not the name that Aristotle chose; he called his investigation "first philosophy" and in some cases "theology."[33] It could be said, therefore, that the realization that theology is not a demonstrative science is as old as Aristotle. The question is whether his understanding of theology is compatible with Judaism's understanding of Torah study so that it would make sense to say that inquiry into the foundations of the Torah is a sacred obligation.

Jerusalem and Athens in the Thought of Maimonides

Except for a short treatise on logic written at an early age, there is nothing in the Maimonidean corpus comparable to Aristotle's *Organon*. But we saw that the *Guide* begins with a predicament very similar to the one Aristotle describes: Joseph is perplexed by conflicting claims from reputable authorities. At first the puzzle seems obvious: Strauss's choice between Jerusalem and Athens; but as the book develops, the puzzle becomes more complex. It is *not* between philosophic demonstration on the one hand and prophetic authority on the other, because Maimonides is enough of a rationalist to admit that in areas where demonstrations are possible, no perplexity arises (*GP* 1.31, p. 66):

> For in all things whose true reality is known through demonstration there is no tug of war and no refusal to accept a thing proven—unless indeed such refusal comes from an ignoramus who offers a resistance that is called resistance to demonstration. Thus you can find groups of people who dispute the doctrine that the earth is spherical and that the sphere has a circular motion. These folk do not enter into our purpose. The things about which there is perplexity are very numerous in divine matters, few in matters pertaining to natural science, and nonexistent in matters pertaining to mathematics.

For Maimonides, the classic example of demonstrably certain knowledge is the existence and unity of God. Throughout the *Guide*, he claims that his position on this matter will be demonstrated, has been demonstrated, or demonstrates a position about which there can be no doubt or dispute.[34] Faced with scores of passages in the Bible that imply that God is corporeal, he maintains that they cannot be interpreted literally and that anyone who so views them is no better than an idolater (*GP* 1.36, p. 84), since anyone who thinks that God is corporeal denies the most basic principle of the religion: that God is one. It is in this sense that philosophy acts as a corrective.

Not surprisingly the question of what can and cannot be demonstrated is critical to understanding Maimonides' conception of phi-

losophy. At *Guide* 1.32 he argues that knowledge of the difference is
a mark of human perfection; later at 1.71 he criticizes the Mutakallimun for ignoring it. All this is of a piece with his insistence that
logic is a prerequisite for metaphysics or divine science.[35] It is significant, then, that once Maimonides gets beyond the existence and
unity of God, his mode of argument changes. Instead of offering a linear proof beginning with assumptions and moving straight to conclusions, he examines competing arguments: three on creation (five
if you count the Epicureans and Mutakallimun), three on prophecy,
and five on providence. In regard to creation, he points out that even
Aristotle did not think he could demonstrate his position.[36] As we
will see in chapter 4, Maimonides' predecessors were anything but
unanimous on what creation is or whether it is reasonable to believe
in it. Thus much of the *Guide* deals with issues that can be discussed
only dialectically.[37]

In fact once we leave the physics of the sublunar realm or the existence and unity of God, the tradition that derives from Athens was
anything but monolithic. Even on the existence of God, there were
competing accounts of how demonstration was to proceed and what
it was supposed to show. Two consequences follow. First, Maimonides claims that what the philosophers discuss under the guise of
physics is equivalent to what the prophet tradition refers to as "the
account of the beginning" (*ma'aseh bereishit*), an obvious reference
to the doctrine of creation, while divine science or metaphysics is
equivalent to "the account of the chariot" (*ma'aseh merkavah*), a reference to Ezekiel's vision. This equivalence is the crux of Maimonides' claim that philosophy is not and never was foreign to Judaism.[38]
But if demonstration is difficult to achieve, so that we cannot be certain what celestial physics or metaphysics commit us to, the job of
reconciling secular knowledge with religious is that much more
complicated than it appears. Under the circumstances, it will not do
to say that philosophy and religion are simply two roads that con-
verge on the same destination; sometimes the destination is unclear
and sometimes there is no convergence.

Second, Maimonides does not contradict himself when he says at
Guide 2.2 that he has no intention to write a treatise on natural science or to provide a summary of what has been said elsewhere.[39] All
he means is that he will take for granted results that have already
been demonstrated. This leaves open the possibility that he will discuss, critically evaluate, and revise theories whose results have not
been demonstrated. In either case, it is safe to say that Joseph would
have reason to be perplexed even if he had never been exposed to the

prophetic tradition: No less an authority than Aristotle maintained that philosophy could tie a person in knots.

In regard to the prophetic tradition, many people have interpreted Maimonides as saying that prophetic awareness is superior to philosophic in the sense that prophets have access to truths unavailable to philosophers.[40] While there is some evidence for this view, I agree with Strauss that it overlooks one critical point: There is for Maimonides no such thing as specifically religious cognition.[41] In other words, all cognition, whether prophetic or philosophic, is subject to the limitations imposed by the human condition. According to Exodus 33:20–23 even Moses, the greatest of all prophets, could not see the face of God and had to settle for something less.[42] In the "Parable of the Palace" (*GP* 3.51, p. 620) Maimonides puts prophets in a category above philosophers not because prophets have special faculties that philosophers lack but because prophets "turn wholly to God" and renounce everything other than God. In Maimonides' words: "Thus it is clear that after apprehension, total devotion to Him and the employment of intellectual thought in constantly loving Him should be aimed at." But he does not say that by virtue of being devoted to God, prophets gain access to new or previously hidden information. As we will see, God is not the sort of thing about which information in the normal sense of the term is available.

There is, of course, one area where prophets have superiority. Maimonides conceives of prophecy as a double overflow: first from God (or the Agent Intellect) to the rational faculty of the prophet's mind, and then from the rational faculty to the imaginative. Thus prophets have all the abstract understanding of philosophers plus dreams and visions that allow them to express that understanding in parabolic terms and to devise rituals that reinforce it. In Kantian terms, they can provide a schematization for the truths of physics and metaphysics. For this reason, prophets are better able to reach large audiences and serve as political leaders.

In his discussion of prophecy at *Guide* 2.38, p. 377, Maimonides indicates that there are some occasions when prophets are able to achieve a higher level of speculative knowledge:

> Know that true prophets indubitably grasp speculative matters; by means of his speculation alone, man is unable to grasp the causes from which what a prophet has come to know necessarily follows. This has a counterpart in their giving information regarding matters with respect to which man, using only common conjecture and divination, is unable to give information.

Although the passage is not as clear as we might like, Maimonides seems to say that prophets sometimes gain an edge over philosophers by starting with the clearness of their vision rather than an investigation of general principles. When he takes up the issue of creation, for example, Maimonides sides with Moses against Plato and Aristotle.[43]

In the rest of *Guide* 2.38 Maimonides continues to talk as if prophets and philosophers have the same faculties and receive the same emanation. The thrust of the passage is that there are times when the prophet has an advantage because he can think both intuitively and discursively, sometimes in regard to the same subject. Here one is reminded of places in the Platonic dialogues where the argument is advanced by appeal to the visions of priests or priestesses.[44] Even in a modern context, it is not hard to imagine a physicist like Albert Einstein working with a thought experiment rather than a set of premises. Still there is no faculty that allows the prophet to ignore the epistemological problems that pertain to earthly existence or pierce the veil of unknowing that surrounds God.[45] Prophecy is the natural perfection of a human being and is subject to all the limitations human beings face.

According to Maimonides, there is one area where prophetic understanding always exceeds philosophic, namely the liveliness of the prophet's imagination. Unfortunately there is also a drawback: The imagination is tied to material things and frequently the source of error. It is, after all, the imagination that is responsible for anthropomorphism and belief in a corporeal God.[46] In some instances, for example *Guide* 2.29, p. 347, Maimonides warns his readers not to solve problems by relying on the imagination alone.[47] At *Guide* 3.51, p. 621, he is more emphatic: "For thought concerning imaginings is not called *knowledge* but *that which cometh into your mind.*" At *Guide* 2.12, p. 280, he goes so far as to identify the imagination with the evil impulse. So while prophets use visual imagery to make themselves understood, we must be careful how this imagery is interpreted. By what procedure can we take references to God's arm, feet, clothes, or throne and derive a philosophic lesson?

Obviously no simple procedure exists. Not only the prophets but the sages who interpret them speak in parables and metaphors. Maimonides himself admits to perplexity in trying to interpret the sayings of Rabbi Eliezer (*GP* 2.26, p. 330). It follows that no matter how much truth it contains, or where it has an edge over philosophy, the prophetic tradition is hardly a model of clarity. Even if Joseph had never studied philosophy, he might still be perplexed about the prin-

ciples of his religion. We saw that while the second commandment
forbids idolatry, the prophets do not hesitate to describe God in corporeal terms.

I suggest that the real perplexity Maimonides has in mind in
writing the *Guide* is not the result of being *between* traditions rep-
resenting faith and reason but of being *in* traditions each of which
stretches human awareness to the limit of its capacity. If so, the issue
is not the rivalry between Jerusalem and Athens as much as the speculative nature of the subjects both address. While philosophy is needed to correct for the anthropomorphism of the prophetic tradition, we
will see later in this study that the prophetic tradition is needed to
correct for the tendency of philosophers to assume that principles
that apply to the sublunar realm also apply to God. In short, once we
get beyond the limited scope of what can be known by demonstration, neither tradition has a dialectical trump card. As Maimonides
points out in the Introduction to book 1 of the *Guide*, truth in these
matters is never fully known to anyone. Thus all we can do is struggle to find glimpses of truth from whatever quarter they may emerge.
In the Introduction to Book 3, Maimonides describes his own method
as one that relies on conjecture and supposition. There are, as Lenn
Goodman asserts, no experts on God.[48]

We may conclude that both traditions call for a critical examination of God and human reason. Once we begin this examination,
the global question "Which side is right?" gives way to more limited
ones like "What arguments need to be reworked?" or "What insights
need to be reformulated?" Contrary to Strauss, Maimonides could be
a Jew *and* a philosopher because he was able to take material from
one tradition and shed light on the other. For Maimonides one cannot
love God unless one also loves wisdom. Recall that to think about
God in the wrong way is not to think about God at all. But one cannot love wisdom unless one displays awe and humility in the face of
a being infinitely greater than oneself. Maimonides did not leave philosophy or religion as he found them. Though he borrows heavily
from rabbinic Judaism and the Aristotelianism of Alfarabi and Avicenna, he feels perfectly justified in reinterpreting the former and de-
parting from the latter.

From a historical perspective, there is nothing startling in the
claim that a great thinker extends the limits of a tradition by asking
new questions and introducing with new modes of thought. So even
if Judaism in its classical period is incompatible with philosophy in
its classical period, there is no reason to think that Maimonides or
anyone else is stuck with a conflict between static bodies of knowl-

edge. Not surprisingly, one of Maimonides' heroes is not a philosopher with a finished doctrine or a mystic who claimed to achieve
union with God but Rabbi Akiva, the man who entered paradise
(*pardes*) and returned in peace because he did not try to comprehend
matters too marvelous for the human intellect (*GP* 1.32, pp. 68–69).
It is noteworthy that Maimonides does not present Akiva as a romantic hero striving for a goal he can never reach. On the contrary,
Akiva *does* achieve his goal when he recognizes that there are limits
he cannot supersede but continues to worship God.

Maimonides' view of Akiva is more than an attempt to court
favor with religious authorities; it is part of a conception of philosophy that sees no incompatibility between the search for knowledge
and the experience of awe, humility, even shame before God (*GP*
3.52, p. 629). In our terms, it is a sobering experience instead of a rap-
turous one, a way of exposing human vanity rather than celebrating
human triumphs. The goal is to get to the point where one is humble enough not to let emotions cloud one's judgment and to see
things as they are. Maimonides describes it (*GP* 1.32, p. 68) as not de-
ceiving yourself into thinking that there is a demonstration in regard
to matters that have not been demonstrated, not hastening to reject
opinions whose contradictories have not been demonstrated, and not
aspiring to apprehend what cannot be apprehended. It is in this sense
that Maimonides thinks philosophy is a sacred obligation and feels
justified in saying that Moses and the patriarchs were philosophers.[49]

Maimonides Our Contemporary

Having looked at Maimonides and considered Strauss's claim of
a natural opposition between philosophy and religion, we must
ask whether our approach to these matters is any different. Not only
does the sacred literature of Judaism contain anthropomorphic descriptions of God, it also contains passages that glorify war, denigrate
women, and cast doubt on the intelligence and moral integrity of gentiles. Do these passages not also need a corrective, or should we simply say that because they appear in authoritative sources, we have no
choice but to accept them at face value? To put the question another
way, is not our urge to do philosophy just as irresistible as Maimonides'? Are there not just as many reasons to think that a Judaism
that ignores philosophy and talks about God in an uncritical way has
shortchanged itself?[50]

As for philosophy itself, reasonable people still disagree about
first principles and how they should be investigated. If Maimonides

restricted the sphere of what could be demonstrated in the twelfth
century, most philosophers would be even more restrictive today.
From Kant onward, the dominant tendency has been for philosophers
to proceed as if no divine matters can be demonstrated and assign all
such issues to the sphere of what it is rational to believe. By the nineteenth century, even the laws of logic and some of the postulates of
mathematics came to be seen as rational choices rather than self-
evident facts. In this day and age there are few people who think that
philosophy can ignore its past and take up issues relating to God de
novo. Rather than proceed in a linear fashion from premise to conclusion, we have no choice but to study texts from several sources
and use one as a check against the other. The tools, then, are not demonstration as much as the ones suggested by Aristotle: interpretation, criticism, and reconstruction.

Needless to say, reconstruction is a dangerous business because
one always runs the risk that the flavor of the original text will be
lost. But it is well to remember that the business of reconstructing
other people's arguments is as old as philosophy itself. Plato did it
with Parmenides and Protagoras; Aristotle with Plato; Maimonides
with Plato, Aristotle, the Asherites, the Mutazilites, the book of Genesis, and many of the prophets and sages. In fact, given the cryptic
way in which Maimonides writes, and the fact that he does not say
everything he can about a particular subject in one place, reconstruction is inevitable.

Though much of the material I will consider in this study comes
from historical sources, my purpose is not only to ask what they say
but where they are trying to take us. What do they teach us about
God and the problems of trying to address such a difficult subject?
More to the point, what would it be like to have a Maimonides who
abandoned his commitment to outdated paradigms like Aristotelian
physics, geocentric astronomy, and hierarchical conceptions of gender but retained his commitment to negative theology and creation
ex nihilo? One way to think of this project is as an exercise in re-
trieval. The Maimonides who believed in geocentric astronomy can
be relegated to the history books, but if I am right, the Maimonides
who believed in negative theology and creation ex nihilo cannot.

To use a metaphor popularized by Richard Rorty, my goal is to
have an imaginary conversation with Maimonides in which he ac-
knowledges his debt to Plato and Aristotle and takes up the objections of people like Aquinas, Kant, and Hegel. Some may think
it necessary to imagine a conversation between Maimonides the
philosopher and Maimonides the rabbi, but I will follow Twersky and

David Hartman in trying to argue that such a division is untenable. Conversation, after all, is the original meaning of *dialectic*.[51] Although this process is fraught with risk, its justification rests on the claim that I am not doing anything that Maimonides and scores of other thinkers did not do with their predecessors. They too stage imaginary debates and revise positions as they go along. They too take insights from different sources and try to bring them together to form a coherent vision of the world. In sum, having a conversation with a thinker from another age is also part of the urge to philosophize.

The vision I wish to defend holds that the first two commandments are, in Maimonides' words, "the great principle on which everything else depends." Since these commandments can be grasped either by reason or by a close reading of the prophetic books, their truth has nothing to do with the election of Israel or any claim of privileged access to God. As we will see, Maimonides regarded them as binding on all humanity. Although Maimonides ascribes will to God in connection with creation, David Novak is right to say that this should not be confused with temporal choice.[52] God's will is eternal and does not change from one moment to the next. There are, then, no specific events in the life of God, nothing that enables one to say that God spoke directly to x, forgave the sins of y, or manifested special love for z. There are important passages in the sacred literature that make such claims, but if Maimonides has taught us anything, it is that they must be reinterpreted in a way that does not compromise God's transcendence. Revelation is not a case of God's choosing to speak with Moses but of Moses' coming to understand the will of God. Repentance is not a case of God's granting mercy to y but of y's deciding to redirect the course of her life. Love is not a case of God's dispensing special favors on z but of z's coming to feel awe and humility in the presence of God.

Clearly this vision has critics. There is a tradition that begins with more literal interpretation of the sacred literature and includes Judah Halevi, Søren Kierkegaard, Franz Rosenzweig, Martin Buber, and Abraham J. Heschel. According to this school of thought, Maimonides has everything reversed. Instead of reinterpreting claims of religious experience to cohere with an abstract conception of God, we should realize that experience is primary and abstraction secondary.[53] Rosenzweig, for example, argues that God's reality is not shown by God's having an absolute nature but by God's reaching out to specific individuals in their individuality.[54] Thus (*SR*, p. 164): "God's love loves where it loves and whom it loves," and (*SR*, p. 381):

"We experience his [God's] existence directly only by virtue of the fact that he loves us and awakens our dead Self to beloved and requiting soul." This is all a way of saying that in religious matters, existence precedes essence: Before we can make sense of God, creation, or redemption, we have to examine our experience of them.

According to my vision, however, the experience of God is never direct. It comes, if at all, after a lifetime of observance, reflection, and conceptual revision. Even at the highest levels, it is plagued by doubt and uncertainty as finite beings try to understand matters beyond their reach. We cannot resolve this issue simply by citing Scripture, because doing so will only raise the question of how Scripture should be interpreted. What I propose, then, is to defend a vision by trying to articulate it. It should be understood, however, that articulation is a process in which success is measured in inches and territory once taken must sometimes be fought for and taken again.

2

The Challenge of Monotheism

Etymologically *mono* + *theism* implies belief in or worship of a single deity. But belief in a single deity is at most a necessary condition for monotheism. A religion that recognized Zeus as the only deity would not be considered monotheistic even if its adherents insisted that besides him, there are no other gods. It matters little whether a person worships a single god or a large number *if* that god is nothing but a glorified version of something found on earth. To qualify as monotheistic, a religion must not only worship one deity but conceive of that deity in a particular way. According to Maimonides (*GP* 1.57, p. 133), to say that God is one is to say that God has no equal. But having no equal does *not* mean that God is the wisest, most durable, or most powerful force in the universe. That much could have been said of Zeus. Rather it means that nothing is comparable to God, can serve as a surrogate for God, or can stand as a rival to God. Thus Isaiah 40:25: "To whom then will you liken Me, that I should be equal?"

Infinite or Finite; Creator or Creation

Behind Maimonides' claim is the conviction that if God were a bigger, stronger, more durable version of humans, in worshipping God we would again be worshipping our own reflection. The crux of monotheism is not only belief in a single deity but belief in a deity

23

who is different from everything else. In one passage (*GP* 1.56, p. 130) he goes so far as to say that it is *not* true that God's power is greater than ours, God's knowledge more extensive, or God's will more universal. It is not true because to say that it is would imply that there is a measure of comparison, that even though God is at the top of the scale, it makes sense to put us both on it. We can compare my strength to that of an Olympic athlete, or an Olympic athlete's to that of a horse or bull. We can compare armies, empires, and the horsepower of automobiles. But we can commit no greater sin against monotheism than to compare any of these capacities to the power to create a whole galaxy out of nothing—or for that matter, to the power to create even one atom out of nothing.

In a word, God's power is infinite. No matter how many times we magnify the strength of a finite creature, we will never arrive at anything more than an enhanced conception of a finite creature and will not even get close to the idea of divinity.[1] In Maimonides' terms (*GP* 1.35, p. 80): "There is absolutely no likeness in any respect whatever between Him and the things created by Him."

Similar considerations apply to the idea of unity. If by *oneness* we mean an accident that attaches to ordinary substances, then following Avicenna, Maimonides insists it is just as ridiculous to say that God is one as it is to say that God is many (*GP* 1.57, p. 132). God's unity must be so unlike everything else that for God and God alone (*GP* 1.51, p. 113),

> there is no oneness at all except in believing that there is one simple essence in which there is no complexity or multiplicity of notions, but one notion only; so that from whatever angle you regard it and from whatever point of view you consider it, you will find that it is one, not divided in any way and by any cause into two notions.

An obvious consequence of divine unity is that God cannot be material, because everything material is divisible. In fact, God cannot admit of any form of composition whether beginning and end, essence and existence, or genus and specific difference.

A more subtle consequence of divine unity is that God cannot be conceived in hierarchical terms. Although the Bible often depicts God as a monarch presiding over a heavenly court, and there are passages where Maimonides himself uses similar comparisons, this way of thinking is misleading if it implies that we can begin on the lower rungs of the scale, determine what accounts for the intervals, and extrapolate to God. As we saw, God is not a superior version of something else. The problem with hierarchical conceptions of reality is that they assume that everything can be measured by one set of criteria. Instead of recognizing two vastly different conceptions of wisdom and power, for example, they imply that God has more of the things that we have, so that the difference between God and us is analogous to the difference between a poor person and a rich one. One of the consequences of Maimonides' negative theology is that the differences between one creature and another are as nothing compared with the overwhelming difference between any creature and God. If it is true that God is "off the scale," then ultimately the only difference that matters is that between God and everything else.[2]

In a later age Hermann Cohen summed up these arguments by saying that the distinguishing feature of monotheism is not oneness but uniqueness (*Einzigheit, RR,* pp. 35–58). Pagan gods struggle against nature or are conceived according to categories that arise out of it: the thunderbolt, the hunt, the harvest, or sexual passion. But the unique God stands apart from nature, which means that categories like wealth, home life, or social function are totally inapplicable. Thus monotheism is not only a claim about God but a claim about the rest of the universe as well: that it owes its existence to something whose perfection it cannot share.

What, then, is the proper relation between God and the created order? If this line of argument is correct, it can only be separation. Physical separation is out of the question because it implies a common space in which God and everything else are located. Rather separation means that whether we take the most powerful ruler, the largest galaxy, or the most towering intellect, God is still in a different category. Note, for example, that the quote from Isaiah cited earlier is preceded by the observation that the nations of the world, the beasts of the field, and the cedars of Lebanon are as nothing before God. So monotheism requires that we look at the universe in terms of a fundamental dichotomy: God and everything else, *Creator* and *creation.* According to Alexander Altmann:[3]

> the different shades of being in all created beings are neutralized, as it were, and reduced to one single level compared with the totally other Being of God. The only ontological distinction which matters from the theological point of view is the one between created and uncreated being.

In view of the overwhelming difference between Creator and creation, it is no accident that much of the symbolism of Judaism consists of a series of bifurcations: God and the created order, heaven and earth, Egypt and the Promised Land, the Sabbath and the other days of the week, Israel and the other nations of the world, milk and meat, wool and flax. The best example of this symbolism is in the prayer said at the close of the Sabbath:

> Blessed are Thou, O Lord our God, Ruler of the Universe, who separates the sacred from the profane, light from darkness, Israel from the other nations, the seventh day from the other six days of labor. Blessed art Thou, O Lord, who separates the sacred from the profane.

Indeed the Hebrew word for holiness (*kedushah*) means to treat as separate. We may conclude that from a theological perspective, everything is either/or, and nothing is both/and.

Separation and Mediation

The most immediate consequence of the either/or principle is that nothing can straddle the fence that separates God from the created order. This does not rule out the possibility of creatures superior to humans, but it does require us to say that if such creatures exist, even they are nothing when compared with God. According to Genesis 1:14–19, the heavenly bodies are part of the created order and nothing more. While they may have enormous influence over weather and crops, they have no powers not granted to them by God.

Like Christianity and Islam, Judaism has an elaborate angelology. But for the most part, care is taken to ensure that angels are not subjects of worship in their own right. In the Bible, angels generally have two functions: to carry messages from heaven to earth, and to enhance the majesty of God by providing a heavenly retinue. It is noteworthy, however, that they do not receive names or separate identities until the book of Daniel (8:16; 9:21), which is very late. Although rabbinic literature contains a dispute on when angels were created, the important point is *that* they were created at all.[4] Like humans, angels do not rival God. Commenting on biblical passages where God appears to address a heavenly court, Maimonides points out that God is not really talking, or deliberating, or consulting the opinions of other beings, "For how could the Creator seek help from that which He created?" (*GP* 2.6, p. 263).

While some accounts make angels closer to God than humans are, there are numerous passages in rabbinic literature where God becomes angry with angels or rejects their advice altogether.[5] It is well to remember that whatever advantages they have, they cannot perform commandments. With one exception, no prayers are directed to them and no ceremonies undertaken on their behalf.[6] Thus the standard view seems to be that expressed at *Berakhot* 13a: "If trouble befall someone, let him not cry to Michael or Gabriel; let him cry to Me and I will answer him at once." This view is reiterated in the Passover *Haggadah*, which reads:

> I will pass through the land of Egypt: I Myself and not an angel. And I will smite every firstborn: I Myself and not a Seraph. And on all the gods of Egypt I will execute judgment: I Myself and not a messenger. I, the Eternal, I am the One, and none other.[7]

There is even a tradition according to which angels are inferior to humans when the latter behave in a righteous fashion.[8]

More important than angels is the prophecy of Moses. According to Exodus 33:11, Moses did not need heavenly messengers and was allowed to speak to God "face to face." In fact, Moses must intercede between God and the people, because the people are afraid that if they see God, they will die (Exodus 20:16).[9] So rather than angels, Moses is the closest thing to a being with one foot in the divine order and one foot in the created one. But here too there is a powerful corrective: He cannot enter the Promised Land. Instead of completing his journey and celebrating the end of over 40 years of leadership, he goes off to die in an unmarked grave. Hence the greatest prophet is only a prophet, not a demigod. He is not even mentioned in the *Haggadah*, which celebrates the Exodus from Egypt. We can therefore agree with Solomon Schechter, who followed in the footsteps of Maimonides, when he said that the establishment of an intermediary is really the setting up of another God and hence the cause of sin.[10]

Yet sinful or not, some sort of intermediary can be found in practically every corner of Jewish philosophy in the form of *logoi, sephirot*, heavenly spheres, and heavenly intelligences.[11] For many medieval thinkers, prophecy is not a direct relation between God and a person but a mediated relation in which forms emanate from God through the heavenly intelligences to the mind of the prophet. But the intelligences do not direct the flow of emanation from one individual to another; they are simply conduits for a kind of causality over which they have no control. In the heavenly realm, they are objects of desire that explain the motion of the spheres in much the way that final causes explain physical motion on earth. In Maimonides' opinion (*GP* 2.7), they exercise free choice; but since they do so in a timeless realm, their will is not analogous to ours. While study of the intelligences may bring us closer to God by acquainting us with heavenly phenomena, it bears repeating that none is an object of worship in its own right.[12] In fact, the view that stars and intelligences control the destiny of people on earth is one of Maimonides' main objections to astrology. It is true, of course, that the intelligences enjoy a knowledge of God superior to ours, but it is well to remember that in Maimonides' opinion their knowledge is also imperfect.[13] In short, the intelligences are part of the created order, obey the laws of the created order, and have no claim to divinity.

Beyond the question of angels or intelligences, there is the question of how to interpret passages that describe God's nearness to things on earth. According to Exodus 40:34-35, when work on the Tabernacle was finished, a cloud covered it and the glory of the Lord filled it so that Moses could not enter.[14] We can take the passage to mean that the Tabernacle reflected the honor of God or that a physical manifestation of God entered the earthly realm and took up space. There is, of course, a long tradition that regards the glory of God as a beam of light that illuminates prophet experience. To take an obvious example, Ezekiel (1:27–28) saw fire and brightness when looking on an image and goes on to claim that the earth was illuminated by the glory of the Lord and that the glory of God filled his house (43: 2–5).

Closely connected with the glory of God is the *Shekhinah* or indwelling presence of God. The root *shakhon* means to settle down or dwell, as in Exodus 29:45: "And I will dwell among the Children of Israel and will be their God." Like the glory of God, the *Shekhinah* is said to shine down on earth, emit light, and occupy space.[15] In other contexts, it goes into exile with Israel, feels pain, sheds tears, and enters or departs the world depending on whether Israel is faithful or unfaithful.[16] In mystical literature, the *Shekhinah,* conceived as feminine, takes on sexual connotations even to the point of having holy intercourse with Moses.[17] Although a famous study of this issue by Joshua Abelson tried to show that the *Shekhinah*, or light that it emits, is understood as an incarnation of God, this conclusion is vigorously disputed by Ephraim Urbach, who maintains, "A survey of all the passages referring to the Shekhinah leaves no doubt that the Shekhinah is no 'hypostasis' and has no separate existence alongside the deity."[18] In fact, Urbach argues that in many cases the *Shekhinah* is nothing but a literary device to allow the rabbis to avoid using the Tetragrammaton.[19]

Maimonides' treatment of the verb *shakhon* follows his interpretation of other verbs that imply corporeality: It must be used figuratively when applied to God (*GP* 1.25, p. 55). Accordingly the noun *Shekhinah* is a colorful way to describe God's providence over the earthly realm: When prophets apprehend the goodness of God, the *Shekhinah* or holy presence comes to them. In other contexts, *Shekhinah* refers to the glory of God, in which case it refers to a beam of light in the created order, not to God in physical form.[20] In either case, Maimonides' analysis of the *Shekhinah* implies that it is not a separate entity with a will or intelligence of its own. Enlarging on Maimonides' position, Steven Schwarzschild argues that the coming and going of the *Shekhinah* are nothing but a figurative way of referring to Israel's willingness to obey the commandments.[21] To say, for example, that the *Shekhinah* comes when the commandments are obeyed and departs when they are not is simply to say that God approves of one and disapproves of the other. Again, there is no need for a hypostasis.

As for God's nearness to human beings, Maimonides insists that it too is a figure of speech. Accordingly there is no difference between a person in the center of the earth and, if it were possible, a person in the highest heavenly sphere (*GP* 1.18, p. 45): "For nearness to Him . . . consists in apprehending Him; remoteness from Him is the lot of him who does not know Him." In short, there is God and our attempt to know God. While knowing involves an emanation from God to the heavenly intelligences to the mind of the prophet, once we leave God, we enter the created order and are no longer dealing with divinity. As we saw, the most that can be said for heavenly intelligences or miraculous beams of light is that they bring us closer to God. According to Schwarzschild: "The intermediaries are almost always only temporary and representational functionaries between the only two real agents involved, namely God and the individual."[22] So while it may be wishful thinking to conclude, as Schwarzschild does, that "pure and austere monotheism always carried the day in the end," it is nonetheless true that the normal way for philosophers to deal with this problem is to push intermediaries to one side of the either/or dichotomy: They are either literary devices to help us think about God or finite beings in the created order.

Along these lines, Maimonides argues that while obedience to a king requires one to treat the king's emissaries with respect, it does not follow that the same is true of God.[23] Worship of the sun, moon, stars, or any supposed vessel or image of God is tantamount to idolatry. It is important to see, however, that the reluctance to accept intermediaries reflects more than a concern for neatness. A genuine intermediary would be something that draws attention away from God. If Moses had been allowed to enter the Promised Land in triumph, if we knew where he was buried and could erect a shrine, a cult would develop around Moses, and sooner or later he would become an object of worship in his own right.

From a practical standpoint, monotheism is opposed to the tendency to glorify and eventually deify political leaders, movie stars, sports figures, and others who demand worship or adoration on their own behalf. One reason to stress the uniqueness of God is to enable people to see that anything other than God is fallible and subject to critique. That is why the Bible does not hesitate to portray major characters like Jacob, Moses, or David in less than flattering ways. In sum, monotheism involves more than fealty to God; it also involves a critical attitude to the things in God's creation.

The strongest statement of this attitude is the second commandment. As was noted earlier, not only are there no other gods besides the true one, but it is wrong to make any likeness of anything that is in heaven, on earth, or below the earth. The issue, then, is not how awesome or beautiful the image is but how nothing other than God can represent the splendor of God. From a philosophic perspective, the second commandment could be extended to say that not only can things in heaven, on earth, or below the earth not serve as objects of worship, neither can things conjured up by the human imagination. Again, nothing can be an object of worship except something truly unique, and by definition there is only one thing in the universe that fits that description.

Monotheism and Skepticism

If we define monotheism in terms of uniqueness and insist on a strict interpretation of the second commandment, we face an immediate difficulty: How do you characterize something truly unique? Recall Maimonides' claim that there is absolutely no likeness in any respect whatever between God and the things created by God. If this is true, every time we look for something in the universe with which to compare God, we will fail. But if there is nothing with which God can be compared, how can we ever know God?

One way to understand the problem is to imagine a spectrum with uniqueness at one end and intelligibility at the other. The more unique God is, the harder it will be for God to fit our concepts or be subsumed under our laws. Thus Isaiah 55:8: "For my thoughts are not your thoughts, Neither are your ways My ways." If our categories always fall short of God, any claim to know God is suspect. As Bahya says, there is an unavoidable paradox: The moment we pretend that God is near to our understanding, we lose God completely.[24]

We can also understand the problem by returning to paganism. Whatever religious problems might arise in worshipping Zeus or Athena, there is at least one problem that does not: intelligibility. Because they are nothing but glorified versions of us, we have no trouble imagining what they look like, where they live, or how they act. But once we deny that God is a glorified version of something else, the only way to identify God is as "wholly other."[25] To follow Baḥya's insight, monotheism puts us in a dilemma where any positive claim of knowledge constitutes proof that we have missed the subject of our inquiry.

We can deal with the dilemma in one of two ways: sacrifice uniqueness in the interest of intelligibility or forgo intelligibility and opt for pure and austere monotheism. Although the typical solution is to take the first option, I want to follow Maimonides by taking the second. We saw that if God does not admit plurality, then categories like genus and species, subject and predicate, matter and form, or essential and accidental do not apply to God. But the issue goes much deeper. According to Maimonides, not only is the attempt to divide God objectionable but so is the attempt to present God under a description. To use his word, all categories or descriptions *particularize* their subject. To say, for example, that God is F is to imply that F-ness is a cause anterior to God or that it makes sense to put God in the same class as other F things. In either case, God's perfection would be conditioned by or conceived through something else and thus be dependent on something else. If it is dependent, then it is no longer unique.

If God does not fall under a category, neither can God manifest any sort of relation. According to Maimonides, relations hold between things in the same or proximate species. Relations, in other words, are accidents that attach to or inhere in things in the same category. We can say that the outermost sphere of the universe is larger than a mustard seed because both are extended; but there is no relation between a quality like heat and a quantity like a hundred cubits long. As Maimonides asks (*GP* 1.52, p. 118): "How then could there be a relation between Him . . . and any of the things created by Him, given the immense difference between them with regard to the true reality of their existence?" As we saw above, it is not true that God's power is greater than ours or God's knowledge more comprehensive than ours. So strictly speaking, all the psalms or prayers that describe God as a father, king, or marriage partner are false.[26] Even to say that God is the wisest king or most merciful father is to measure God by human standards.

It is well known that Maimonides regards statements like "God is wise" or "God is powerful" as disguised negations. In a nutshell "God is powerful" means "God does not lack power nor does God manifest it in a conventional way." It says, in other words, that while God is not deficient, the true nature of divine power is beyond our comprehension. Thus terms like *knowledge, power, will,* and *life* are predicated of God and us in a completely equivocal way (*GP* 1.56, p. 131): "so that their meaning when they are predicated of Him is in no way like their meaning in other applications." The term *knowledge,* for example, typically identifies an achievement of the human mind. As applied to us, it refers to something different from what is referred to by *power* or *will*; but as applied to God, none of these terms can refer to a perfection distinct from that referred to by the others. Thus (*GP* 1.57, p. 132): "He exists, but not through an existence other than His essence; and similarly He lives, but not through life; He is powerful, but not through power; He knows, but not through knowledge." The idea is that if God is powerful *through* power or wise *through* knowledge, once again God would depend on something else.

In fact, Maimonides is so rigorous on the issue of particularizing God that he thinks even negative predicates are guilty of it to some extent. Basically negative predicates have two advantages. The first is that they do not measure God's perfection in human terms; instead of putting God at the top of a scale, they deny that God is even on it. The second is that they do not add anything to God's essence by piling up multiple descriptions. If God's knowledge and power are both beyond our comprehension, we have no grounds for thinking that they refer to two faculties rather than one. Thus Maimonides (*GP* 1.60, p. 145) affirms that someone who thinks that God has positive attributes has not understood God imperfectly but abandoned belief in God altogether.

Still there is a respect in which negative predicates also subsume God under a category.[27] According to Maimonides (*GP* 1.58, p. 134), "The attributes of negation have in this respect something in common with the attributes of affirmation, for the former undoubtedly bring about some particularization." In this connection, he asks us to imagine a situation where we know that something is in a house but not what it is. If we learn that it is neither a mineral nor a vegetable, we can infer that it is an animal. By denying that a subject falls under one category, negative predicates typically imply that it falls under a different one. Clearly this will not work for God. By turning to the negative formulation, we are not identifying God by process of elimination but claiming that any attempt at identification fails. The reason is that even a claim like "God is not inanimate" subsumes God under a category and puts God in a class with other things. Once God falls under a description, even a description that applies to only one thing, there is no possibility of uniqueness in Maimonides' sense.

Similar considerations apply to the claim that there is an essence of God. According to Aristotle, the essence of a thing is what it is in itself (*kath hauto*), and only things whose formula is a definition can have an essence.[28] Definitions, according to the usual account, involve genus and specific difference. Since God, as Avicenna argued, cannot fall under a genus, no definition of God is possible. Maimonides therefore feels confident in saying (*GP* 1.52, p. 115), "It is well known among all people engaged in speculation, who understand what they say, that God cannot be defined." If no definition, then no essence either. In short, there is no "what-ness" connected with God, nothing that allows us to bring God within the scope of a category. We should be clear about the radical nature of Maimonides' position. To say that God cannot be defined is to say that even claims like "God is pure intellect" or "God is pure activity," though helpful up to a point, are misleading, for while they distinguish God from other things, they still try to make God fall within conceptual boundaries, to condition the unconditioned.

Although God does not have an essence in the usual sense of the term, any reader of the *Guide* can see that Maimonides talks about essence in connection with God throughout the chapters on negative theology. On several occasions he reminds us that God's essence is simple and nothing can be superadded to it. In discussing Exodus 33, he points out that even Moses could not know God's essence as it really is. At *Guide* 1.61, p. 147, he claims that God's proper name (the Tetragrammaton) "gives a clear indication of His essence." Since Maimonides connects the Tetragrammaton with necessary existence, it would seem that, like Avicenna, he regards necessary existence as God's distinguishing characteristic.[29] Yet how can this be if God cannot be defined? Is the essence of a necessary being just its existence, or is it better to say that it does not have an essence at all?

One solution is to say that Maimonides typically uses *essence* in two senses: one (*māhiyya*) to talk about contingent things, where existence is superadded to essence; another (*dhāt*) to talk about the absolute identity of essence and existence in God.[30] But we must keep in mind that even the strong sense of the term puts God in a category that we can characterize. It is significant, then, that after saying that God exists but not through an existence other than the divine essence, Maimonides makes a larger point about the limits of religious language (*GP* 1.57, pp. 132–33):

These subtle notions that very clearly elude the mind cannot be considered through the instrumentality of the customary words, which are the greatest among the causes leading unto error. For the bounds of expression in all languages are very narrow indeed, so that we cannot represent this notion to ourselves except through a certain looseness of expression. Thus when we wish to indicate that the deity is not many, the one who makes the statement cannot say anything but that He is one, even though "one" and "many" are some of the subdivisions of quantity. For this reason we give the gist of the notion and give the mind the correct direction toward the true reality of the matter.

I suggest that what is true of *one* and *many* is also true of *essence* even in the strong sense: Maimonides says that nothing can be superadded to God's essence in order to emphasize that God is different from everything else. His claim is intended to rule out unacceptable alternatives and direct the mind to the unique nature of the subject. But strictly speaking, God does not have an essence in a sense that we can understand. So Maimonides must use terms in one context that he rejects in another. As Plotinus remarks (*EN* 6.8.13), "Our inquiry obliges us to use terms not strictly applicable."[31]

The idea of pointing the mind in the right direction also helps to explain how Maimonides would square negative theology with the view that God's existence can be demonstrated.[32] The answer is that while "God exists" is true and enables us to recognize that the universe contains more than contingent beings, it has nothing in common with ordinary existential propositions. In the first place, it does not have a subject/predicate structure. Although it appears to mention two things, it cannot really do so because God's existence is not separate from God. In the second place, "God" does not refer to a something we can define or comprehend. In a statement like "Bill Clinton exists," there are a number of descriptions I can use to present Bill Clinton to my mind. But we have seen that there are no descriptions that will allow me to do the same with God.[33] In the last analysis, "God exists" would have to be interpreted negatively, and its negativity would have to be qualified so as not to put God in a class with something else. The same is true of descriptions like "God thinks" or "God is the ground of being." They enable us to see something important and to reject obvious falsehoods. But *as* descriptions they are objectionable in principle.

It follows that Maimonides' view of religious language is heuristic: It is a tool to help *us* focus attention or come to important insights, but it is always imprecise and can never culminate in literal truth. As Maimonides points out in discussing the claim that God's relation to the world is like that of a captain to a ship (*GP* 1.58, p.

137), such descriptions "lead the mind toward the view that He . . . governs the existent things" but are not a true likeness because again God "has nothing in common with them in any respect." Even negations only (*GP* 1.58, p. 135) "conduct the mind toward the utmost reach that man may attain in the apprehension of Him." As we saw, the closest Maimonides comes to something that refers to God in an unequivocal way is the Tetragrammaton, which according to Jewish tradition is not supposed to be pronounced.[34]

I will have more to say about religious language in the next chapter. For the present it is enough to realize that once we get beyond its liturgical or pedagogical function, once the mind has been turned away from the material realm toward God, the purpose of religious language is to reveal its own inadequacy. A person may have to labor in a science for years to see that its terms and categories apply only to the created order (*GP* 1.59, p. 138). In the words of Anton Pegis, "Man must come to *unsay* the whole universe in order to say that *God exists* properly."[35] In this way, religious wisdom is really a kind of learned ignorance. What separates the wise person from the fool is that the former realizes that only God can comprehend God.

In some respects, Maimonides' view of language resembles the one expressed by Wittgenstein at the end of the *Tractatus*:[36]

> My propositions serve as elucidations in the following way: Anyone who understands me eventually recognizes them as nonsensical, when he has used them—as steps—to climb up beyond them. (He must, so to speak, throw away the ladder after he has climbed up it.) He must transcend these propositions, and then he will see the world aright. What we cannot speak about, we must pass over in silence.

Obviously Maimonides would not say that every claim we make about God is nonsensical. But he would say that the claims we make about God are best understood as steps on the way to something higher: a perspective from which we see that strictly speaking nothing we say about God can be true. After reflecting on the deficiencies of religious language, Maimonides (*GP* 1.59, p. 139) also encourages the reader to pass over the subject in silence, quoting Psalm 65:2: "Silence is praise to thee."[37]

We can understand silence as the price we pay for uniqueness. If God is truly unique, any attempt to praise or characterize God can only end in failure. Maimonides sums up his position by proclaiming (*GP* 1.59, p. 137): "Glory . . . to Him who is such that when the intellects contemplate His essence, their apprehension turns into incapacity; and when they contemplate the proceeding of His actions from His will, their knowledge turns into ignorance; and when the tongues aspire to magnify Him by means of attributive qualifications, all eloquence turns into weariness and incapacity." To be sure, silence runs the risk of atheism; to say nothing is to encourage some people to think there is no point in taking up the subject in the first place. But atheism, as Levinas remarks, is a risk that has to be run, because only through the process of denying inadequate conceptions of God can we reach the idea of true transcendence.[38]

Having emphasized the limits of human knowledge, Maimonides could make it easy on himself by claiming that what reason cannot comprehend, revelation can. In other words, he could argue that there are extrarational modes of access to God that have provided him or others with a special kind of enlightenment. But it is important to see that he does not pursue this option and is willing to live with the consequences of his position. Twice in the *Guide* (3. Introduction, p. 416; 3.51, p. 624) he tells the reader that he has not had a prophetic experience of his own. In keeping with his skepticism, he begins the *Guide* on a hesitant note, apologizing for what he intends to do (*GP* 1. Introduction, p. 16): "God . . . knows that I have never ceased to be exceedingly apprehensive about setting down those things that I wish to set down in this Treatise." His apprehension does not apply to the existence and unity of God, topics so central to Judaism that even general audiences must accept them (*GP* 1.35, pp. 79–80). But God's existence and unity must still be interpreted negatively or else we will again put God on the same level as creatures.[39]

We saw that once we get beyond existence and unity to "obscure matters," Maimonides' teaching is full of reservations. The issues he discusses are not completely known to anyone, which means that the reader cannot expect full coverage and must settle for scattered insights that will "appear, flash, and then be hidden again." The reason we can have only scattered insights is that matter acts as a dark veil over the human mind, preventing it from apprehending the true nature of immaterial reality (*GP* 3.9, pp. 436–37).[40] All we can hope for, then, are a few insights from which we can try to put together a provisional theory. Like the prisoner in Plato's cave who sees the sun and returns to tell his fellow prisoners about it, those who are fortunate enough to receive these insights have trouble communicating them to others (*GP* 1. Introduction, p. 8): "Know that whenever one of the perfect wishes to mention, either orally or in writing, something that he understands of these *secrets*, according to the degree of his perfection, he is unable to explain with complete clarity and coherence even the portion that he has apprehended."

Monotheism and Religion

We come to what may be the greatest problem of all: the possibility that monotheism in the strict sense may not be the essence of Judaism but a separate doctrine to which Judaism is only partly related. Can Judaism accommodate a timeless, changeless, unitary being whose greatness is best appreciated in silent devotion? In some ways this is the Jerusalem versus Athens question all over again. Critics charge that Maimonides has done away with the personal side of God, found philosophic messages in texts that are completely innocent of philosophy, undermined the institution of prayer, and put too much faith in the power of reason. Defenders answer that if Judaism is to be more than a series of rituals, if it is really committed to a worldview that everyone ought to consider, then the foundations of that worldview have to be articulated in a philosophically acceptable way, which is to say a way that plays down superstition, cultural or ethnic chauvinism, and claims of privileged access to God.

There is no need to review the history of this debate, because it breaks out in every age. We saw that Rita Gross argued that it is impossible to pray to or receive commandments from a nonpersonal ultimate. Essentially the same point is made by more traditional theologians who do not share Strauss's view of Jerusalem and Athens. According to David Burrell:[41]

> The clean alternative is simply to assert God to be *other than* the world, holding on quite firmly to the reality of the world in which we live. This can be considered Maimonides' position . . . but one always feels in such cases that one's religious self holds one's mind captive. For it takes but a little reflection to realize that God cannot be *that* neatly other if we are to use the name *creator*, or if divinity is to be in any way accessible to our discourse.

And Steven Katz:[42]

> If we take these claims for apophantic theology seriously, two problems, one philosophical, the other theological, arise: Philosophically the issue is how can the "x of x's" retain any meaning given the embargo on content for all predications about the ultimate. Theologically the concern is how can God, conceived so radically apophantically, be the object, or subject, of covenantal relationship, the revealer of Torah and mitzvot, the Judge or Redeemer of souls, the One to whom we address prayers and supplications?

To these questions I add one of my own: Can we seek God in ever widening spheres of negation, or does worship inevitably lead to a "god" with one foot in heaven and one foot on earth?

Obviously these issues are too broad to be addressed in a single chapter. We should keep in mind, however, that Maimonides would begin by emphasizing one point: Tradition supports him. Granted that the sacred books do not support him if we understand them at a surface level. There is no doubt that the Bible seems to present a God whose emotions change from one moment to the next and whose promises and threats establish the boundaries of moral discourse. But Maimonides would reply that Judaism is heir to a body of learning that rejects surface meaning and looks for insights that can withstand the give and take of dialectical scrutiny. In other words, he would reply that there is no reason why we have to take this conception of God as primary and measure everything else against it.

One hardly needs to point out that many of Maimonides' interpretations of the Bible would not hold up if judged by the standards of modern historical scholarship; but the same could be said for the interpretations of the rabbis, the mystics, and many of Maimonides' fiercest opponents. For all its virtues, modern historical analysis makes no claim to be sacred. But that is exactly what Maimonides does claim. At the beginning of the *Guide* he says that he is going to discuss the secrets of the Torah, or what he calls the science of the Law, in its true sense (*GP* 1. Introduction, pp. 5–9). When all is said and done, the science converges on one point: that the primary intention of the Law consists in people apprehending God and not worshipping anything but God (*GP* 3.28, p. 512; 3.32, p. 530).[43] That is why Maimonides refuses to compromise on the question of God's transcendence. In Judaism, as in most religions, there is a duty to love God (Deuteronomy 6:5). Once the otherness of God is surrendered, once our image of God is measured in human terms, love of God would become a form of self-love, and everything sacred in the religion would be lost.

To the person who objects that Maimonides' view provides little in the way of comfort or consolation, the gist of Maimonides' answer is that comfort and consolation, though desirable, are not the be-all and end-all of religious life. As a rabbi and a physician, he was certainly in a position to see suffering and pain on a regular basis. And no student of Jewish law could doubt that caring for the sick and comforting mourners are divine commandments. But a religion whose primary function is making people feel comfortable would soon become a travesty.

Beyond the issue of comfort is that of truth. If Maimonides is right, the highest obligation we have is to pursue truth even if what we discover threatens our self-image and causes anxiety. As he is fond of pointing out, Judaism does not ask people to starve themselves, beat themselves, or jeopardize their health. But it does require them to achieve a certain amount of theoretical sophistication, at least enough to recognize that we are only a small part of a vast universe. Viewing God as a friend, love partner, or protection agency may provide comfort in the short run, but in the long run it is to take solace in a life of fantasy.

Reduced to simplest terms, monotheism tries to purge us of the need to see our own image reflected everywhere in the universe. Rather than bringing God and humans closer together, its purpose is to emphasize the infinite distance that separates them. To return to Akiva and the parable of the rabbis who entered *pardes*, monotheism asks us to confront the wholly other *as* other without losing our sanity or composure. Recall that after hearing the voice of the Almighty, Job repented in silence. Without achieving union with God or looking for kinship between God and himself, he sought and found a higher form of holiness than what he had known before. In Maimonides' opinion, this form of holiness is the goal to which all the holidays, rituals, and sacred books point even if it does not look that way to the average worshipper. In sum, monotheism is justified by the truth of its vision rather than by the number of its adherents.

Monotheism as Enslavement: Hegel's Critique of Judaism

Despite Maimonides' sincerity in trying to prevent spurious worship, his view of religion remains controversial. As long as the gap between God and humans is infinite and unmediated, then some people will object, as Hegel did, that we cannot help but feel a profound sense of estrangement when we reach out for a God we can never embrace.[44] Faced with an opposition we cannot surmount or even comprehend, we have no choice but to stand in awe of God and, like Job, submit to the dictates of an alien will. Not surprisingly, estrangement soon manifests itself as enslavement. The point of worship is to glorify God and stress that next to God we are nothing. For Hegel, this idea of God is not only mysterious but severely, even oppressively, abstract. Lacking any sensuous manifestation, God is never present and never really revealed. In the end, all we have is an empty conception of divinity and a people who believe they have been cho-

sen as its servants. Because God is always other and never understood, God's commandments will always be arbitrary and unyielding.
In this scheme, the human attempt to please God will always fall
short of its goal, with the consequence that Judaism is a religion that
culminates in sorrow and regret.

From Hegel's standpoint, the only way to avoid this plight is to
abandon the idea of God as an undifferentiated "other" and overcome
the opposition on which it is based. The goal, then, is to spell out the
historical process by which the implicit unity between God and
human becomes actual and definite. In considering Hegel's criticism,
it is important to remember that by *God* he does not mean an all-
powerful being existing separate from the world but rather absolute
spirit or *Geist*. The characteristic feature of spirit is to become conscious of itself through history, which in Hegel's system means that
humans become ever more conscious of or articulate about the idea
of divinity.[45] "God is God," Hegel tells us, "insofar as he knows himself; his knowing himself is, furthermore, a self-consciousness in
man and man's knowledge *of* God that goes on to man's knowing
himself *in* God."[48] Or more succinctly (*LPR* 3, pp. 303–4): "The Spirit
of Man, whereby he knows God, is simply the Spirit of God himself."

It follows that for Hegel, the medieval position that says we can
know *that* God is but not *what* God is cannot be right. As long as we
are in the dark about what God is, spirit would remain undeveloped
and God less than absolute. In short, an unknowable God is concep-
tually impossible. Like Plotinus, Hegel believes in a reunion of the
finite with the infinite; but unlike Plotinus, he does not believe that
the infinite is indifferent to the process by which reunion occurs.
Until the process is complete, there is a sense in which God is not yet
God, not fully self-aware. Revelation is the process by which God is
no longer (*LPR* 2, p. 328) "a Being above and beyond this world" but
a being that attains consciousness of itself in our consciousness of
ourselves.

In concert with many thinkers in the romantic age, Hegel also accepted the idea of a fundamental dichotomy between Athens and
Jerusalem and disparaged the latter.[47] Judaism, on this account, is a
religion of slaves who took no delight in the visual arts and remained
in fear of a tyrannical God. Since tyranny is the result of separation,
it must be corrected by reconciliation. The first step in the process of
reconciliation is for humans to take confidence in themselves by
coming to see themselves in God. Instead of worshipping a distant
God, they worship a god who shares their needs, habits, emotions,
and political relations. According to Hegel (*LPR* 2, pp. 257–58):

> In this religion there is nothing incomprehensible, nothing which cannot be understood; there is no kind of content in the god which is not known to man, or which he does not find or know in himself. The confidence of man in the gods is at the same time confidence in himself.

Despite its anthropomorphism, Greek religion therefore represents a more advanced stage in the development of spirit than Jewish monotheism does. From Hebrew and Greek religion, we move to a "synthesis" in Roman religion, but the real synthesis or reconciliation between God and humans does not occur until we get to "absolute" religion, which means Christianity.

If the characteristic feature of Greek religion is that humans see themselves in God, the characteristic feature of Christianity is, in Hegel's eyes, the reverse: God becomes human, and in the process each side of the original opposition (*LPR* 2, p. 347) "recognizes itself, finds itself and its essential nature in the other." As Hegel puts it a bit later (*LPR* 3, p. 73), "Man appears as God and God as Man." It is here that the unity of divine and human natures becomes actual and the estrangement or unhappiness caused by their separation vanishes.[48] Overall the drama can be seen as one in which God creates humans, humans sin against God and fall away, humans and God are reunited in the person of Christ, Christ dies but his body lives on in the form of the Church. In this way religion is a sensuous representation of the movement of thought toward self-consciousness and culminates in the establishment of an institution that universalizes the incarnation by freeing it from dependence on one person. It is not that Hegel's God has one foot in heaven and one foot on earth but that the categories of heaven and earth have been overcome and replaced by that of Spirit.

There are essentially two ways for a Jew to respond to this analysis. The first is to follow Fackenheim in saying that while Judaism insists on the radical otherness of God, it also insists on the nearness and intimacy of God and must hold the two sides of this contradiction in some sort of dialectical tension.[49] According to Fackenheim, God, though other than the world, "enters into the world" and "descends to meet man."[50] Not surprisingly, he puts a great deal of weight on the midrashim that deal with God's *Shekhinah*.[51]

The second alternative is to follow Schwarzschild in saying that the separation between God and the world cannot be overcome and that any attempt to compromise God's transcendence or explain God's entry into the world is misguided.[52] Again Judaism contains a variety of currents, so the question is what aspect of the religion one wants to follow. While Hegel's view of Judaism is obviously simplistic, he certainly put his finger on the right question: Is the distinctive feature of the religion that the gap between God and the world cannot be overcome or that it can? Should prayer, repentance, love, and other ways of bringing us "near" to God be understood as closing the gap or as reinforcing it?

It is clear that in this debate, Maimonides is on the side of Schwarzschild, for what Hegel sees as the great weakness of Judaism, Maimonides sees as its underlying strength: clean lines of demarcation and no attempt to overcome opposition. What Hegel regards as a state of estrangement and unhappiness, Maimonides would regard as an honest assessment of the human condition—or at least one unfettered by romantic assumptions about "man's confidence in himself." For Maimonides, the need to see ourselves in God is a denial of religion rather than an attempt to bring it to a new level of understanding. Maimonides would be unmoved by the claim that since God's otherness is grasped by humans, the activity of grasping it is something more than human.[53] For Maimonides, otherness means the denial of essence and ultimately the acceptance of silence. There is, then, no possibility of seeing ourselves in the other.

Reduced to simplest terms, the debate between Maimonides and Hegel is a debate between a logic of either/or and a logic of both/and. The issue is whether a religion based on either/or is viable—whether, as Levinas put it, we should exit Hegel's system by moving backward through the very door by which Hegel thinks we enter it.[54] Clearly separation creates problems from both a theoretical and a practical perspective. How can God create the world and not have something in common with it? What sense can we give to the claim that holiness consists in becoming like God? More pointedly, can we still talk about prayer, repentance, and love of God in a meaningful way? This is another way of asking whether my account of monotheism is compatible with a religion that can accommodate classical doctrines and meaningful rituals, a religion that people can practice. And if it can, what sort of religion will it be? Does it hold out an ideal that some of Maimonides' staunchest defenders regard as unattainable? Will it avoid the estrangement that Hegel thinks is practically synonymous with Judaism? These questions will be the focal point of the remaining chapters.

3

Speaking of and to God

In the previous chapter we saw that from a philosophic perspective, many of the things people say about God are suspect and that ultimately all talk about God "turns into weariness and incapacity." On a practical level, one does not show respect by treating God as a spoiled child whose anger can be assuaged by flattery. Along these lines, Maimonides (*GP* 1.59, p. 140) relates the story of the person who addressed God as the Great, Valiant, Terrible, Mighty, Strong, Tremendous, and Powerful but was rebuked by Rabbi Ḥaninah for doing so.[1] According to the moral of the story, to praise God in this way is like praising a king who possesses millions of pieces of gold for possessing silver.[2]

Still, any person with religious sensibilities knows that it is nearly impossible to preserve a tradition or invoke a feeling of reverence without prayer. Accordingly Maimonides not only accepts the ritual of daily prayer but regards it as mandatory. In the *Mishneh Torah*, he tells us, "The obligation in this precept [prayer] is that every person should daily, according to his ability, offer up supplication and prayer; first uttering praises of God, then with humble supplication and petition asking for all that he needs, and finally offering praise and thanksgiving to the Eternal for the benefits already bestowed upon him in rich measure."[3] My purpose in this chapter is not to discuss the efficacy of prayer or anything else related to the question of how or if we can influence God; that issue will be taken up later.[4] For the present, it is enough to say that Maimonides insists that genuine worship be completely disinterested.[5] My purpose in this chapter is to ask how the language of prayer can be meaningful, and if it is, what meaning it has.

The issue at hand has been aptly described by Marvin Fox:[6]

> Considered from the perspective of the philosophical doctrines of the *Guide*, conventional prayer would seem to be a meaningless and even improper activity. Praise of God is impossible, because we have neither the language nor the knowledge to speak about Him in any meaningful way.

If this is true, if prayer not only produces no immediate results but is a batch of nonsense, then the tension between Maimonides' conception of monotheism and his commitment to Judaism would be unresolvable. To the question "Is monotheism compatible with religion in anything like its traditional form?" we would have to answer no. As Fox notes, Maimonides does not restrict the obligation to pray to the masses; it applies to everyone regardless of the level of learning. But then we must ask how the masses, the educated few, or anyone else can praise God in a meaningful way.

Maimonides and Aquinas on Negative Predication

Maimonides' initial response is to reiterate the well-known rabbinic dictum, "Torah speaks in the language of the descendants of Adam." In other words, the sacred books are not written in a philosophically precise vocabulary but in language that everyone can understand. So it is hardly surprising that the sacred books call God a king, master, father, or marriage partner and ascribe properties that follow from these descriptions. Nor is it surprising that the sacred books make free use of corporeal imagery, for most people assume that anything that is not corporeal is imaginary. All this is a way of saying that the language of prayer cannot be interpreted in a literal fashion. Thus far Maimonides' response is hardly controversial. "The wise thinker," Baḥya tells us (*DH* 1, p. 105), "will endeavor to strip the husk of the terms—their materialistic meaning—from the kernel, and will raise his conception, step by step, till he will at last attain to as much knowledge of the truth as his intellect is capable of apprehending."[7]

The second response is to point out that we cannot take every adjective that occurs in prayer and assume that God has an attribute corresponding to it. If, for example, there were a separate attribute for mercy, graciousness, steadfastness, and so on, our idea of God would be nothing but a bundle of attributes. In Maimonides' opinion (*GP* 1.53, pp. 119–20), belief in multiple attributes is part of the same mistake that causes belief in corporeality: reading sacred texts in a literal fashion. Again, no one but the most extreme fundamentalist would disagree.

Where Maimonides' doctrine becomes controversial is on the issue of negative theology. Is it true that when we say "God lives," all we mean is "God does not lack animation nor is God alive according to a conventional understanding of the term"? We saw that while negative predicates still particularize God to some extent, they have one advantage over positive ones (*GP* 1.59, p. 139): "Negation does not give knowledge in any respect of the true reality of the thing." In other words, it does not furnish any knowledge of the thing's essence. But if this is all we mean, religious language is an extravagant way to make a very simple point: that God's perfection is beyond our understanding.

Before we turn to the specifics of Aquinas' critique of Maimonides, it will be helpful to consider their points of agreement. Aquinas agrees that God is "altogether simple, not divided in any way" (*ST* 1.11.4). He agrees that God's essence as it is in itself is unknowable in this life (*ST* 1.12.11–12).[8] And he agrees that the divine names cannot be univocal because, when used of creatures, a word like *wise* is superadded to the essence of the subject but is not superadded when used of God (*ST* 1.13.5). In one passage (*ST* I. 3. intro), he even accepts the gist of negative theology, saying, "Now because we cannot know what God is, but rather what He is not, we have no means for considering how God is, but rather how He is not." His disagreement with Maimonides concerns the claim that divine names are *purely* equivocal. Behind Maimonides' view is the belief that God does not resemble creatures in *any* respect; if no resemblance, then no common thread of meaning.

Aquinas therefore offers two criticisms of Maimonides (*ST* 1.13.2).[9] The first is that the theory cannot account for why certain names are used of God but others are not. To this criticism Maimonides has an easy response: Religious language has to appeal to a general audience. Thus the sacred books do not attribute to God any qualities that ordinary people would regard as a deficiency or privation (*GP* 1.26, p. 56). If they did, people would form a negative opinion of God and cease to obey the Law. So even though terms like *stupid* or *cowardly* might mean something completely different when applied to God than they do when applied to us, the issue is moot because the prophetic tradition does not sanction their use.

This criticism could be pressed further by pointing out, as Gersonides does, that we still need to know *why* the prophetic tradition does not sanction their use.[10] Unless there is some similarity between the meaning of these terms when used to describe imperfections in us and imperfections in God, we have no basis for denying them of God. If there is a similarity with respect to negative terms, why should there not also be one with respect to positive terms? Why, in other words, should we not say that there is a core meaning to *wise* or *merciful* when used of a sage and of God?

Maimonides' answer is that denying imperfections of God is true and valuable *up to a point*. He himself never fails to insist that God is not corporeal. But the proposition "God is not corporeal" cannot be true as it stands. For if we take it as literally true, we would have to say that God is in the same category as numbers, heavenly intelligences, and other things that have no material component. As we saw, even negative predicates particularize God to some degree. The proposition "God is not corporeal" would have to be analyzed as "God is not corporeal in the way that normal objects of experience are or *in*corporeal in the way that abstract or heavenly entities are." In other words, negating corporeality of God is fundamentally different from negating it of anything else. In God's case, the denial not only rejects the predicate in question but puts God outside the scope of the predicate or anything like it. To the question "How do we know which negations to make?" Maimonides' answer is that at one level we negate predicates that suggest imperfection to the average worshipper, but at another level we negate all predicates.[11] In either case, there is no common core of meaning once we take into account the full extent of the negation.

Aquinas' second criticism, as David Burrell points out, is not based on metaphysics as much as it is on religious practice: that Maimonides' view is "against the intention of those who speak of God."[12] In other words, Maimonides' attempt to translate what look like affirmative statements into negations is too radical an assault on ordinary usage. According to Aquinas, those who praise God for being wise mean more than that God does not lack wisdom or possess it in a conventional way.

There is a sense in which Aquinas is right: Maimonides does not think he is bound by ordinary usage. Unlike the *Summa*, the *Guide* is not written for a general audience but for an observant Jew who has been exposed to the sciences. In fact, Maimonides goes to great lengths to ensure that general audiences will not read his work. While Judaism mandates daily prayer, it forbids one to discuss speculative matters in public.[13] One reason for the prohibition is that, unlike Christianity, Judaism does not have formal articles of faith.[14] Without a body of official doctrine to fall back on, it is hard to know how people will understand terms like *God, creation,* or *providence.* Needless to say, loose talk can have a damaging effect. The result is that Judaism discourages people from discussing these things except in a highly structured environment.

We saw that on the subject of ordinary usage (*GP* 1.57, p. 132), Maimonides believes that the customary words are "the greatest among the causes leading to error" and therefore "the bounds of expression in all languages are very narrow indeed." And we saw that he is quite scornful of "poets and preachers" whose utterances "constitute an absolute denial of faith, while other utterances contain such rubbish and such perverse imaginings as to make men laugh when they hear them." To support his position, he quotes Ecclesiastes 5:1: "For God is in heaven and you upon the earth; therefore let your words be few." Or, as the mishnaic tractate *Pirkei Avot* (3.17) puts it: "Silence is a fence to wisdom."[15]

Whether perfect worship is possible for a human being is another question, but Maimonides would hardly shudder at the thought that he had raised doubts about a sizable chunk of religious discourse. Provided we were careful to explain what motivated these doubts, he would be proud of it. Another way to see this point is to recognize that for Maimonides, existing habits of speech are not a given.[16] They are instead patterns of thought that the wise person must understand and eventually reject. Aquinas, on the other hand, is not willing to take such a radical step. Though he agrees that the bounds of expression in all languages are limited, he still thinks we can agree that the essence of God is unknowable and leave many of our linguistic practices intact. The goal for Aquinas is to show how positive predicates can be meaningful without compromising God's uniqueness.[17]

Analogy

Aquinas' solution to the problem of religious language is the doctrine of analogy, the crux of which is a distinction between the perfections that are signified (*res significata*) and the mode of signification (*modus significandi*). With respect to what is signified, the divine names are used properly of God—in fact, more properly of God than of creatures because God contains all perfections in a preeminent fashion. But the mode of signification is imperfect because it belongs most properly to us. The latter point is what enables

Burrell to say that "Aquinas' resolution of the matter retains a generous dose of the 'unknowing' that Maimonides sought to secure."[18] For while it is true and meaningful to say *that* God is wise, our understanding of *what* wisdom is in God remains inadequate. As Aquinas reminds us (*ST* 1.13.5), the term *wise* when applied to God "leaves the thing signified as uncomprehended and as exceeding the signification of the name."[19] So all we get from Aquinas is the ability to talk about, not comprehend, a being whose perfection is not proportionate to ours.[20] We can signify without knowing how or why the signification is true. Again from Burrell, the purpose of the divine names is to point beyond us and our mode of signifying to something greater.

Another way to understand Aquinas' position is to recall his objection to Maimonides: Negative theology is against the *intention* of those who speak of God. The divine names are part of a language spoken by humans. As such, they have no magical power: The name is still disproportionate to the thing named. But when used properly, divine names allow the speaker to intend something more than negation. In Aquinas' words: "In the signification of names, that from which the name is derived is different sometimes from what it is intended to signify." The fact that *wise* may be derived from our experience does not prevent us from using it to signify perfect wisdom in God.[21] We saw that Maimonides also believes that religious language can "give the mind the correct direction" or "conduct the mind toward the utmost reach that man may attain." The difference is that Maimonides would insist that the speakers and their mode of signification are too imperfect for pointing fully to succeed; hence the qualification *the utmost reach that man may attain.*

Why can pointing not succeed? The difference between Maimonides and Aquinas on language is symptomatic of a greater difference on metaphysics. Aquinas takes issue with the claim that God does not resemble creatures in any respect. It is true that the likeness of creatures to God is imperfect because "it does not represent the same thing even generically." But where Maimonides argues that two things in different genera bear no relation to each other, Aquinas disagrees. The basis of Aquinas' opposition is the idea that if God is the cause of creatures, creatures must bear some similarity to God (*ST* 1.13.5): "Whatever is said of God and creatures is said according as there is some relation of the creature to God as to its principle and cause." Earlier (*ST* 1.13.2) Aquinas clarifies this relation by saying that every creature represents God and is like God insofar as it possesses some perfection. Creatures and God exist together in a community that allows speakers of the language to predicate terms by analogy. Analogy, then, is a mean between complete equivocation and simple univocation. If univocation would imply that God is too much like us, complete equivocation would lead to some form of skepticism.

From Maimonides' standpoint, skepticism is not necessarily a bad thing. Once the average person is persuaded that God is not corporeal and that the sacred books are not committed to anthropomorphism, most of the battle is won. As for the educated few, all we can expect are momentary flashes of insight. Again, Aquinas is more optimistic. The goal of the *Summa* is to set forth the truth of sacred doctrine "briefly and clearly." The reason for doing so is that the subject has been cluttered with too many useless questions or disputations. We saw, however, that Maimonides warns the reader that even when a person of extraordinary talents tries to set forth "something that he understands . . . he is unable to explain with complete clarity and coherence even the portion that he has apprehended."

To return to metaphysics, Aquinas has to explain how two things in different genera can be related, or more precisely, how one thing that does not fall within any genus is related to things that do. According to Aristotle, relations typically have correlates with which they are interdependent: The existence of a master necessitates the existence of a slave, and the existence of the double necessitates the existence of the half.[22] But it cannot be the case that God's existence is in any way dependent on that of creatures. Aquinas points out, however, that Aristotle made an exception for knowledge and its object. Clearly the object is independent of and unaffected by our knowing it. Aquinas concludes that the relation between God and creatures is "mixed" in the sense that creatures are related to God even though God bears no real relation to creatures, only a relation of reason (*rationem*).[23] This means that while the resemblance of creatures to God is a fact about them, the resemblance of God to creatures is something that arises only in our minds when we intend to signify God's perfection.

Maimonides, of course, does not admit any relation between God and creatures and continues to insist that all language obscures the primary fact of God's simplicity. For Maimonides, all relations are accidents, and God cannot be the subject of accidents (*GP* 1.52, p. 118): "Even if it is not an accident with regard to His essence . . . nevertheless it is, generally speaking, some sort of accident." But despite his preference for silence, Maimonides must still confront the issue of prayer. Even if prayer poses a danger and should be preceded by a warning, Maimonides cannot say that it is meaningless. After all, Judaism requires it, and he himself engaged in it. So while prayer may not be the highest form of worship, it is still a legitimate one.

Attributes of Action

Maimonides' solution to the problem is to abandon the category of relation and try to work with that of action. In commenting on Exodus 33:18–19, where Moses is allowed to see the ways of God, Maimonides introduces the idea of an attribute of action (*GP* 1.54, p. 125):

> It thus has become clear to you that the *ways* and the *characteristics* are identical. They are the actions proceeding from God . . . in reference to the world. Accordingly, whenever one of His actions is apprehended, the attribute from which the action proceeds is predicated of Him . . . and the name deriving from that attribute is applied to Him. For instance, one apprehends the kindness of His governance in the production of the embryos of living beings, the bringing of various faculties to existence in them and those who rear them after birth—faculties that preserve them from destruction and annihilation and protect them against harm and are useful to them in all the doings that are necessary to them. Now actions of this kind proceed from us only after we feel a certain affection and compassion, and this is the meaning of mercy. God . . . is said to be *merciful*, just as it is said, *Like a father is merciful to his children.*

Before going further, we must take account of two points. The first is that attributes of action are not based on an underlying similarity between God and us. As this quotation makes clear, moral actions in us proceed from affections or emotions. But God cannot possess affections or emotions of any kind. So the meaning is not that God possesses moral qualilities analogous to ours but that God performs actions which resemble actions that proceed from moral qualities in us. In other words, if there is a comparison, it is not between God and us but between the outcome of divine activity and the outcome of ours.[24]

The second is that attributes of action are not properties of God's essence but of what God has made or done. Note, for example, that at *GP* 1.54, Maimonides refrains from saying God *is* merciful and says instead that God is *called* merciful or *said* to be merciful. The difference indicates that even though we may praise God, it is still true that God is not a subject of predication. According to Maimonides (*GP* 1.53, p. 122), "These attributes too are not to be considered in reference to His essence, but in reference to the things that are created." Thus Maimonides connects the attributes of action with Genesis 1:31: "And God saw everything He had made, and, behold, it was very good." So far from telling us something about God, the attributes of action are observable features of the world around us. That is why Moses was allowed to see them and we are able to emulate them.

Seymour Feldman is therefore right to say that Maimonides does not regard God's actions as accidents that inhere in their subject in Aristotle's sense of the term.[25] Rather than aptitudes of the soul, God's attributes of action are events that proceed from God as heat proceeds from a fire (*GP* 1.53, p. 120). Just as the activity of one fire hardens, softens, cooks, bleaches, and blackens depending on the things around it, so, Maimonides argues, a unified God can be merciful, gracious, forgiving, and so on depending on the things that receive the consequences of divine activity.

The attributes of action enable us to say we can know God, *if* we admit that our knowledge is always a step removed: Our knowledge deals with the ways divinity manifests itself in the natural order rather than with the "essence" of divinity or divinity as it is in itself. Recall that at Exodus 33:23, Moses was permitted to see God's back but not God's face. Knowing God through attributes of action in this way would be like knowing a fire from the things that it hardens, softens, and bleaches. But even this example can be misleading. Fire is an earthly phenomenon. As such it has an identifiable nature or essence that is causally connected to the surrounding air. While it is true that one cause can have multiple effects, causality is a relation, and relation, as we saw, is an accident. Maimonides' point is that action does not come from wells or springs in God but proceeds from God without destroying divine simplicity. The fire example would be better if, after seeing the hardening, softening, and bleaching, we resisted the temptation to ask how they were produced or what the thing that produced them is like. This is another way of saying that the fire example works only if we accept the general thrust of Maimonides' negative theology. In modern terms, God is the one who makes merciful and gracious things happen even though strictly speaking God is not merciful or gracious.

It may be objected that both Maimonides and Aquinas stretch our linguistic intuitions to some extent. Where one asks us to accept the idea of a mixed relation or asymmetrical resemblance between God and creatures, the other asks us to make a critical distinction between "God *is* Q" and "Q-like things proceed from God."[26] To the question "How do they proceed from God?" Maimonides has no answer except to say that God remains simple despite the fact that there are a variety of things in the world that give us reason to praise God. As we will see in the next chapter, the details of how the world was created are as mysterious as the essence of the Creator. The best we can do to understand creation is to think of it as something God has done rather than something that establishes a bridge between God and other things. In short God creates the world but does not enter into relation with it.

Maimonides would be the first to admit that by denying that God *is* merciful and gracious, he is proposing something that sounds strange, even heretical, to untrained ears. We saw, however, that all language distorts divine simplicity to some extent. Maimonides' goal is to introduce as little distortion as possible, to show that we can praise God as the eternal source of mercy and graciousness without lapsing into anthropomorphism. We can praise God if we realize that doing so is not like heaping compliments on a queen or a commanding officer. Praise of God is either a step removed or a process designed to teach us that ultimately God is beyond praise. Awareness of these qualifications may make us more self-conscious about praying, more willing to see that prayer is a complex activity that raises questions about language and its limitations. But the fact that prayer causes us to reflect on our limitations does not imply that it is meaningless or that people who derive satisfaction from it are stupid. So far from separating the "masses" from the "educated few," prayer breaks down the division by allowing us to see that everyone faces the same difficulties so that ultimately (*GP* 1.58, p. 137) "all eloquence turns into weariness and incapacity."

While prayer is meaningful, we do not have to say that it represents the last word in religious discourse. Since it contains visual imagery, evocative terminology, and any number of positive attributes, the language of prayer can never be as perspicuous as the language of negation. We saw that in Maimonides' opinion, even the language of negation falls short of a studied silence. All are valid as ways of turning the mind away from temporal existence and preparing it to contemplate eternal. The fact that there are problems associated with some of the intermediate stages does not mean that we are justified in short-circuiting the process and turning to contemplation right away. Nor does it mean that once contemplation is achieved, prayer is no longer necessary: The obligation to pray applies to everyone.

Surely the greatest mistake we can make is to insist that because prayer is meaningful to us, because *we* derive comfort or edification from praising God, God must fit our categories and be understood according to our terms. The greatest mistake, in other words, is to think that because we can talk about God, God can be our friend, partner, or personal advisor. On this point, Maimonides and Aquinas are in complete agreement. Though Aquinas speaks of a community between God and us, this fact should not prevent us from seeing that it is a community by analogy, with all the limitations that idea imposes. For both thinkers, *how* God is wise, merciful, or gracious is beyond our comprehension.

It could be said, therefore, that prayer puts us in the presence of an other who insists on otherness. If it did not raise special problems, prayer would encourage us to think of God as ordinary and to believe that we can call on God the way we call on room service in a fancy hotel. By asking us to praise something completely different from ourselves, prayer also asks us to see ourselves from a higher perspective. In the words of Ehud Benor: "Recognition of the greatness of God that surpasses all existence, awareness of the ultimate dependence of all that is on the being of God, and acknowledgment of the pure graciousness of the divine sustenance of the universe are necessary elements of the intellectual love of God as it is conceived by Maimonides."[27]

Language as a Form of Idolatry

At this point, it might be helpful if we looked at Maimonides not with respect to his differences with Aquinas but with respect to his similarity with Plato. In a well-known passage in the *Seventh Letter* (341b–c), Plato says that no one who really understood philosophy would write a book about it because:

> This knowledge can never be put into words like other subjects; but is generated by living with the matter itself and from many conversations. Then like a flashing light when a fire is kindled, it is born in the soul and nourishes itself.

Although some scholars have taken this remark to imply dissatisfaction with *written* language and gone on to argue that Plato had a secret doctrine that he shared with a few close associates, the better and more interesting reading is that he is expressing a dissatisfaction with all language, written and oral.[28]

To be sure, Plato does not think it is possible to achieve this kind of illumination without extensive philosophic training: Hence the reference to conversation (*sunousia*). In fact, he goes on to say that he has claimed many times before that for every real being, there are

three things that are necessary if we are to achieve knowledge: the
name, the definition, and the physical or plastic image (*eidolon*). He
then puts knowledge, reason, and right opinion in a fourth category
and the object itself in a fifth. When the first three are "rubbed together" and tested with teacher and pupil asking and answering questions, then, if we stretch reason and knowledge to the limit, it is
barely possible that the object will be illuminated (344b). Clearly,
then, the object itself is distinct from its definition or from the knowledge we use to apprehend it. All we can do by rubbing names, definitions, and images together is compare theories and arguments in a
dialectical fashion, hoping to put ourselves in a position where the
object itself will shine forth. It follows that the things other than
the object are really instruments by which the object is presented
or disclosed. As Socrates says in an autobiographical section of the
Phaedo (99e), in his early years he was afraid of being blinded by
looking directly at things with his eyes, so like people who view an
eclipse by examining its reflection in water, he decided to take
refuge in *logoi*.

The problem is that instruments that present something to the
mind run the risk of calling attention to themselves rather than to
the reality they depict. This is especially true if one believes, as Plato
does, that language is inherently unstable (343a–b). So the instruments we use to study reality all have what Gadamer terms "an intrinsic distortion tendency." As Plato describes it, they "present to
the soul in discourse and examples something it is not seeking,"
what the thing is like (*to poion ti*) rather than what it is (*to ti*). This is
another way of saying that all the instruments at our disposal are fallible: Even knowledge, which Plato thinks is closest in affinity to the
object itself (342d), leaves us short of the burst of light that is born in
the soul after years of living with the reality and conversing about it.

Maimonides would be sympathetic to this account for several
reasons. Although he is not talking about an object with an essence,
he would agree that while prayer, attributes of action, and negative
attributes all serve a legitimate function, they too distort the nature
of their subject by introducing grammatical complexity and some
form of particularization. When not understood properly, they draw
the mind to themselves rather than the reality to which they are supposed to point. As he puts it (*GP* 2.5, p. 260): "He who praises through
speech only makes known what he has represented to himself." As
we saw earlier, belief in positive attributes is the result of reading sacred texts too literally (*GP* 1.53, pp. 119–20). For Maimonides, too,

language is an instrument that if used properly over a long period can direct the mind to something nonlinguistic. But he never tires of pointing out that fallibility and confusion are part of the human condition. His way of overcoming this distortion is to lead the reader in the direction of silence.

Still, the reference to images and modes of presentation shows exactly what is at stake. Note, for example, that Plato treats names, definitions, images, and knowledge as if they were similar. The thing they have in common is that they are devices other than the original that we use to try to grasp the original. It follows that if religious language does not "give the mind the correct direction toward the true reality" (*GP* 1.57, p. 133), if lavish praise attracts attention away from the thing itself, then even the most sincere praise can become a nonplastic idol, a way of serving an imitator or surrogate. The same is true of knowledge if we take something that is a human accomplishment and treat it as if it were something more.

It is noteworthy that while he warned about the limitations of language, Plato was still able to embark on a brilliant literary career; he was able to write in a way that calls attention to the limitations of communication. Rather than write essays, he wrote dialogues; rather than leave people with the impression that they understood the subject, he often left them with the impression that they had to continue the search. As he says in the *Seventh Letter* (341e), his writing is not intended for the multitude but for those who could "with a little guidance discover the truth for themselves." It is difficult to read this passage and not think of Maimonides' warning that he cannot be completely explicit and can only furnish a well-trained and attentive student with "chapter headings" (*GP* 1. Introduction, pp. 6–7). The difference is that Maimonides must still deal with prayer as an obligatory ritual while Plato does not. Plato's philosopher-kings may have to go back down to the cave and converse with others, but there is nothing to suggest that they themselves must continue to repeat the words, definitions, and dialectical exercises that got them there in the first place.

Prayer as a Concession

Until now we have looked at prayer as a legitimate, if not optimal, form of worship. But more needs to be said on this subject. Unlike religious thinkers in the nineteenth century, Maimonides does not view human history as an upward movement beginning with pagan-

ism and culminating in monotheism. Since human beings incline toward the things to which they are habituated (*GP* 1.31, p. 67), a resur-
gence of paganism is always possible. Not surprisingly, he accepts a
long-standing tradition according to which the Israelites adopted the
religious practices of their captors during the Egyptian captivity: [29]

> When the Israelites had stayed a long while in Egypt, they relapsed,
> learned the practices of their neighbors, and, like them, worshipped idols,
> with the exception of the tribe of Levi, that steadfastly kept the charge
> of the patriarch [Abraham]. This tribe of Levi never practiced idolatry.
> The doctrine implanted by Abraham would, in a very short time, have
> been uprooted, and Jacob's descendants would have lapsed into the error
> and perversities universally prevalent. But because of God's love for us
> and because He kept the oath made to our ancestor Abraham, He ap-
> pointed Moses to be our teacher.

According to Maimonides, there was no philosophic problem with
Abraham's understanding of monotheism; but because it relied too
heavily on abstract arguments, he failed as a legislator and did not
leave a lasting impression in people's minds.

From Maimonides' perspective, Abraham's failure underscored
the need for Moses. Since people became so accustomed to erroneous
beliefs and practices, Moses could not ask them to make a sudden
transition from a pagan religion to a monotheistic one and had to settle for gradual improvement (*GP* 3.32, p. 526). That is why the religion Moses instituted contained a luxurious sanctuary, priestly vestments, fast days, animal sacrifice, and other practices that resembled
what the people saw in Egypt. It is noteworthy that one of the things
Maimonides mentions in this connection is prayer. At *GP* 3.32, p.
526, he says that if Moses had claimed that the Law forbade prayer,
fasting, or any effort to call on God in times of need, and if it went on
to say that worship should consist solely of meditation, it would
have been rejected. Thus prayer is a way to give the people something
with which they were accustomed.

Unfortunately Moses' attempt to turn the people's hearts to God
met with another relapse. In the *Mishneh Torah* (2, Laws of Prayer,
1.4), Maimonides argues that during the age of Nebuchadnezzar the
people mingled with other nations, so no one could express anything
clearly in a single language or recount the praises of the Lord in Hebrew. Finally, in Rabbi Gamliel's time, the heretics increased and
tried to get the people to turn away from God.[30] In Maimonides'
opinion, the only reasonable response was to standardize the language of prayer so that everyone from the eloquent to the slow of
speech could praise God without introducing foreign elements.

Though prayer in the biblical period had been relatively open and spontaneous, the rabbis had no choice but to replace it with statutory prayer in the hope that they could prevent yet another relapse and, in Twersky's words, try to "restore the original monotheism."[31]

What are we to make of this account? Since Maimonides never doubts that silent contemplation is the highest form of worship, we are again left with the conclusion that prayer, though not ultimate, is at least legitimate. In the context of public worship, where social differences between people count for nothing, it may even be a great equalizer.[32] But we are also left with the conclusion that ultimately the function of prayer is not to lift people to a higher level of awareness but to prevent them from falling to lower ones. In the words of Hermann Cohen (*RR*, p. 375), prayer is an idealization of "the highest end in life," which is the human need to seek redemption from sin. Thus (*RR*, p. 399): "Whoever has the mastery of true prayer loses earthly fears and earthly heaviness in his ascent to infinity." But Cohen reflects the optimism of his time. The thrust of Maimonides' position is that prayer as we know it was a response to deteriorating conditions. The difference between them is analogous to that between political theorists who see the state as a way to allow people to perfect their nature as rational agents and those who see it as an attempt to prevent the outbreak of anarchy.

We can appreciate the difference by recognizing that people have a natural desire to praise God, beseech God, or cry out to God in times of need. According to Fox:[33]

> Prayer is a basic and irrepressible expression of the human spirit. Perhaps the pure intellect that has advanced to the true intellectual apprehension of God no longer needs ordinary prayer. . . . The ideal praise of God may well be, as Maimonides suggests, the wordless praise of the spheres, but how can this ideal ever be realized in actual human lives? Our apprehension is imperfect at best, and our dependence on language is deep. We cannot conceptualize without language, although we are fully aware that our conceptions are defective and our language inaccurate with respect to God.

Although Fox may be too optimistic in saying that we are "fully aware" that our language is defective, he is certainly right in saying that our dependence on language is deep. Where Cohen (*RR*, p. 371) sees the language of prayer as "the proper expression of reason," Maimonides clearly does not. To repeat: Even the highest intellects only get a few flashes of insight and have difficulty communicating them. If they have difficulty, how much more will the rest of us have?

From Maimonides' perspective, the situation is this. We all need

language to begin to think about God. Even the best language introduces distortions, and there is no guarantee that everything we hear
will be the best. How do you satisfy the need to talk both to and
about God at the same time that you put up a defense against "poets
and preachers" who run on at the mouth? From a contemporary perspective, how do you encourage people to pray but prevent them
from taking the unfortunate connotations of their language to heart?
On the one hand, you have to give people something important to
say; on the other hand, you cannot encourage them to think that
prayer is a context where more is necessarily better.

Maimonides' solution is to fall back on tradition. The human
need to talk to and about God is satisfied by repeating highly structured phrases. Since the language of prayer is fixed, people are not
free to introduce new and even more misleading characterizations of
a God who is radically simple. Thus the only attributes we are
justified in using are those found in the Torah or sanctioned by rabbinic authority (*GP* 1.59, pp. 142):

> You accordingly ought not to set forth in any respect the attributes of
> God in an affirmative way—with a view, as you think, to magnifying
> Him—and ought not to go beyond that which has been inserted in the
> prayers and *benedictions* by the *men of the Great Synagogue*. For this is
> sufficient from the point of view of necessity; in fact, as *Rabbi Ḥaninah*
> said, it is amply sufficient. But regarding the other attributes that occur
> in the books of the prophets and are recited during the perusal of these
> books . . . they are attributes of action or . . . they indicate the negation
> of their nonexistence in God.

It should be understood that Maimonides is not talking about the
things one can say to God in personal confession but the attributes
one can predicate of God in statutory prayer. His claim is that
making God the subject of attributes is a necessity we must live
with as long as the number of attributes is limited. It would be better if we did not make God the subject of attributes at all, but
under the circumstances, a fixed set of attributes is preferable to
carte blanche. Once we allowed people to go beyond the traditional
benedictions, our concept of God would become nothing but a
loose grab bag of descriptions people associate with divinity. By
contrast, one can easily imagine Maimonides agreeing with Mies
van der Rohe that less is more.

Most of the attributes mentioned in statutory prayer are attributes of action involving gender-neutral descriptions such as mercy,
graciousness, justice, healing the sick, or making peace. While it

is true that God is described as "great" and "mighty," Maimonides would reply that divine power and greatness have nothing in common with the human variety and that any attempt to extrapolate from military or political leaders to God is completely misguided.[34] Statutory prayer does refer to God as "God of our fathers" and "shield of Abraham." Though Maimonides himself does not allow for alterations, the addition of "God of our mothers" and "protector of Sarah" would do little to change his overall view of prayer, because whatever formula we employ, we will confront the same problem: Strictly speaking, all formulas are false.

Like animal sacrifice, prayer is a concession.[35] Obviously God does not need food to survive or the smell of incense to be pleased. Nor for that matter did people need sacrifice to achieve holiness. Maimonides (*GP* 3.32, pp. 330–31) therefore quotes Jeremiah 7:22–23 ("For I spoke not unto your fathers, nor commanded them in the day that I brought them out of the land Egypt, concerning burnt offerings or sacrifices") in claiming that the Ten Commandments make no mention of sacrifice and that in general sacrifices are not part of the first intention of the Law, which is to worship God and nothing else. But sacrifice was meaningful to people in the ancient world because it allowed them to pay tribute to God and to acknowledge the importance of God in their lives. At its best, sacrifice enabled people to overcome the burden of guilt and reinstate themselves in the holy order. So even though sacrifice is not really necessary, a religion without it would have struck people as a contradiction in terms (*GP* 3.32, p. 526).

In time people came to realize that sacrifice is subject to abuse and that, even if done properly, it does not always focus attention on the most important aspect of the religion: love of God. Hence the emergence of prayer, which has the advantage of not requiring priests or luxurious sanctuaries and makes greater demands on the sincerity of the individual. Here too people can pay tribute to God, acknowledge the sovereignty of God, and seek redemption from God. Not only is prayer a response to emotions like awe or gratitude, it is a way of evoking and sustaining them. As Benor points out, prayer can be viewed as formative. The person who praises God for making peace is encouraged to adopt peace as a goal; the person who offers thanks to God is encouraged to feel grateful, and so on. As Benor puts it: "In learning to will that which is desirable in itself, the worshipper is learning to desire the kind of things that can be thought to have been primordially programmed by God into the general structure of providence."[36] Prayer, then, is both a cause and an effect, both a way of asking for things and a way of making us reflect on what we have asked for.

But even if one gains mastery in Cohen's sense, prayer is still a means to an end rather than the end itself.[37] Like sacrifice, it is our way of gaining the courage and integrity to love a God we cannot see. Because it is not an end in itself, prayer is a two-edged sword. If it can give you the courage to stand before God, it can also give you the boldness to think that God is at your beck and call; if it allows you to reinstate yourself, it can also make you think that God is easily appeased. Note, for example, that one of the problems with sacrifice is that it was not always accompanied by improvement in behavior. Unfortunately the same is true of prayer.

More important from Maimonides' perspective, prayer contains attributes that describe God in the only terms people can understand—their own. God is great, mighty, exalted, healer of the sick, maker of peace, shield of Abraham, and our partner throughout the ages. Part of the reason for skepticism is that despite the enormous differences between monotheism and paganism, from a psychological standpoint the line separating them can be very thin. You can read a prayer a thousand times, read it in an attentive and reverent frame of mind, but if you find yourself praying to a superhuman figure with multiple perfections, in Maimonides' opinion you are no closer to God than a pagan Greek who worshipped Zeus. So one of the most important decisions in your life, perhaps the single most important, can rest on something as precarious as your response to a series of metaphors. That is why we must be careful which metaphors are used and whether people are clear that they are in fact metaphors. As I argued earlier, it is not enough to say "as it were" and assume everything will be fine.

From the skeptic's point of view, the justification for prayer is that, great as its dangers may be, the dangers of avoiding it are even greater. On the issue of heresy, we saw that Maimonides meant business: A person who does not accept the unity and incorporeality of God is cut off from Israel and has no chance of redemption.[38] Although few people hold such a radical view today, there is no getting around the fact that even the most perfect prayer carries no guarantee that it will be interpreted correctly. And while a person may not be cut off from Israel and despised for an incorrect interpretation, if I am right, he or she certainly will miss the greatest contribution the religion has to offer.

While statutory prayer exists at the expense of spontaneity, it is questionable whether spontaneity is necessary for spiritual growth. Surely it is possible to read the works of Shakespeare and come to the conclusion that he did a better job of expressing your own feelings about love, hate, and fear than you could do yourself. One does not need widespread experience to see that much the same is true of the prophets and religious language. I have already argued that it is a mistake to think that we can relate to God with the same innocence that we attribute to Moses and the patriarchs. Our rituals, attitudes, and expectations are informed by the writings of people whose eloquence and clarity of vision have stood as a paradigm for two millennia. Take away the Psalms, for example, and few if any worshippers would be able to call on the vocabulary now at their disposal. But even if we could inspire the same emotions as those touched by the prophets, or write with the same force and vividness, there is still the question of distortion. Allow people to introduce anything they want and you run the risk of introducing more egregious forms of multiplicity.

Contemplation as a Religious Ideal

We saw that for Maimonides, the highest form of worship is contemplative rather than verbal. In the Parable of the Palace (*GP* 3.51, p. 620) he tells us that after people achieve mastery of divine science or metaphysics, there is a small group who put their thought to work and "turn wholly toward God . . . renounce what is other than He, and direct all the acts of their intellect toward an examination of the beings with a view to drawing from them proof with regard to Him, so as to know His governance of them in whatever way it is possible."[39] He then tells us that worship at this level, what the rabbis call *worship of the heart*, is the result of loving God and that love "can only be engaged in after apprehension has been achieved." Such worship, which is achieved mostly in solitude and isolation, is contrasted with the activity of people who think and frequently talk about God on the basis of imagination or beliefs adopted on someone else's authority.

In fact, Maimonides goes on to say that when extraordinary individuals like Moses and the patriarchs talk to others or are occupied with bodily necessities, inwardly their thoughts are turned toward God. They may deal with affairs of this world, but they are completely detached and perform their activities in a dispassionate way. I will not dwell on the question of whether such a state can be

reached by anyone in this life. For present purposes, all we need to
know is that Maimonides holds out the possibility that a person can
go beyond the apprehension of physics and metaphysics to complete
devotion to God.[40] In what follows, *prophet* will refer to a person in
the latter category.

What interests me is the question of why prophets must still engage in prayer. If you are aware of the pitfalls of language, what is to
be gained by repeating the usual praises and benedictions? The question is all the more important because Maimonides insists (*GP* 3.51,
p. 620) that for those who have apprehended the true realities, the
more they think of God, the more their worship increases.[41] I take
this to mean that not only does pure worship or worship of the heart
increase, but traditional worship does as well. So while prophets may
kick away the ladder in the sense of recognizing the limitations of
worship at lower levels, they do not kick it away in the sense of aban-
doning the obligations it imposes.

The simple answer to the question of prayer is to compare prophets with philosopher-kings and say that since the former must establish a community devoted to the worship of God, they have no choice
but to return to the multitude and set a good example. But this answer is misleading because it assumes that the worship of prophets
would be of no intrinsic value to prophets themselves and is undertaken merely to impress others.

A better answer is to begin by asking what prophets are thinking
about during their moments of solitude and isolation. From what we
have seen, they would have to begin with one of two things: (1) God's
attributes of action, or as Maimonides calls it, God's "governance" of
the created order, and (2) negative predicates and God's ultimate unknowability. From things Maimonides says elsewhere, we can conclude that prophets would have mastery of the sacred books, ability
to demonstrate the existence and unity of God, and advanced training in physics, astronomy, and mathematics. Alternatively they
would have no interest in personal matters or anything else pertaining to the earthly realm. But because of the "dark veil" that matter
imposes on them, their knowledge would still be speculative in some
places and incomplete in others. Note, for example, that when Maimonides describes the intellectual preparation needed to become a
prophet, he does so with numerous qualifications (*GP* 3.51, p. 619):

> He, however, who has achieved demonstration, to the extent that that is
> possible, of everything that may be demonstrated; and who has ascer-
> tained in divine matters, to the extent that that is possible, everything

that may be ascertained; and who has come close to certainty in those matters in which one can come close to it—has come to be with the ruler in the inner part of the habitation.

I take this to mean that unlike philosopher-kings, who see the sun without looking at images or reflections, prophets will have moments of self-doubt—not about their fortunes or place in society but about matters in which certainty is beyond the reach of the human intellect.[42] In fact, prophets will probably have more doubts than others, because in this context it is the fool who claims to know for certain.

It should be understood that by self-doubt I do not mean sadness or depression but a dispassionate assessment of what one knows and where one stands. In the *Mishneh Torah* (1, Basic Principles, 4. 12) Maimonides describes it as follows:[43]

> When a man reflects on these things, studies all these created beings, from the angels and spheres down to human beings and so on, and realizes the divine wisdom manifested in them all, his love for God will increase, his soul will thirst, his very flesh will yearn to love God. He will be filled with fear and trembling, as he becomes conscious of his lowly condition, poverty, and insignificance, and compares himself with any of the great and holy bodies; still more when he compares himself with any one of the pure forms that are incorporeal and have never had association with any corporeal substance. He will then realize that he is a vessel full of shame, dishonor, and reproach, empty and deficient.

We will be making a big mistake unless we see that just as love of God is different from romantic love, the shame, dishonor, and reproach Maimonides is talking about in this passage are of a different order than the emotions one would feel if embarrassed at a social gathering.[44] Maimonides is talking not about falling short of customs imposed by one's fellow human beings, but of failing to reach knowledge that one desperately wants to have. But the fact remains that despite reaching the highest point in the spiritual ladder, prophets will experience a profound sense of inadequacy.[45] As we saw, even Moses did not get everything he wanted.

Though a prophet may not need prayer to call forth feelings of reverence, and would not be foolish enough to think that worship ends when statutory prayer is completed, there is no reason to think that praise or expressions of thanksgiving from the mouth of a prophet will be forced or insincere. While others may offer praise to obtain health, prosperity, and personal satisfaction, the prophet will offer praise for God's governance of the entire created order. The prophet, in other words, will not ask God to make momentary changes in that order but will see it as a manifestation of God's mercy and graciousness. Where others experience fear and trembling at the prospect of death or misfortune, the prophet will experience fear and trembling when contemplating the vastness of heaven and the contingency of her own existence. As we will see later on, existence is something we get from God but not something we have a right to claim. It is, as one might say, a gift, and for that reason it is perfectly appropriate for even the wisest of people to offer thanksgiving for it.

In regard to petition, statutory prayers ask for things like guidance, forgiveness, redemption, health, prosperity, and salvation. But each request ends with an expression of gratitude praising God as the One who gives what the worshipper has asked for. For the prophet, petition will be a way not of seeking special favors but of drawing attention to the structure of the world in which God has placed us. In short, there will be no presumption that praise of God is tied to specific performance.[46] Finally, if the majority of worshippers need courage to love a God they cannot see, it is not out of the question that prophets will need courage to love a God whose greatness they admit they cannot comprehend.[47] I suggest, therefore, that it does not take an extraordinary act of imagination to picture a prophet reading a psalm or thanking God in the required way.

In this respect, religion is no different from science. Both laypeople and specialists talk about atoms, the flow of electrons, or cellular walls despite the fact that these expressions are metaphors that cannot survive literal interpretation. Though a physicist could explain why electrons do not really move through a circuit the way water flows through a pipe, it does not follow that physicists are compromising their principles by using these expressions or that they have to look on the speech of laypeople as nonsense. Metaphors provide convenient ways to talk about complex phenomena. Beyond the issue of convenience, there is a point made earlier: Sometimes we understand a thing better when we begin with intuitive knowledge rather than with abstract propositional knowledge. So while a prophet will follow Maimonides in recognizing the limitations of language and will see that the expressions used to praise God are not literally true, there is no reason why he cannot take this fact in stride. To return to Fox's criticism, the prophet does not have to think that conventional prayer is a meaningless and improper activity. Although not the same as a technical vocabulary, the language of prayer is perfectly suited to the function it is supposed to perform.

What kind of religion is Maimonides proposing? The answer is a religion that puts acceptance of a worldview ahead of everything else.

Rather than eliminate ritual, it attempts to make ritual serve a higher end. Although it may not be a religion that large numbers of people are ready to practice, this fact should not disturb us. The important point is that there is nothing in his conception of religion that robs one of spiritual integrity. Worship of the heart in Maimonides' sense is a legitimate goal even if it is not an easy one to achieve. In any case, Maimonides does not force us to choose between a religion grounded in mythology and a philosophy that regards all worship as a noble lie. His goal is not to undermine popular religion but to put it on the right course, a course that stays clear of images that appeal to human vanity and sets its sights on something higher.

In support of this view, he assumes that the average worshipper can be brought to see that God is not material and cannot be a bigger, better version of a human being. This is another way of saying that the average worshipper at least can recognize that talking to God is not like talking to a commanding officer. If physicists and laypeople can talk to each other about electrons, why can prophets and average worshippers not pray together in the course of a service? Perhaps Maimonides asks too much of the average worshipper. Perhaps even the minimal degree of awareness needed to reject anthropomorphism is too demanding. But if this is true, it is not just Maimonides who has failed but a significant part of Judaism's claim to be a monotheistic religion.

4

The Problem of Creation

Thus far I have argued that monotheism is based on a separation between God and the created order. If the separation is as severe as Maimonides thinks, if God and creatures have nothing in common in any respect, another puzzle emerges: How can we maintain that the created order owes its existence to God? How can God create the world without having anything in common with it?

Following Aristotle, the scholastics held that causality is a relation in which the cause passes an attribute to the effect, as fire passes heat to an iron bar.[1] An immediate consequence of this view is that causal connection implies similarity between the thing that contributes the attribute and the thing that receives it. In the words of Maimonides (*GP* 2.22, p. 317):[2]

> Any thing at random does not proceed from any other thing at random, but there subsists necessarily a certain conformity between the cause and its effect. Even in the case of accidents, one accident at random does not proceed from any other accident at random. . . . Similarly, form does not proceed from matter nor matter from form.

It was, after all, the inherent similarity between God and creatures that made Aquinas say that creatures represent God insofar as they possess some perfection. We saw, however, that Maimonides does not accept this view.[3] If not, how can he maintain that God is responsible for the created order?

While the problem of creation originated from a scholastic understanding of causality, it is hardly unique to the philosophy of that period. Knowledge of causal connections is based on experience of

66

spatial/temporal phenomena. Even for some early modern thinkers, the cause must be contiguous with its effect. How, then, can we maintain that a being who is neither spatial nor temporal is the cause of things that are? The answer is that we cannot. According to Kant, causality is a relation that applies only to things in the phenomenal realm; thus any attempt to extend causality to cover the relation between noumena and phenomena constitutes a misuse of reason.[4] If he is right, creation is not a causal connection, and there are no grounds for thinking that the creation of the world can be understood by looking at events that occur within it. As Aquinas said in a similar vein: "Creation cannot be called change except metaphorically."[5]

For philosophers in the Neoplatonic tradition, the standard way to deal with the problem of creation is to introduce a form of causality that is not limited to spatial/temporal phenomena and to put a series of intermediaries between God and earthly matter.[6] According to this account, the world derives from successive emanations in the following way. God is engaged in self-thinking thought and generates the first intelligence. The first intelligence thinks about itself and God and generates the outermost sphere of the universe and the second intelligence. The second intelligence thinks about itself and the first intelligence and also generates a sphere and additional intelligence. This process is repeated until we reach the Active Intellect, which is the last stage in the heavenly realm. From there the forms of the sublunar realm are generated, and with them, the intelligence of human beings.

But it is rare that a problem can be solved by introducing additional entities. Even though the first intelligence is neither spatial nor temporal, it is still part of the created order. We will see that if the division between Creator and creation is as sharp as Maimonides thinks, emanation does not solve the problem of how a being that is simple and necessary can be the source of something that is complex and contingent. It is noteworthy that while Maimonides invokes emanation to explain prophecy, which involves the transmission of forms from one intelligence to another, he does not use it to explain the creation of the world as a whole.[7]

Though it is widely held that Maimonides' treatment of creation is one of his greatest achievements, there is little agreement among scholars about what that achievement consists in. The traditional interpretation holds that he defends a version of creation ex nihilo.[8] The normal estericist interpretation holds that he defends a version of necessary emanation from an eternal and unchanging

source.[9] Another group holds that he defends a Neoplatonic view
according to which the world was created from preexisting matter.[10] In opposition to all three, Sarah Klein-Braslavy holds that he
maintained a skeptical *epoche* that does not commit itself to any
view in particular.[11]

Why so much confusion on so central a point? The answer is not
just Maimonides' cryptic writing style but the tendency of scholars
to look at his discussion of creation in isolation from his commitment to negative theology. In a nutshell, I want to argue that his view
of creation is based on (1) maximum separation between God and the
created order, and (2) an inherent skepticism according to which we
have reason to believe in a creation that is both ex nihilo and de novo
but have no way to know or even guess what the details of creation
are. This implies that Maimonides' treatment of creation parallels
his treatment of God in that we have reason to believe *that* it occurred but no way to understand *how*. For Maimonides the "how?"
of creation, by which I mean how God brought the world into existence, is just as mysterious as the "what?" of God.[12] In fact, the two
are linked, because if we do not know what God is, we cannot know
by what means God conferred existence on things. While there may
be something to gain by learning what creation is not, there is nothing to gain by trying to speculate about an event that is completely
beyond the limits of human experience. Perhaps this is why Judaism
regards creation as an esoteric subject best discussed in private.

The Historical Background

At the beginning of Book 2 of the *Guide*, Maimonides claims to
demonstrate that the existence of the world presupposes a timeless,
changeless, unitary being who is neither a body nor a force in a body.
On this issue, there is no difference between the prophetic and philosophic traditions (*GP* 2.33, p. 364)—at least as Maimonides understands them. What differences there are concern the question of whether
the being presupposed by the world should be understood as an agent
capable of spontaneous action or as the source of a necessary causal
process like emanation. This in turn leads to the question of whether
the world is contingent or the outcome of a process that could have
produced only one result. Thus creation, to use Davidson's term,
goes "hand in hand" with God's possessing free will.[13] And free will
goes hand in hand with commandment and revelation, essential parts
of the biblical worldview.

On the other hand, eternity goes hand in hand with necessity. If everything comes to be as the result of a necessary process that leaves no room for choice, ideas like commandment and revelation have to be seriously reinterpreted. Not surprisingly, Maimonides claims (*GP* 2.25, pp. 328–29) that eternity undermines the foundation of the Law while creation upholds it.[14] In broad terms, the debate is between something approximating the biblical conception of God and something approximating Plotinus' conception of the One.[15] According to the first, the existence of the Creator does not necessitate the existence of creation; according to the second, it does.

Maimonides, of course, never mentions Plotinus and ascribes the theory of eternal emanation to Aristotle.[16] Since the historical Aristotle does not invoke emanation, it is clear that what Maimonides has in mind is Aristotle as interpreted by Arabic Neoplatonists like Alfarabi and Avicenna. In view of his negative theology, Maimonides has no hope of demonstrating that one of these positions is true and the other false. Once we admit that God is unknowable, the issue is not whether we can demonstrate that God created the world but whether it is reasonable to believe it. Maimonides' task, then, is to show that creation is possible in the sense that no arguments force us to give it up and some arguments count in its favor.

So interpreted, his approach to creation is reminiscent of Kant's approach to free will. Since we cannot know that the will is free, the question for Kant is whether we are justified in assuming it is in order to satisfy the demands of morality. Put otherwise, the question is whether freedom is possible, not whether it is certain. In Kant's words (*CPR* B xxix), "Morality does not, indeed, require that freedom should be understood, but only that it should not contradict itself."[17] Rather than prove the existence of freedom directly, Kant's strategy is to turn the tables on his opponents. In the *Foundations of the Metaphysics of Morals* (459), he tells us that "where determination according to natural laws comes to an end, there too all explanation ceases and nothing remains but defense, i.e., refutation of the objections of those who pretend to have seen more deeply into the essence of things." It is his opponents, then, who overstep the limits of reason by assuming that because freedom has no natural explanation, it makes no sense. His reply is that since we have been given no reason to think that natural causes exhaust the realm of possibility, his opponents' arguments do nothing to show that belief in freedom has to be given up. Since it does not have to be given up and morality presupposes it, a rational person can accept it.

This response clearly derives from Maimonides, whose primary strategy is stated at *Guide* 2.17, p. 298:

> For at present we do not wish to establish as true that the world is created in time. But what we wish to establish is the possibility of its being created in time. Now this contention cannot be proved to be impossible by inferences drawn from the nature of what exists.

Like Kant, all Maimonides has to do to put his opponents on the defensive is show that creation is coherent even if we do not understand, and may never understand, the details of how it happened.[18]

When it comes to the history of the dispute, Maimonides claims (*GP* 1.71, p. 180) that philosophers have been discussing creation for 3,000 years and have still not resolved the issue. Later (*GP* 2.15, p. 291), he argues that even Aristotle realized he had no demonstration (*burhān*) of eternity and had to rely on mere arguments. With so much indecision, it is tempting to think that we can turn to the Bible for help. If this were true, Maimonides would be in a position to say, with Aquinas, that creation has to be taken on faith alone.[19] But it is characteristic of Maimonides to be just as skeptical of the religious tradition as he is of the philosophic.

Even without Maimonides' warnings about the ambiguity of prophetic language, it is clear that the opening lines of Genesis raise more questions than they answer.

> In the beginning God created the heaven and the earth. Now the earth was unformed and void, and darkness was upon the face of the deep; and the spirit of God hovered over the face of the waters.

To begin with, there is a long-standing dispute on whether the opening line should be read "In the beginning, God created . . ." or "When God was creating . . . ." There is also a problem with the word *bara* (created). Since it is used only of divine creation and has no human analogue, it is difficult to know exactly what it refers to.[20] The words *tohu vavohu* (unformed and void) are grammatical nonsense. And what are we to make of the water over which the spirit of God hovers? Does God bring the world into being and *then* impose order, or is the imposition of order synonymous with the act of creation itself? We will see that Maimonides has his own interpretation of these verses, but he openly admits that some rabbinic sages took them in very different ways.[21]

As for Maimonides' predecessors, Saadia believed in creation ex nihilo while Ibn Gabirol believed in a preexisting material. Among his successors, Abravanel believed in creation ex nihilo, Gersonides in creation from a preexisting material, and Moses of Narbonne in eternity. To repeat: Judaism does not have formal articles of faith. We can therefore agree with Marvin Fox that "there was no internal Jewish pressure on Maimonides to reach a single, fixed conclusion with respect to the problem of creation."[22] The issue, then, is not one of trying to balance the claims of faith against those of reason but of examining arguments from both ends of the spectrum to see if the idea of creation is coherent.

The Three Primary Alternatives

The three alternatives discussed at *Guide* 2.13 are attributed to Moses, Plato, and Aristotle. The theory of Moses holds that every existent other than God was brought into existence "after having been purely and absolutely nonexistent" and that "through His will and His volition" God "brought into existence out of nothing all the beings as they are, time itself being one of the created things." It also holds that God acted alone "without the help of angels, spheres, or intelligences." So in addition to free will, Moses' theory is committed to a radical separation between Creator and creation. If this theory is true, God is the only thing in the universe that is eternal and the only thing responsible for creation.[23]

What does it mean to say that God brought the world into existence *after* pure and absolute nonexistence? Since Maimonides agrees with Aristotle that time is an accident dependent on motion, and motion presupposes something that moves, the idea of a temporal succession "before" creation is incoherent. As Maimonides points out, the claim that God "was" before creation, where "was" indicates the passing of time, derives from the imagination and cannot be true. We can say that God exists prior to creation, but this expression involves logical rather than temporal priority. All it means is that the world exists in time and presupposes God while God is outside of time and presupposes nothing.[24]

Harry Wolfson argues that Maimonides often describes creation ex nihilo as creation *after* nothing (*ba'd al-'adam*), not to indicate temporal passage but to avoid a possible misunderstanding.[25] Grammatically "God created the world out of nothing" resembles "Susan made the statue out of bronze." So unless one is careful, "nothing" will appear to be the material cause of being. But if nothing is pure and absolute, it cannot be the material cause of anything; it is, after all, nothing.[26] Put otherwise, creation ex nihilo does not mean that God transformed nothing into something. It means instead that without God, nothing—not angels, spheres, or prime matter—would exist. According to Wolfson, Maimonides' "after nothing" is therefore the equivalent of Aquinas' *post non esse*. For both thinkers the point is not that creation involves the passage of time but that creation ex nihilo is not creation *from* something in the normal sense.

It is well known that Maimonides does not use a single expression to designate creation ex nihilo. After telling us that the Mosaic position asserts that the world was "after pure and absolute nonexistence," he starts to talk about creation "not from a thing" (*la min shay'*) or "from no thing" (*min la shay'*). Sometimes he abandons the "after nothing" formula entirely and talks about creation "out of nothing."[27] As Klein-Braslavy points out, he also drops the qualification "pure and absolute" when discussing the verb *bara* at *Guide* 2.30.[28]

Part of the problem is that the philosophic tradition did not reach a consensus on how nothing should be understood. The realization that *nothing* need not be absolute and in some respects can "be" is as old as Plato's *Sophist*.[29] Thus the Greek *to me on* can mean either "the nonexistent" or "matter."[30] The same ambiguity applies to the term *'adam*, which is why Maimonides feels the need to say "pure and absolute" when introducing the Mosaic position. Why would a philosopher who wrote with care begin with one expression and then shift to others?

The simple answer is that having told us that the Mosaic theory is committed to full-blown creation ex nihilo, he is under no obligation to keep repeating the same phrase. Note, for example, that by the time he gets to *Guide* 2.30, the "after nothing" formula is no longer essential because he has given several arguments to show that creation should not be confused with change. Given Maimonides' skepticism about language, he may have wanted to avoid a fixed vocabulary, or he may have thought that several expressions would drive the point home better than one. Aquinas, who has no taint of esotericism, did not settle on a single expression either.

I suggest that the real issue is not terminological but philosophic: Must creation have a material cause? The answer is yes *if* creation is a causal process analogous to change. Following Aristotle, most scholastics conceived of change as a process in which something loses one attribute and gains another. This implies a substrate that remains the same throughout, the subject of the change. If this is the paradigm we use to explain creation, the suggestion that absolute nonexistence can gain or lose an attribute and therefore be the subject of change is absurd. But again we must ask why the creation of the world as a whole must resemble individual changes that take place within it. The thrust of Maimonides' argument is that nothing requires us to think it does.

In addition to an exchange of attributes, change involves movement of the subject from potency to act. In Maimonides' words (*GP* 2.14, p. 287): "The possibility of its changing precedes in time the change itself." But as he goes on to show in a later chapter (*GP* 2.17, p. 297), when we talk about creation ex nihilo, we are working with a different model, so that "neither the senses nor the intellect point to something that must be preceded by its possibility."[31] Again creation is unique, and any attempt to explain it with reference to natural processes begs the question. Consider an example. Though wood is flamm*able* before an agent actualizes its potential to burn, it does not follow that before creation, the world existed in an unformed state waiting for God to actualize its potential in a similar way.[32] If creation is unique, it does not involve the transition from potency to act and would not require a trigger mechanism or preexisting material substratum. This does not mean that to believe in creation ex nihilo one has to give up belief in prime matter. A person can still hold, as Maimonides appears to, that prime matter is that out of which all other material things are formed. After all, changes that take place *within* the created order do require a material cause. It simply means that God created material things as well as the source from which they are generated.[33]

What Maimonides has done is to refute an argument against creation that derives from Aristotle's *Physics* 8.1. Before the world existed, it was possible for it to exist. Possibility requires a material cause. Therefore there had to be a material cause for creation. His response is that the existence of possibility before the fact applies only to things that already exist or, in Maimonides' words, to "being that is stabilized."[34] Thus any application of this principle to creation oversteps the limits of reason. In a nutshell, creation does not follow the same pattern as human reproduction, the building of a house, or the growth of an acorn into an oak tree. It is not the shedding of one attribute and acquisition of another. Rather than a change in what exists, it is the origin of existence in the most radical sense. To say that God created the universe out of nothing implies that God's action bears no resemblance to anything we have seen or are capable of doing on our own.

There is one more issue to be discussed if we are to grasp the Mosaic position. We saw that for Maimonides, time is an accident dependent on motion. Hence creation is not a temporal act that takes place *in* time or a process that can be measured *by* time; it is the origin of time and motion together. As Maimonides tells us again and again: "Time is a created and generated thing." The problem is that when Maimonides says that the world is created anew (*hudūth*), Pines' translation has him say that the world was created "in time." The result is that there are a number of passages where Maimonides appears to contradict himself in the most egregious fashion, saying first that time is created and second that creation takes place *in* time.[35]

The problem can be resolved if we take Maimonides to be talking about creation de novo, which is to say creation that involves a radical beginning of time and motion together. To say that time is not absolute and depends on motion is perfectly compatible with saying that neither time nor motion are eternal. Or, as Richard Sorabji put it: "[T]alk of a beginning of time or of motion does not imply some earlier *time* at which they were absent."[36] All it implies is that a context in which time and motion can be measured has existed for finitely as opposed to infinitely many years. So there is nothing incoherent in saying (1) the age of the world is finite, (2) time is consequent on motion, and (3) there is no time before creation.

On the basis of arguments in the *Physics* (8.1) and *Metaphysics* (12.6), Aristotle would reject (2) and accept (1); but that does not mean that (1) and (2) are incompatible. According to Aristotle, time is composed of moments. A moment is a midpoint between "before" and "after." So if there were a first moment, there would have to be time before the first moment, which is absurd. Therefore the idea of a first moment is absurd. As a statement of what we normally mean by a moment of time, Aristotle is clearly right: A moment is a point in a continuum. But why should normal usage force us to deny the possibility of a first moment? To put the question another way, why is the idea of a moment that has no time before it incoherent? To repeat: It is not that this moment has empty time before it; it simply marks the beginning of time. Why, in other words, can we not follow Gersonides and use "before" in two different ways: one to mark a midpoint in the way Aristotle suggests and one to mark a limit as in "Before the first moment, there was no time?"[37] Along similar lines Aquinas argues that denying the existence of time before the first moment is on a par with saying "Above the heavens, there is nothing." In neither case do we generate absurdity.

The first person to point out the problem with Aristotle's view was Philoponus, who argued that the belief that every moment is a midpoint between two other moments assumes what Aristotle is trying to prove—that the world is eternal.[38] To avoid the charge of circularity, Aristotle would have to show that there cannot be a first moment because there cannot be a first motion. He attempts to do this by arguing that motion requires the actualization of a potentiality. Since actuality, in Aristotle's opinion, is prior to potentiality in time, there must be something already actual for something else to move from potency to act.[39] In this case, there must be something already moving if something else is to exercise its potential for motion. If so, there must have been a motion before the first motion. Therefore the idea of a first motion is absurd, so motion is eternal. But if motion is eternal, time is eternal as well. The problem with this argument is its reliance on the categories of act and potency. If we accept explanation according to act and potency as the only option, and admit the priority of the former to the latter, the deck is stacked against spontaneity. But as we saw above, and will see in greater detail below, there is no reason to think that these categories are the only ones available.

Unfortunately some of Maimonides' commentators seem to think that because he believed in the dependence of time on motion, he could not accept the Mosaic position.[40] In other words, they argue that by *creation* Maimonides can only mean the eternal dependence of the world on God. I hope to show that this view is wrong both textually and philosophically. There is no question that Maimonides accepts the dependence of time on motion. If the Mosaic theory were incompatible with so elementary a point, it is hard to see what Maimonides would gain by discussing it for nearly fifteen chapters. Recall that the purpose of dialectic is to consider positions that reasonable people either can or do hold. At the very least, the Mosaic position falls into this category, which means that its view of time and motion is perfectly acceptable.[41]

At the close of *Guide* 2.13 Maimonides says that the Mosaic position is committed to two things: (1) "That there is nothing eternal in any way at all existing simultaneously with God," and (2) "That the bringing into existence of a being out of nonexistence is for the deity not an impossibility." Thus the Mosaic position is committed to a creation that is both ex nihilo and de novo.[42] From my perspective, the importance of these claims is that they assert complete separation between God and the created order. The Platonic position accepts the latter type of creation but not the former; the Aristotelian position accepts neither. So not only is Maimonides defending the idea of a religion that involves commandment and revelation, he is still defending a rigorous view of monotheism.

Maimonides tells us that philosophers reject creation ex nihilo
on the grounds that it is absurd: To say that God can create the world
from nothing is like saying that God can create a square whose diag-
onal is equal to the side. We saw that the philosophers were right if
we take creation ex nihilo to mean that God transforms nothing into
something or that nonexistence *becomes* existence. From nothing
we will only get nothing. But the Mosaic position does not hold that
nonexistence is transformed or becomes something else. Rather it
holds that God is the only factor responsible for creation. And this
position, though not self-evident, is hardly absurd.[43] Contrary to
what Maimonides tells us, there was a long tradition of philosophers
who did affirm it.[44]

Maimonides relates that to avoid creation ex nihilo, "the philosophers of whom we have heard reports" believe in "a certain matter
that is eternal as the deity is eternal." In other words, they choose to
compromise God's uniqueness by introducing another factor in creation that is related to God "as, for instance, clay toward a potter or
iron toward a smith." Given a spectrum with uniqueness on one side
and intelligibility on the other, the philosophers opt for intelligibility.
In fact, the crux of the philosophers' opinion is that God can be understood according to principles derived from our experience of
earthly phenomena.

The philosophers' objection would be valid if it could be shown
that creation must have a material cause. But why should this be the
case? Why should we assume that creation is a bigger version of generation or reproduction? Certainly the thrust of Maimonides' negative theology counts against this idea. I bring up negative theology
because it is often assumed that Maimonides juxtaposes a religious
tradition, which is given to flights of fancy, with a philosophic one,
which is based on a critical understanding of the issues. But in the
case of creation, the problem is not that the philosophers are too critical but that they are not critical enough: They assume that principles that apply to our experience of one part of the world must also
apply to God and the creation of the world as a whole.[45]

Maimonides divides the philosophers into two groups corresponding to Plato and Aristotle. The Platonic position holds that the world
was created from matter and that the heavens are subject to generation and destruction just like things on earth. After describing it,
Maimonides says that it is not the same as his because he believes
that "the heaven was generated out of nothing after a state of absolute nonexistence." Later, at *Guide* 2.25, p. 329, he continues to
say that "we shall not favor this opinion."

Finally we come to the position of Aristotle, who, like Plato, believes in eternal matter. But unlike Plato, Aristotle believes that the heavens are not subject to generation or destruction; the world as well as time and motion are eternal. Moreover, God is not subject to change in any way, so "it is impossible that a volition should undergo a change in Him or a new will arise in Him." In our terms, God cannot act spontaneously. As Maimonides characterizes the Aristotelian position, it consists of variations on a theme we encountered above: A new volition in God means change in God; change requires transition from potency to act; a transition of this sort is impossible in a perfect being. In one respect the Aristotelian position recognizes creation; it just defines creation as the eternal information of matter by a necessary causal process. According to *Guide* 2.16, p. 194, none of the three positions is free of difficulties, but "just as a certain disgrace attaches to us because of the belief in the creation in time, an even greater disgrace attaches to the belief in eternity."

Arguments for the Possibility of Creation

Maimonides' first line of argument against the Aristotelian position is that it assumes we can begin with knowledge of the world in its present state and reason backwards to knowledge of its origin. Against Aristotle he asserts (*GP* 2.17, p. 295):

> No inference can be drawn in any respect from the nature of a thing after it has been generated, has attained its final state, and has achieved stability in its most perfect state, to the state of that thing while it moved toward being generated.

In support of this principle, he asks us to imagine that a male child is taken from his mother after several months and put on an island. Upon his reaching maturity, there would be no way for him to infer anything about reproduction or gestation. Told that he spent the first nine months of his life in the belly of another human being where he received food and air through a tube, he might respond with disbelief.

To evaluate this argument, several points need to be kept in mind. First, the analogy between the birth of a child and the creation of the universe is imperfect, since the former takes place in space and time and is plainly visible.[46] If Maimonides' argument is valid, *any* analogy between the creation of the universe and the occurrence of a specific event in it will fail. But the analogy does not have to succeed in every respect for Maimonides to make his point: If we cannot infer something as simple as the circumstances of a child's birth from knowledge of the adult, it is all the more true that we cannot infer the details of creation from knowledge of the universe in its present state. If one inference is questionable, the other is outrageous.

Second, this argument does not show that creation must be explained by principles different from the ones that apply to the world in its present state; it simply shows that there is no reason to think that creation must be explained by the same principles. As we saw above, creation does not have to involve a transition from potency to act. Though potency and act apply to changes that take place within the world, the Aristotelians have offered no proof that they must apply to the origin of the world as well. The Aristotelians could always respond with an argument from ignorance: "If creation does not involve a transition from potency to act, what does it involve?" But Maimonides does not have to answer this question. At this stage, all he has to say is that Aristotle has assumed something that is open to doubt. Thus *Guide* 2.17, p. 298: "I shall accordingly show you, in a following chapter, how doubts can be cast on these methods so that no proof whatever can be established as correct by means of them."

The primary area of doubt concerns volition. According to Maimonides (*GP* 2.18, p. 301), the essence of the will consists in its ability to will or not will.[47] It should also be kept in mind that Maimonides is talking about the *possibility* to will and not will, not the *fact* of changing one's mind. In a being that responds to external stimuli, willing one thing now and a different thing later would involve change and therefore some kind of imperfection. But there is no reason why we have to think of God's will along the lines of a person looking at a menu and deciding what to eat for dinner. Accordingly, "The fact that it may wish one thing now and another thing tomorrow does not constitute a change in its essence and does not call for another cause." In short, God could will in a purely autonomous fashion. This does not imply arbitrariness, as Algazali suggested, but the absence of reliance on external impediments or inducements. Once external factors are out of the picture, we no longer have to regard the will as an effect of something else: It can be completely self-determined, so that the only thing operating on the will is the will itself. It follows that a being who wills in a purely autonomous fashion is not analogous to a being who wills as a result of change. The upshot is that there is no reason why we cannot admit the possibility of free will in an eternal being, and once we have free will, we can have purpose or intention as well.

What does it mean to say that a being can will one thing now and a different thing later without changing its essence? Although Maimonides does not provide much in the way of detail, he seems to be getting at a point made by Philoponus and taken up by Algazali and Aquinas: that willing change is not the same as changing one's will.[48] To use one of Aquinas' examples, if a doctor asks a patient to wait a day before taking a particular drug, it does not follow that the doctor has to will one thing today and a different thing tomorrow; it simply means that the doctor wants the patient to proceed in due course.[49] This situation is altogether different from one in which the doctor prescribes one treatment, sees that it does not work, and shifts to another treatment later on. For natural causes a delayed effect of this sort is impossible: Given the existence of the cause, the effect must follow. But for an agent with will, the determining factor is not the existence of the agent but the agent's intention to realize a particular end. Thus anyone who says that the eternity of the world follows from the eternity of the Creator assumes that the only way to think of the Creator is with categories taken from natural science. Once we admit that the reach of natural science is limited, there is no reason why we cannot think of God as free. Once we think of God as free, a distinction emerges between the act of will and the object willed in the act.[50] Though the former is unchanging, it does not follow that the latter is.

This does not mean that Maimonides knows what God's will is or how it operates. Nor does it mean that he has smuggled in the idea of a personal God while no one was watching. From the knowledge at our disposal and the limited perspective we have, there is no way we can infer the ultimate purpose God has in mind. The only thing Maimonides has shown is that one can give a coherent account of will and purpose in God and therefore that the Aristotelian arguments against will and purpose are not convincing (*GP* 2.18, p. 299).[51] In short, he has shown that spontaneity is possible in God and therefore creation de novo is possible as well.

Arguments for the Likelihood of Creation

Beyond the issue of whether creation de novo is possible, Maimonides presents a series of arguments from the *Kalam* designed to show that it is the best explanation of the available evidence. Although he rejects these arguments as *proofs* of creation, he feels free to use them as considerations that count in its favor.[52] The first claims that if we start with an unchanging God and a necessary causal process, we might be able to account for the existence of *a* world but not for the distinctive features of this one, in particular the orbits of the planets.[53] According to the received wisdom, each sphere was supposed to impart regular motion to the one below it. But this theory broke down in a number of cases (*GP* 2.19, p. 307):

> For we see that in the case of some spheres, the swifter of motion is above the slower; that in the case of others, the slower of motion is above the swifter; and that, again in another case, the motions of the spheres are of equal velocity though one be above the other. There are also other very grave matters if regarded from the point of view that these things are as they are in virtue of necessity.

The key word is *necessity*. According to Maimonides (*GP* 2.19, pp. 302–3), anyone who believes in the eternity of the world is committed to the view that whatever proceeds from God does so by necessity. Maimonides objects that if we cannot explain something as visible as planetary orbits, we have no demonstration and thus "the matter, as he [Aristotle] sets it out, does not follow an order for which necessity can be claimed."[54]

It should be noted that Maimonides has no quarrel with Aristotle on the physics of the sublunar realm. In fact, he claims that anyone who does not accept causal explanations of earthly phenomena is a fool. The reason is that causal explanations of earthly phenomena allow people to explain what they observe. What do you do when the available explanations lead you to expect something very different from what you observe? The problem is all the more difficult given that the motion of heavenly bodies is not random. Ptolemaic astronomy allowed people to form a reasonably good idea of where the planets would be. The difficulty, which Maimonides (*GP* 2. 24, p. 326) calls "the true perplexity," is that Ptolemy's epicycles and eccentric orbits could not be reconciled with Aristotle's claim that all heavenly bodies rotate in uniform circular motion around a common center. In Maimonides' opinion, epicycles and eccentric orbits are "entirely outside the bounds of reasoning and opposed to all that has been made clear in natural science." Thus there was the appearance of order coupled with the failure of existing theories to account for it. His answer is to drop scientific explanations and turn to a form of voluntarism. The heavenly bodies behave as they do because a being that is endowed with will and purpose designed them that way (*GP* 2.19, p. 308): "For we say that there is a being that has particularized, just as it willed, every sphere in regard to its motion and rapidity." To say that the heavenly bodies reflect will and purpose is to say that, from what we can tell, their order and arrangement could be different. The argument, then, is that without a satisfactory scientific explanation, there is no reason to think that the order and arrangement we observe are inevitable.

Isaac Husik objected to this argument on the grounds that Maimonides is no better off than his opponents.[55] Asked why Mercury moves this way and Jupiter that, all Maimonides can say is that God willed it to happen. To be sure, his "explanation" can never be disconfirmed; but for that very reason, it has no explanatory power. If the Aristotelians are in a quandary about how to explain planetary behavior, Maimonides is no better. Yet surely Husik missed the point. Maimonides does not claim to have a naturalistic explanation for planetary orbits. On the contrary, his point is that all naturalistic explanations known to him are inadequate. In fact, he is skeptical about the possibility of ever having an explanation that saves the phenomena. At *Guide* 2.24, pp. 326–27, he admits bewilderment and concludes that "regarding all that is in the heavens, man grasps nothing but a small measure of what is mathematical."[56] All that the argument from particularity claims is that heavenly phenomena are compatible with free will but not with emanation from an unchanging source. For if the theory of emanation were true, there should be no anomalies or contingencies at all. The argument from particularity does not purport to explain why God chose one arrangement rather than another.

This is, to say the least, a highly provisional argument. Maimonides admits at the end of *Guide* 2.24 that phenomena that seem irregular to him might be adequately explained by a new theory. But his concession has to be viewed in light of two facts. First, Maimonides is very doubtful that such a theory will be developed, since it would strain the limits of human knowledge as he understands them. Second, even if such a theory were to appear, it might make emanation from an unchanging source more plausible but would still not guarantee its truth.

Lacking an adequate astronomical theory, the Aristotelian position is clearly on the defensive. Suppose, for example, that a person who had never seen the motion of the heavenly bodies were told that they emanated from a perfect being by a causal process that does not allow for will or purpose. Suppose she were also told that motion proceeds from the outer to the inner spheres. Surely she would never expect to find data so confusing that even the best theories run into obstacles.

It is true, as Warren Harvey points out, that Maimonides talks about divine volition when he introduces the Aristotelian position at *Guide* 2.13: "All that exists has been brought into existence, in the state in which it is at present, by God through His volition."[57] But in the chapters that follow, Maimonides goes on to argue that strictly speaking, a will that lacks the possibility of spontaneous action is no will at all. As we saw, volition is the ability to will or not will. Insofar as the world proceeds from God by necessity (*GP* 2.20, p. 314), "this is not called purpose, and the motion of purpose is not included in it." To use Maimonides' example, this would be like saying that a person willed to have two arms and two legs. In fact, earlier in the same chapter he considers the possibility that necessary emanation could be combined with the idea of will and purpose, but he rejects it as a contradiction in terms. Once we grant that the world proceeds from God by necessity, everything from the motion of the heavenly bodies to the size of a fly's wing would be fixed for all eternity (*GP* 2.22, p. 319). Note, however, that while the particularity argument may tip the scales in favor of creation de novo, it does not address the question of creation ex nihilo. As things stand, a Platonist could use the same argument to support creation from a preexisting material.

A second but related argument takes the issue of particularity further. If we begin with God and a necessary causal process, not only can we not account for the motion of heavenly bodies, we cannot account for metaphysical complexity of any kind. Underlying this argument is an assumption that Maimonides claims is shared by Aristotle and everyone else (*GP* 2.22, p. 317): "It is impossible that anything but a single simple thing should proceed from a simple thing."[58] This assumption is an instance of the principle that the effect must be similar to the cause, or as Maimonides puts it, exhibit "a certain conformity." It might make sense to suppose that a simple intelligence could proceed from God by a causal process or that one simple intelligence could proceed from another simple intelligence. But even if there were a thousand stages in the process, the final product would have to be simple. And even if the final product were an intelligence contemplating other intelligences, we would still not have anything like the complexity we observe around us. How, then, can a sphere, which is a composite of matter and form and which contains a star that is also composite, proceed from something simple? Maimonides' answer is that it cannot, and that the only way to explain complexity in a causal fashion is to start with something complex.

What is the alternative? Again Maimonides claims that the particularity of the world is compatible with will and purpose but not with necessity. Yet this argument makes a bigger claim than the previous one: Unless God willed it, the universe would not contain any composite beings at all. In other words, we cannot explain the existence of spheres and stars, much less the existence of the sublunar realm, by supposing that forms emanate from God, because matter, which is the source of complexity, cannot proceed from form. As Maimonides asks (*GP* 2.22, p. 318): "What relation can there be between matter and that which being separate has no matter at all?"

Unlike the previous argument, this one seeks to show that the world is not eternal *and* that every composite being in the world owes its existence to the will of God. As Davidson remarks, the latter appears to support creation ex nihilo.[59] If God is simple and immaterial, no causal relation can explain the origin of a complex world. The only way we can explain it is to invoke something that does not imply similarity between the source of existence and the things that proceed from it. As we saw, an act of will can have properties very different from the object willed. It is possible to will now something that will not be realized for years to come or to will something that can never be realized. The decision to buy a house, for example, can be simple and instantaneous even though the object willed is often a mass of complications. Maimonides' hope is that by shifting to a voluntaristic explanation, he can hold on to divine simplicity and worldly complexity at the same time. The problem is that he can do so only by making the efficacy of God's will a mystery: Though the source of existence, it remains distinct from existence in every possible way.

When he first introduced the subject of creation, Maimonides set out to defend two things: creation de novo and creation ex nihilo. He admits that the arguments supporting creation de novo are not decisive but makes three claims on their behalf: (1) they establish the possibility of creation de novo, (2) they take into account the limits of human knowledge and do not require us to provide a natural explanation for everything we see, and (3) by defending free will in God, they uphold the foundation of the Law. Because they are tied to an outdated astronomy, the particularity arguments are no longer valid.

But if the scientific revolution rendered part of Maimonides' position obsolete, it provided support for other parts. In today's world few people believe that explanation in terms of act and potency is the only option available or that the eternity of the universe can be established a priori. In fact, the evidence at our disposal now points to a temporal origin between 10 and 12 billion years ago. If we accept the relativity of space and time, then the idea of a common frame of reference between God and various parts of an expanding universe may be not only false but incoherent. It may also be incoherent to suppose that everything in the universe is moving at the same speed or can be measured by the same clock.[60]

Still, we should be cautious in concluding that Maimonides would run to embrace the big bang theory. Maimonides took the newness of the world as evidence of free will in God, but modern science draws no such inference.[61] More important, his warning about reasoning from the world in its present state to the circumstances of its origin has lost none of its validity. Scientific principles presuppose space and time. Once space and time exist, we can use those principles to explain how something goes from one state of its development to another. If Maimonides is right, we cannot use scientific principles to explain the origin of space and time in the most radical sense.

Pushing scientific explanations back to a point where temperatures were many billions of times greater than anything known to exist at present is a speculative endeavor to be sure. Even from a scientific standpoint, we may question whether the origin of the universe can be explained by conventional means. Thus Alan Guth seems to echo Maimonides in warning about the dangers of extrapolation:[62]

> If one continues the extrapolation backwards in time, one comes to a point of infinite density, infinite pressure, and infinite temperature—the instant of the big bang explosion itself, the time that in the laconic language of cosmologists is usually called "$t = 0$." It is also frequently called a *singularity*, a mathematical word that refers to the infinite values of the density, pressure, and temperature. It is often said—in both popular-level books and in textbooks—that this singularity marks the beginning of the universe, the beginning of time itself. Perhaps this is so, but any honest cosmologist would admit that our knowledge here is very shaky. The extrapolation to arbitrarily high temperatures takes us far beyond the physics that we understand, so there is no good reason to trust it. The true history of the universe, going back to "$t = 0$," remains a mystery that we are probably still far from unraveling.

As Guth goes on to explain in a footnote, if the extrapolation to $t = 0$ is not trustworthy, then a description like "one second after the big bang" is ambiguous. In fact, it is not even clear that time measurements, which are relative to each other, have any bearing on the idea of a "time zero" at all. But the issue involves more than speculation. According to Maimonides, there is no reason why we have to think of the origin of all causal sequences as a causal sequence obeying the same set of laws.

Maimonides' appeal to will and purpose is a bad account of the existence of the world *if* we interpret it as an attempt to provide the kind of explanation science does. A more generous reading would say that it is an attempt not to do science in the normal sense but rather to answer general questions about the universe in which science operates. On one side, he faced the Mutakallimun, who denied all causal connection and explained everything by direct appeal to the will of God. According to *Guide* 1.73, p. 202, "They assert that when a man moves a pen, it is not the man who moves it; for the motion occurring in the pen is an accident created by God in the pen." On the other side, he faced the Aristotelians, who argued that all observable phenomena can be explained by reference to laws that cannot possibly be otherwise. In Maimonides' world, there are causal connections worth investigating, but they are contingent and proceed from God's decision to create an orderly world. Though much of that order is beyond our comprehension, we are best advised to pursue scientific explanations as far as they go and recognize that at some point we will not be able to go any further. In Maimonides' world, then, scientific explanations are possible but not ultimate: They advance our understanding of the world but do not exhaust it.

Maimonides was not the first and will hardly be the last thinker to use the limit of scientific knowledge as grounds for affirming the possibility of free will. If the evidence for the big bang is compelling, he would accept it without hesitation. But honesty would force him to say that creation in his sense of the term still cannot be demonstrated because scientific principles are not designed to take us from a spatial/temporal world to a nonspatial/nontemporal origin. The issues at stake have nothing to do with Athens versus Jerusalem but with the limits of human knowledge and how to cope with them. Maimonides' contribution to this issue is to show that the question of origin is unlike any other question we may ask. To return to a familiar theme, the question of origin is unique, which means that the answers we give are always speculative.

A Courteous Bow to Platonism

In regard to creation ex nihilo, Maimonides is more guarded. After saying that he rejects the Platonic view at *Guide* 2.13, he claims at 2.25 that it is permissible to believe it. From his standpoint, the Platonic view has two points in its favor: (1) it affirms or at least is compatible with creation de novo, and (2) it is a reasonable interpretation of what Maimonides describes as "many obscure passages" in the Torah and rabbinic literature. The passages he is talking about are noteworthy for visual imagery designed to appeal to the imagination. We saw that the opening lines of Genesis refer to darkness, a body of water, *tohu vavohu*, and the spirit of God hovering over the water. The sayings of Rabbi Eliezer talk about creation from God's garment and the snow under God's throne (*GP* 2.26, pp. 330–31). One way to make sense of these passages is to say that water or snow are colorful expressions used to refer to preexistent matter and therefore lend themselves to the Platonic view of creation.

At *Guide* 2.25, pp. 328–29, Maimonides says that he would not interpret Genesis according to its external sense if the Aristotelian and Platonic views could be demonstrated. Since in his opinion they cannot be demonstrated, the external sense is to be preferred.[63] That raises the question of what the external sense is. In my view it is the position Maimonides ascribes to Moses: a creation that is de novo and ex nihilo.[64] The issue of how to interpret the opening lines of Genesis is raised again at *Guide* 2.30, where Maimonides repeats that time cannot have a temporal beginning because it is itself a created thing; thus God does not precede the world in a temporal sense. He goes on to say that the first word of Genesis (*bereishit*) suggests creation de novo, a remark that implies again that creation de novo is not a temporal process but the origin of time in the most radical way.[65]

He then argues that the preposition *et* should be taken to mean that God created, together with the heavens, everything that is in the heavens, and together with the earth, everything that is in the earth; in short, "everything was created simultaneously; then gradually all things became differentiated." If so, *creation* in the proper sense applies to the first act, which is simple and instantaneous.[66] Anything that happens after that involves categories like hot/cold, fast/slow, large/small, or high/low, but not the category of existence pure and simple.

The mention of elements, prime matter, and various form of chaos takes us back to the issue of hierarchy. We can explain the elements out of which things are composed, distinguish heavenly matter from earthly matter, describe the actions of the stars and intelligences, or reach all the way down to prime matter; in a modern context we can talk about hydrogen, helium, and enormous energy levels. But in the end, the only difference that matters is the ultimate one between Creator and creation. Along these lines, Maimonides (*GP* 2.30, p. 358) takes the word *bara* to refer to bringing the whole world into existence out of nonexistence. If I am right in taking nonexistence as *complete* nonexistence, these considerations point in the direction of creation ex nihilo, the other half of the Mosaic position.

Why, then, does he allow people to believe the Platonic view? I submit that the answer has less to do with esotericism than with human psychology: The imagination balks at the idea of creation ex nihilo. Since it is tied to material things, it cannot conceive of creation except as a causal process that involves an agent and a patient. But if you understand creation ex nihilo, you will see that images like darkness, swirling waters, or exploding galaxies not only do not help, they introduce a number of distortions by suggesting that creation is a process occurring in space and time rather than the origin of space and time in the most radical sense. According to Maimonides (*GP* 2.12, pp. 279–80), "Just as the imagination cannot represent to itself an existent other than a body or a force in a body, the imagination cannot represent to itself an action taking place otherwise than through the immediate contact of an agent or at a certain distance and from one particular direction." Along with space and time, distance and direction have no relevance to creation in Maimonides' sense. As Saadia pointed out before Maimonides, our only access to the idea of creation is through reason.[67] The problem is that the level of reason needed to understand these arguments is rare, while the doctrine of creation is too important to give up.

Recognizing that not everyone would be able to accept creation ex nihilo, but wanting to preserve a workable idea of creation and a respect for rabbinic interpreters, Maimonides himself makes a concession: Though Platonism may not be correct on every point, it does not do serious damage to the biblical text and it preserves the idea of divine volition. This is another way to say that ultimately, divine volition and creation de novo are the real point. A person who accepts them can still view existence as a gift and still accept the possibility of revelation and commandment. Maimonides is willing to challenge rabbinic authority when he is sure that it contradicts something known to be true. In the case of creation ex nihilo, the only thing Rabbi Eliezer's sayings contradict is a strong probability. Thus Maimonides has little choice but to allow them as an acceptable if not optimal reading of a notoriously obscure text.

Creation, Separation, and the Sabbath

Let us recall the problem with which we began: Causality is a relation linking two things in the same category; hence God cannot be the cause of the world. In Maimonides' discussion of creation, he follows the same line he established in his negative theology: Because causality involves similarity, it cannot account for the emergence of a complex world from a simple God. The alternative is to look at creation as an act, keeping in mind that attributes of action are not qualities that inhere in their subject. As we saw, multiple attributes can proceed from a simple source. Again the "how" of creation is beyond our comprehension. The point is that however we think of it, creation must preserve the freedom and uniqueness of the Creator.

Although it may seem that the distinction between creation as cause and creation as act is merely semantic, in fact the two lead to very different views of the world. The doctrine of emanation explains the procession of the sublunar realm from God by positing a series of intermediaries. What emanation gives us is a continuum in which God does not act directly on earthly matter but indirectly through a series of causal connections. Because the continuum does not contain any radical jumps, there is no reason why principles that apply to things in lower stages should not apply to things in higher—even to God in some respects. That is why the Aristotelians explain God in terms of act and potency. We saw, however, that Maimonides' view is different: Everything is created simultaneously by an act of God, and all differences between created things are neutralized before God. This act is a unique moment in the history of the world and cannot be understood by extrapolation from the present. Nor can the Actor be understood by looking at potters, blacksmiths, or overflowing fountains. Rather than a continuum between God and creation, there is an unbridgeable gap; rather than a causal force, a free agent, though once again free in a unique and purely autonomous way.[68]

If God is free, the created order does not exist by necessity. In religious terms, existence is a gift. By *gift* I mean something we cannot get for ourselves and have no right to claim from God, something that God must choose to give us. In the terminology of scholasticism, existence is an accident.[69] From the idea of an accident or gift, there is a smooth transition to the celebration of the Sabbath, a day set aside to commemorate creation de novo and the Exodus from Egypt.[70] We saw that the Sabbath ends with a prayer praising God as the one who separates light from darkness, the sacred from the profane, and the Sabbath from the other six days of the week. In keeping with rabbinic tradition, Maimonides argues that observance of the Sabbath and abstention from idolatry are each equivalent to the sum total of all the other commandments.[71] As we saw, belief in creation is the foundation of the Law.

The commandment mandating rest on the Sabbath is noteworthy for several reasons (Exodus 20:8–11):

> Remember the Sabbath day, to keep it holy. Six days shalt thou labor, and do all thy work, but the seventh day is a Sabbath unto the Lord thy God; in it thou shalt not do any manner of work, thou, nor thy son, nor thy daughter, nor thy manservant, nor thy maidservant, nor thy cattle, nor thy stranger that is within thy gates; for in six days the Lord made heaven and earth, the sea, and all that is in them, and rested on the seventh day; wherefore the Lord blessed the Sabbath day, and hallowed it.

How could a perfect being rest? Maimonides argues at *Guide* 1.67 that rest does not necessarily imply fatigue: It can also mean to refrain, as in "He refrained from saying anything." Maimonides therefore takes "God rested on the seventh day" to mean that on every day of the first six, events occurred that did not correspond to natural laws as we now understand them; but on the seventh, natural laws became permanent and are still in place. He then concludes by returning to the idea of divine volition: "Accordingly it means that His purpose was perfected and all His will realized."

Why is rest important for us? It is not that Judaism looks askance at work or glorifies indolence. Adam and Eve were given work in the Garden of Eden (Genesis 2:15), and there is an old tradition that maintains that study of the Torah should be combined with a worldly occupation.[72] From our perspective, work typically introduces hierarchical relations by distinguishing rich from poor, employer from employee, and native born from stranger. But rest dissolves these relations and with them the forms of inequality to which they often lead. According to the commandment, not only must people at every level of the social scale rest on the Sabbath, but beasts of burden and, according to Leviticus 25:4, the land as well. On this day, then, we are asked to relate to the rest of creation not as superiors but as partners, or more specifically, as fellow creatures. It could be said, therefore, that on the Sabbath more than any other day, we are asked to live according to the principle that all differences are neutralized before God.

My purpose in mentioning the Sabbath is not to engage in a homiletical exercise but to return to the question "Is a rigorous definition of monotheism compatible with a religion people can practice?" Clearly the symbolism involved in the Sabbath is consistent with the ideas underlying the Mosaic account of creation: freedom and separation. Instead of bringing God into the world by identifying a sacred dwelling place or earthly manifestation, it defines a period of time in which we are asked to reflect on the uniqueness of God's activity. When the Sabbath is over, God is still in heaven and we are still on earth. While there is an old tradition that holds that the Sabbath provides a taste of the world to come, Maimonides claims that the person who observes it to the best of his ability obtains a reward in this life above and beyond anything in the next.[73]

The irony is that the Sabbath does not ask one to endure pain, forgo pleasure, or put forth superhuman effort. According to the standard interpretation, it asks one to remember creation and the Exodus from Egypt, observe the ban on work, and take delight. I submit that there is nothing in Maimonides' definition of monotheism that compromises the integrity of the Sabbath, and nothing in observance of the Sabbath that calls monotheism into question. That does not mean that one can be deduced from the other, but it is false to say that as a philosopher, Maimonides upheld views of God at odds with his religious practice. Once we look upon existence as a gift, the whole system by which we praise God, offer supplications to God, and celebrate our place in God's creation begins to make sense. Not surprisingly, Maimonides lists belief in creation as a pillar of the Law, second in importance only to belief in the existence and unity of God.[74] Though his esotericism is notorious, it is hard to believe that a man who devoted much of his life to the exposition of the Law would make such a claim if he were not convinced that creation underlies the whole system of commandment and obligation.

5

Imitatio Dei

Until now we have considered an understanding of monotheism based on a radical separation between God and everything else. God is eternal, everything else is created; God is beyond our ability to praise, everything else is within it. Not only does separation create metaphysical problems, it creates a religious problem of immense proportions, for the Bible does not say we should simply recognize the uniqueness of God and be content with our finitude; it says quite clearly that we should strive to emulate God. Thus Leviticus 19:2: "You shall be holy; for I the Lord your God am holy."

In the hands of philosophers, the commandment to be holy has been taken to mean that we should not only perform certain actions but perform them in order to become like God.[1] In other words, the imitation of God is the ultimate goal of human life. According to Maimonides (*GP* 1.54, p. 128): "For the utmost virtue of man is to become like unto Him . . . as far as he is able; which means that we should make our actions like unto His, as the sages make clear when interpreting the verse *You shall be holy*."[2] Important as it is, this commandment is problematic given Maimonides' stress on God's uniqueness. How do you imitate something you cannot comprehend? Can a person or group of people actually fulfill this commandment, or will holiness always be beyond our reach? And if the commandment can be fulfilled, what does it require of us—to perfect our nature as human beings or to set our sights on a level of perfection significantly more than human? In general Maimonides' approach to *imitatio Dei* is deflationary in the sense that he does not think it imposes an obligation above and beyond the 613 original commandments.[3]

In this chapter I will consider both a medieval and a modern response to these questions. Before getting to specifics, I want to introduce a principle that will guide everything that follows: A commandment that cannot be fulfilled is a contradiction in terms. While the purpose of the commandments is to elevate human behavior, nothing is achieved if the goal is so high that no one can reach it. Thus Moses tells the Israelites at Deuteronomy 30:11–14 that the Law is not too difficult for them, not in heaven, and not beyond the sea; rather it is in their mouths and their hearts so that they may do it. Although this passage has been subject to any number of interpretations, the simple meaning is that the difficulty of fulfilling the law is not a valid excuse for ignoring it: Since the Law *can* be fulfilled, people are under an obligation to do so. As students of modern philosophy will observe, this principle is nothing but a version of the Kantian dictum that *ought* implies *can*.

Here I must add an important qualification. To say that the Law can be fulfilled is not necessarily to say that I can fulfill it on my own. It may be that the effort required to obey the law is so great that it requires a community, a nation, or a nation over an extended period of time. But no matter how one conceives the task, it must be realizable by someone or some group at some date. I say realiz*able*, not real*ized*, because even if the Law is never fulfilled, all we need to maintain its imperative force is the assurance that it can be. As Schwarzschild put it: "For progress to be possible there must be a logical guarantee of the eventual attainability of the goal of the progress."[4] If the goal is not attainable, if it outstrips even the most generous estimate of human capacity, then so far from providing hope for a better world, religion would only provide despair or what Hegel termed alienation. "God," as Cohen (*RR*, 207) tells us, "can assign no task that would be a labor of Sisyphus." Sisyphus was a tragic hero; unless religion explains how our situation is different from his, it would consign us to the same fate.

Mystical Union

One way to interpret *imitatio Dei* is through the doctrine of mystical union. Simply stated, the doctrine holds that the process of imitating God culminates in a condition where the soul becomes so Godlike that it annuls its finitude and ceases to understand itself as an entity distinct from God. From a metaphysical standpoint, mystical union is the reverse of emanation. If all things proceed from God by a series of continuous connections, it is possible to say that in some respect all things reflect the perfection of their source and eventually will return to it. According to Plotinus (*EN* 5.2.1):

> "The One is all things and no one of them"; the source of all things is not all things; and yet it is all things in a transcendental sense—all things, so to speak, having run back to it: or, more correctly, not all as yet are within it, they will be.

In regard to human beings, return to the source is described in the following way (*EN* 6.9.10):[5]

> The man is changed, no longer himself or self-belonging; he is merged with the Supreme, sunken into it, one with it: centre coincides with centre, for centres of circles, even here below, are one when they unite, and two when they separate; and it is in this sense that we now (after the vision) speak of the Supreme as separate. This is why the vision baffles telling; we cannot detach the Supreme to state it; if we have seen something thus detached we have failed of the Supreme which is to be known only as one with ourselves.

Elsewhere (*EN* 6.9.9) Plotinus claims that the soul, in ecstasy, is "raised to Godhood or, better, knowing its Godhood, all aflame." Invoking another metaphor, he describes this condition as a pregnancy where the soul is filled with God because "this state is its first and its final [*arche kai telos*], because from God it comes, its good lies There, and, once turned to God again, it is what it was." In this way God is both the source of our existence and the end of our spiritual journey.

To the question "How can a finite being lose its finitude?" Plotinus replies that it can lose it because there is a basic kinship or similarity (*suggenei*) between us and God.[6] Since our existence is derived from God, there has to be some feature of God that we reflect. Holiness can then be understood as a process by which we recognize this similarity and seek to enhance it. This is another way of saying that holiness is a way of making the soul so simple and unified that all awareness of duality between it and God is left behind.

There is, of course, a rich mystical tradition in Judaism. But according to the classical study of Jewish mysticism by Gershom Scholem, the number of Jews who claimed to achieve complete union with God is quite small.[7] In Scholem's words:

> It is only in extremely rare cases that ecstasy signifies actual union with God in which the human individuality abandons itself to the rapture of complete submersion in the divine stream. Even in this ecstatic frame of

mind, the Jewish mystic almost invariably retains a sense of the distance between the Creator and His creature. The latter is joined to the former, and the point where the two meet is of the greatest interest to the mystic, but he does not regard it as constituting anything so extravagant as identity of Creator and creature.

Accordingly Scholem argues that the Hebrew term *devekut* (adhesion) stands for a "being-with-God" or a union of the divine and human wills but still retains what he calls "a proper sense of the distance, or, if you like, of incommensurateness." Along the same lines, Salo Baron maintains that even confirmed mystics in the Jewish tradition sought community with God rather than actual union and would have regarded any claims of unity as "execrable blasphemies."[8] Cohen (*RR*, 164) too regards the idea of union as "unchaste" and insists repeatedly that holiness does not mean loss of finitude.[9] In recent years, sweeping generalizations like those of Scholem and Baron have been challenged by Moshe Idel.[10] But even if we agree with Idel's approach and accept the idea that some mystics did believe in union with God, there is no getting around the fact that canonical Judaism does not envision a time when all finitude will be absorbed into a primordial unity and the difference between God and creation will be overcome.

Like Plotinus, Maimonides sees the acquisition of knowledge as an activity that links the mind to what it knows and describes knowledge as a form of union or conjunction (*ittiṣāl*).[11] This is another way of saying that knowledge occurs when there is an identity between the form that shapes the object and the form that activates our intelligence.[12] After stressing that love of God is proportional to knowledge of God, he claims (*GP* 3.51, pp. 623–24) that Moses and the patriarchs, the most perfect individuals who ever lived, achieved union with God and were kissed by God.[13] But it is hardly the case that he has given up the claim that God is separate from and bears no resemblance to the created order. It is still true, for example, that (*GP* 1.59, p. 139) "none but He Himself can apprehend what He is." Strictly speaking, the union Maimonides is talking about in these passages is not between humans and God but between humans and the Agent Intellect, which he describes as (*GP* 3.52, p. 629) "the intellect that overflows toward us and is the bond between us and Him."[14] In *Perek Ḥelek* (sixth principle) it is the Agent Intellect to which the soul of the prophet clings. For Maimonides, then, the highest achievement for a human being is to have an intellect that contemplates the universe as the lowest of the heavenly intelligences does. Here too contact is at best fleeting and imperfect.

It could be said, therefore, that while Jews sought ecstasy or closeness to God, or imagined themselves sitting at the foot of God, complete loss of human identity cannot help but arouse suspicion. Thus the doctrine of *imitatio Dei* normally begins by accepting finitude and does not ask how to deify human life but rather how to sanctify it. But that raises the same question: How can a finite being imitate something with which it has nothing in common?

The Medieval Argument: Maimonides on Imitatio Dei

Although Maimonides does not mention the *"ought* implies *can"* principle in so many words, it is implied by many of the things he says about human perfection. Our goal is to achieve demonstration *to the extent that it is possible*, to ascertain *to the extent that it is possible* everything that may be ascertained, and to become like God *as far as possible*. Even prophets know God's governance "in whatever way it is possible" (*GP* 3.51, p. 620).

In fact, Maimonides' view of the limits of human knowledge applies not only to this life but to the next. According to Maimonides, immortality is a direct consequence of intellectual perfection. In *Perek Ḥelek*, he claims that the ultimate human good is for the soul to be forever involved with God, and he concludes by saying:

> When one becomes fully human, he acquires the nature of a perfect human being; there is no external power to deny his soul eternal life. His soul thus attains the eternal life it has come to know, which is the world to come.

Maimonides tries to establish doctrinal requirements for what it means to be fully human and does not reflect a modern view of religious tolerance. I will have more to say on both issues in the remaining chapters. For the present, it is interesting to note that while we may regard his requirements as a major achievement, it is likely that he regarded them as minimal, for the line from which he derives his position says quite clearly, "*All* Israel have a share in the world to come."

In other words, Maimonides thought he was saying that a person does not have to be a prophet, sage, or guru to merit salvation; all a person has to do is assent to basic principles about God, prophecy, and providence. The "reward" given to those who merit salvation is also intellectual: They shed the material component of their nature and are able to contemplate the heavenly realm without interruption.[15] There is some ambiguity about whether we will be able to apprehend things in the next life that were hidden in this one or whether we will merely sustain the most intense level of concentration achieved on earth.[16] But either way, Maimonides denies something many religious thinkers regard as essential: that it is possible to make spiritual or intellectual progress in the next life. Rather than move from lower to higher levels of apprehension, the soul, like the heavenly intelligences, "remains in one and the same state" (*GP* 3.51, p. 629). Put otherwise, death means that the soul no longer participates in experiences that are transient or terminable. So there is no point *after* death where we come to know God with perfect clarity or get reabsorbed into God in a mystical experience.[17]

If there is no reabsorption, what becomes of *imitatio Dei*? The answer is that Maimonides accepts the traditional view but gives it a new twist. In Judaism people are commanded not only to do what God says but, in a deeper sense, to walk in God's ways (Deuteronomy 10:12; 13:5). According to the standard interpretation, to walk in God's ways means to perform actions like those that God performs. Thus *Sotah* 14a:

> What does the text "You shall walk after the Lord your God" (Deuteronomy 13:5) mean? . . . The meaning is to follow the attributes of the Holy One . . . as He clothed the naked (Genesis 3:21), so do you clothe the naked; as He visited the sick (Genesis 18:1), so do you visit the sick; as He comforted mourners (Genesis 25:11), so do you comfort mourners; as He buried the dead (Deuteronomy 34:6), so do you bury the dead.

Note, as Kellner does, that this passage contains very little in the way of metaphysics: There is nothing that says that by clothing the naked or visiting the sick, we will shed our mortal nature and become like God.[18]

Since he insists that humans and God have nothing in common, why does Maimonides opt for a metaphysical interpretation? Why not say that holiness consists in clothing the naked, visiting the sick, and comforting mourners, and drop the issue of whether there is any respect in which we can become *like* God? In a nutshell, the reason is that Maimonides accepts enough of the Platonic worldview to regard earthly matter as the source of evil and sees *imitatio Dei* as a way of freeing ourselves from the ties of matter. We saw that matter acts like a dark veil that prevents us from apprehending immaterial things as they really are and causes all acts of disobedience.

Not only is matter a constant distraction, but it is a cause of moral and intellectual contamination. In Maimonides' opinion, it is filthy, shameful, and humiliating. Insofar as it causes the mind to think in spatial/temporal terms, it is responsible for idolatry. Not surprisingly, he concludes that (*GP* 3.8, p. 433) "the commandments and prohibitions of the Law are only intended to quell all the impulses of matter." Thus all the commandments aim at holiness insofar as they get us to control or even to feel shame over the material component of our existence. That is why one does not have to be a guru or a diviner or anything of the sort to be holy; all one has to do is perform the commandments we have.

To control the impulses of matter is to purify the soul and enable it to devote as little attention as possible to bodily functions like the desire for food, drink, or sex. When bodily functions rule, he tells us in another chapter, the longing for speculation is abolished, the body is corrupted, sorrows multiply, and death comes prematurely (*GP* 3.33, p. 532). Quelling the impulses of matter is therefore a necessary condition for seeking truth and promoting social harmony. The search for truth culminates in the study of physics and metaphysics, the subjects addressed in the *Guide*. The study of physics and metaphysics, in turn, makes one reflect on the spheres, which are composed of heavenly matter, and eventually on God, who is not composed of matter at all.

In this scheme, performing the commandments is not just a way of pleasing God but a way of redirecting human energy and seeking human perfection. For all intents and purposes, holiness is another name for purification, which can be described as the process of loosening one's ties to the earthly realm and focusing on the eternal. In Maimonides' words, true perfection consists in (*GP* 3.54, p. 635):

> ... the acquisition of the rational virtues—I refer to the conception of the intelligibles, which teach true opinions concerning the divine things. This is in true reality the ultimate end; this is what gives the individual true perfection, a perfection belonging to him alone; and it gives him permanent perdurance; through it man is man.

We saw that as the process of purification reaches its final goal, people turn wholly to God so as to know God's governance of the universe in whatever way possible. In Maimonides' opinion, this condition is marked by loss of interest in bodily functions as well as humility, awe, reverence, and shame before God.

In regard to shame and humility, Maimonides points out that when God first spoke to Moses at the burning bush, Moses hid his face because he was afraid (Exodus 3:6). By contrast the nobles of Israel tried to look on or apprehend God too quickly (Exodus 24:10–11), with the result that their vision of God contained a material compo-

nent and was therefore imperfect. As for bodily functions, Maimonides reiterates that when Moses was on the mountain with God,
he went without food or water for forty days and nights.

In assessing Maimonides' view of human perfection, we should
keep in mind that he is not working in the context of a Cartesian
epistemology. For Maimonides knowledge is not a matter of clearness and distinctness of representations in the mind but of contact or
assimilation between knower and object known. If there is contact,
then there must be some type of similarity. As Baḥya put it: "The
soul is a simple, spiritual entity which inclines to what resembles it
among similar spiritual entities and, in accordance with its nature,
removes itself from its opposites in gross bodies."[19] It follows that a
soul that is still preoccupied with material things cannot approach or
comprehend the spiritual entities to which it is naturally disposed
and thus cannot achieve holiness.

Behind Maimonides, Baḥya, and Plotinus stands Plato. In a famous passage in the *Seventh Letter*, Plato tells us that knowledge
never takes root in an alien nature, so that neither quickness of learning nor a good memory can make someone see something to which
his soul is not inclined.[20] To have any hope of receiving the illumination necessary to achieve knowledge of something like justice, the
soul must "live with" it and develop an affinity for it.[21] While quickness of learning and a good memory are necessary conditions for illumination, Plato insists they have to be combined with moral qualities like patience, humility, and persistence to allow the soul to gain
what it seeks. Without the proper upbringing, the soul may be adept
at manipulating words and symbols, but, in Plato's opinion, it will
not be accustomed to truth and is likely to be satisfied with the first
image suggested to it (*Seventh Letter* 343c). Overall not only must
the soul have the opportunity to think, it must make the decision to
turn away from material things and devote itself to the apprehension
of spiritual.

The assumption that underlies Plato's view is that contemplation
is a form of attachment or association in which the soul clings to the
object with which it has established kinship. Sometimes he compares
the acquisition of knowledge to initiation in a religious cult, sometimes to entry into a holy shrine.[22] In either case, his metaphors for
apprehension all imply some type of symmetry between the knower
and the object known. The knower must resemble the object to become attached to it; but in Plato's opinion, it is impossible to become
attached to an object without taking on some of its characteristics.
To think about eternal beauty or justice is to participate in the eter-

nal order and become beautiful and just oneself. According to *Republic* 500b–d:[23]

> The man whose thoughts are truly directed to real existences, Adiemantus, does not have time to look down upon the affairs of men, and by contending with them to be filled with malice and ill-will. As he looks upon and contemplates things that are ordered and ever the same, that do no wrong to, and are not wronged by, each other, being all in a rational order, he imitates them and tries to become as like them as he can. Or do you think one can consort with things one admires without imitating them in one's own person?—Not possibly.
>
> So the philosopher, who consorts with what is divine and ordered, himself becomes godlike and ordered as far as a man can.

In this respect, Plato's view is an elaboration of the old Greek aphorism "Like knows like." From Plato's perspective, contemplation resembles love in the sense that the soul is naturally disposed to cling to the object of knowledge, occupy itself with it, and pattern its life after it. That is why Plato's epistemology is so well suited to metaphors suggesting ritual purity. Since an unjust soul will never be able to think about justice, it is a waste of time to teach philosophy to someone who is not properly initiated.[24] In the Republic, the guardians are not exposed to philosophy until they have completed a rigorous program of music, gymnastics, and mathematics.

Not surprisingly, Maimonides (*GP* 1.18), who is very much a part of the Platonic tradition, regards closeness or touching as a metaphor for apprehension and typically associates apprehension with love or desire.[25] In view of his negative theology, a person cannot become like God by sharing an attribute or belonging to the same species. The problem is not that our attributes fall short of God's but that strictly speaking God does not have attributes and cannot be subsumed under a species. Since the difference between God and us is not one of degree, it remains inviolate no matter how spiritual or contemplative we become.

But a person can become like God—or more precisely, like the heavenly realm—in a much weaker sense when earthly matters cease to be important and spiritual or eternal ones predominate. The hope is that once the soul contemplates the vastness of the heavenly realm, it will begin to appreciate the insignificance of earthly matters and feel a sense of awe.[26] The culmination of this process occurs when a person becomes so focused on heavenly matters that he or she is "kissed by God" and passes directly into the next world (*GP* 3.51, p. 628). To repeat: Direct contact or union with God is impossible, so that when Maimonides talks about people being kissed by God, he really has in mind contact with the Agent Intellect. In any case, *imitatio Dei* is a process of purification by which the soul transforms itself from an earth-centered existence to a heaven-centered one. Since our grasp of the heavens is limited, the process is also one in which the soul comes to accept its own insignificance and to abandon any form of self-promotion or self-assertion. At *Guide* 3.11, p. 441, Maimonides assures us that once we reach this point, "enmity and hatred are removed and the inflicting of harm by people on one another is abolished." But a soul that reaches it still does not have perfect apprehension and cannot be a subject of worship in its own right. In the end, all it can be is a human soul that has reached the highest level of perfection available to it.

Imitatio Dei *and Human Perfection*

A modern reader is likely to object that Maimonides' intellectualism goes too far. Not only is total detachment from earthly endeavors not possible from our standpoint, it may not be desirable. What happened to clothing the naked and visiting the sick? Maimonides tempers his intellectualism by saying that prophecy is a two-sided phenomenon involving both the rational and the imaginative faculties. Since the imagination is tied to the material world, the prophet will have not only true opinions on speculative matters but "general directives for the well-being of men in relations with one another" (*GP* 2.36, p. 372). As I will argue in a later chapter, Maimonides believed that political stability is not enough to ensure perfect governance; a leader must also be concerned with people's spiritual needs, which means their worship of an immaterial being.

Though we cannot share an essential attribute with God, according to Maimonides, we can try to imitate God's attributes of action; that is, a ruler can try to show justice and mercy in the appropriate circumstances and see to it that people in need are adequately provided for.[27] We saw that while God is called merciful and gracious, these qualities do not spring from internal dispositions. Therefore all we can imitate by being merciful and gracious are actions, not the actor. Maimonides adds that if God does not act on the basis of internal dispositions, we should discipline ourselves so that we do not either. In other words, a ruler should strive to act in a way that eschews passion and emotion and should decide issues solely on the merits of the case. If the ruler shows mercy or vengeance, he should do so not because he *feels* merciful or vengeful but because one person deserves one response while another person deserves another.

This is another way of saying that *imitatio Dei* implies disinterest or, as we might say, impartiality. So while the record of Moses' prophetic activity contains commandments that reinforce speculative judgments about the existence and unity of God, it also contains commandments that set forth a model of behavior and the foundations of a just society.

Overall Maimonides sees human perfection along the following lines. Performance of the commandments cleanses the soul by quelling the impulses of matter and causing it to act in a humble and dispassionate way. Eventually the soul will be motivated to study physics and metaphysics and reflect on the heavenly realm. To the degree that it reflects on the heavenly realm, it establishes contact with the Agent Intellect and participates in the divine overflow.[28] This overflow first reaches the rational faculty of the prophet and then overflows to the imaginative. Once the prophet's faculties are aroused, he turns to God in an act of total devotion. Having achieved this state, the prophet is able to create or oversee a harmonious community just as God, in a manner unknown to us, creates and oversees a harmonious world.[29] In this way Maimonides' conception of the prophet has both a theoretical and practical component and bears an obvious similarity to Plato's philosopher-king.[30]

But even if the comparison with philosopher-kings is valid, problems remain. Though prophecy has a practical component, Maimonides clearly says that the prophet's rational perfection is superior. Hence the claim that even though Moses tended to practical matters, inwardly his heart was turned to God (*GP* 3.51, pp. 621–23). In this section of the *Guide* he also claims several times that true prophets apprehend God not with the imagination but with the intellect.[31] This claim implies that while imaginative visions may be needed to communicate with the greater community, for the most part the prophet does not need them and may even shun them.[32] Maimonides' usual claim is that true holiness, the first intention of the Law, is an intellectual perfection and requires an act of apprehension.[33] Unlike moral perfection, intellectual perfection pertains to the agent alone and does not involve the agent with other people (*GP* 3.54, p. 635). Finally there is Maimonides' emphatic assertion (*GP* 3.27, p. 511) that the ultimate perfection for humans is intellectual and does not involve moral qualities or moral knowledge:

> His [a human being's] ultimate perfection is to become rational in actu, I mean to have an intellect in actu; this would consist in his knowing everything concerning all the beings that it is within the capacity of man to know in accordance with his ultimate perfection. It is clear that to

this ultimate perfection there does not belong either actions or moral
qualities and that it consists only of opinions toward which speculation
has led and that investigation has rendered compulsory.

To say that human perfection is attainment of an intellect in actu is
to say it is an intellect that apprehends theoretical subjects rather
than practical. In regard to the latter, Maimonides argues that the distinction between good and bad is based on commonly accepted beliefs rather than truths grasped by the intellect.[34]

This evidence has not stopped a group of scholars from main-
taining that no matter what Maimonides says about intellectual perfection, the practical dimension of human perfection is still primary.
The argument has both a political and a moral version. The political
version is to concede that Maimonides regards human perfection as
intellectual but to point out that when you take into account all the
limits he puts on knowledge, in particular the unknowability of God
and the heavenly realm, then, like Kant, he is really defending the practical life over the contemplative. Note, for example, the qualification
expressed in the above passage: knowing everything *that it is within
the capacity of man to know.* We saw that at *Guide* 1.54, p. 128, he
says that the utmost virtue is to become like God as far as we are
able, "which means that we should makes our actions like His." In
the same way he concludes the *Guide* by saying that we should glory
in the apprehension of God and in the knowledge of God's attributes
of action.

In an influential article, Pines argues that since Maimonides
thought metaphysical knowledge is all but impossible, the superiority of the contemplative life "may appear as less than evident."[35] If, to
use Plato's metaphor, we cannot get very far out of the cave, our only
hope of becoming like God is to organize a just and merciful society
within it. Along the same lines, Lawrence Berman argues that "just
as God acts in the realm of nature, so the philosopher acts in the
realm of voluntary things, and it is his duty to found an ideal state
and preserve it."[36]

The ethical version is similar to the political but puts more stress
on personal morality than on the founding of an ideal state. Given
Maimonides' negative theology, in particular the claim that God does
not have an essence, the only thing we can know about God is the attributes of action, which is to say the goodness of God as manifested
in the created order. According to Steven Schwarzschild, "Maimonides'
exegesis is clear: Humanity's purpose is to 'know' God, but the God
who is to be known is knowable only insofar as He practices grace,
justice, and righteousness in the world, and to know Him is synony-

mous with imitating these practices."[37] In this connection, it is significant that Maimonides claims in the Parable of the Palace (*GP* 3.51, p. 620) that the prophets who have entered the ruler's council turn toward God "so as to know His governance"—another reference to attributes of action.[38] Moreover, the very last sentence of the *Guide* clearly says that after the perfect individual has achieved the highest level of apprehension, she will always have moral qualities in mind "through assimilation to His actions."

Schwarzschild's view is essentially a restatement of Cohen's and is based on the claim that negative theology amounts to a rejection of metaphysics in favor of ethics. "The place of being," in Cohen's (*RR*, p. 94) words, "is taken by action."[39] For Cohen this means that (*RR*, p. 96) "holiness becomes *morality*," which in turn (*RR*, p. 98) "becomes the embodiment of the thirteen characteristics of God," another reference to the attributes of action. Thus coming to know God is not like trying to identify an unknown chemical in a laboratory. If the prophet tries to know God, it is not to find out what God is but to establish a paradigm for behavior. In this sense, knowledge *of* God is really a form of devotion *to* God.[40] From devotion we get the idea of service or worship, which takes us out of the realm of theory and into the realm of practice. Cohen therefore takes Maimonides to mean that negative theology goes hand in hand with the principle of *imitatio Dei*.

Cohen is right to say that knowledge involves devotion. But it is far from clear that Maimonides understood devotion as purely practical. Certainly there are important passages where he describes negative theology as an achievement in its own right rather than a reason for turning from theory to praxis. It is, after all, Moses' awareness of negation that makes him the wisest and humblest person on earth (*GP* 1.59, pp. 137–38). The attributes of action are God's concession to Moses, and in a way Maimonides' concession to us. They allow us to make sense of the language of prayer and to set our sights on the proper values. But Maimonides never doubts that the attributes of action are a step removed from God, and therefore mention of them is secondary to the highest tribute and best level of perfection, which is silent contemplation.

The same conclusion arises from Maimonides' claim that even when doing mundane chores, Moses' heart was turned to God. According to *Guide* 3.51, pp. 621–22, "Excellent men begrudge the times in which they are turned away from Him by other occupations." Perhaps there is a good ethical reason for this: Because such people begrudge the times when they are turned away from God, they are the only ones who can be trusted not to use that time to advance their own interests. Still, Maimonides describes prophets as people who participate in practical matters "with their limbs only." In the world to come, when we no longer have to worry about interruptions, the only action available to us will be contemplation. In itself contemplation is the highest end; but owing to the necessities of the human condition, it must be accompanied by a practical component as well. So the question of whether the highest end is contemplation or is contemplation plus action depends to a large extent on what standpoint we pick.

Faced with this duality, Guttmann opts for a compromise: While moral virtue is a means to intellectual, once intellectual virtue is achieved, moral virtue takes on a new dimension so that "ethics, though previously subordinate to knowledge, has now become the ultimate meaning and purpose of the knowledge of God."[41] There is no question that Maimonides thinks ethical behavior will take on a deeper meaning as theoretical knowledge increases, or that the latter will spill over into the former, but where is the evidence that ethics will become the *ultimate* meaning of the knowledge of God?

Aside from the question of standpoint, the reason there is so much confusion on this issue is that when we get to experiences like awe, reverence, and complete devotion to God, the distinction between theoretical and practical knowledge breaks down. According to Kant (*CPR*, B ix), reason is either theoretical or practical depending on whether it seeks to determine an object or to realize it. The distinction is relevant when the issue is a scientific conception of the world versus our sense of ourselves as free agents. But neither category captures Maimonides' claim that God is reached through ascending spheres of negation. In the first place, the point of negative theology is that God *cannot* be determined, that when reason tries to subsume God under a genus or locate God in logical space, it runs up against inviolable limits. In the second place, commandment and obligation do not actually put us in touch with God but rather with God's governance of the created order. Strictly speaking, God is not a moral agent, not gracious or merciful, but the infinite and unknowable source from which mercy and graciousness in the world proceed.

To stand in awe of this source is not to have an object or a specific end in view but to confess that all objects and ends that we can fathom fall short, and therefore that the only legitimate response is, like Job, to repent in silence. There are, of course, practical overtones to this experience because it means giving up a self-centered view of the world and coming to terms with finitude. Thus Maimonides (*GP* 3.23, p. 493) interprets Job 42:6 ("wherefore I abhor myself and repent . . .") to mean "wherefore I abhor all that I used to desire. . . ." But there is no reason to think that Job's surrender to God is a simple case of determining an object or of emulating a paradigm. It is instead a limiting experience beyond the reach of metaphysical or ethical categories as we normally understand them. To the degree that it culminates in silence, it is neither the acquisition of discursive knowledge nor a way of interacting with other people.

What is it? We can call it a form of contemplation, but this description is incomplete, because Maimonides also understands it as a form of devotion. It is not the contemplation of propositions, because all propositions distort the simplicity of God. Though it does not involve other people directly, Maimonides never doubts that it will overflow into a life of humility, spiritual purity, and concern for the welfare of others.[42] Clearly it is hard to say where the theoretical component begins and the practical component ends. Cohen is wrong to describe negative theology as the rejection of metaphysics for ethics, because in Maimonides' mind metaphysics gets closer to God than anything else. Certainly there is nothing in the *Guide* claiming that will rather than thought is the medium through which we achieve the highest perfection. But it would be equally wrong to say that negative theology represents the rejection of ethics for metaphysics, because even metaphysics falls short. In fact, it is the rejection of everything other than God, which is to say everything other than what is beyond all attempts at classification. It is, then, a special kind of contemplation, devotion, and rejection in one experience. Though it is not the governing of a society or the doing of good deeds, it invariably leads to them. Though it is not the sharing of an attribute with God, it is as heaven-like or heaven-centered as we can become.

So far from minimizing the difference between God and humans, Maimonides' understanding of *imitatio Dei* reinforces it. In his treatment of people like Moses, Job, or Rabbi Akiva, he never tires of pointing out that even the heroic few have to respect limits. To use a term that Hegel employs in reference to Kant, the fundamental principle in Maimonides' philosophy is "the absoluteness of finitude."[43] Unless this principle is accepted, either God would be mundanized or humans deified. In either case, holiness in the sense of feeling awe and shame before God would be impossible.

As usual, Maimonides' conclusion has a sobering effect. Like Plato's philosopher-kings, the perfect individual has to juggle the desire to contemplate God's transcendence with the need to tend to the affairs of a community. Though the former is primary, the second is still necessary. Even in moments of contemplation, the perfect individual does not get an answer to every question, pursues a goal most people not only cannot achieve but have difficulty understanding, and receives no material reward other than an occasional flash of insight. There is a joy that comes with this life, but it is the joy of intense devotion rather than ecstatic celebration. In the words of Alfred Ivry, the few people who achieve perfection in Maimonides' sense "are not granted any traditional panaceas: No personal after-life awaits the philosopher, no significant immortality: no punishments, but no rewards as usually conceived."[44] As I will argue in a later chapter, the whole issue of reward and punishment ceases to matter.

While this condition may be difficult to achieve, and by Maimonides' own admission (*GP* 3.51, p. 624) is beyond his reach, there is nothing in his description that makes it impossible in principle. Since prophecy is the natural perfection of the human species, it cannot involve powers humans do not have. Accordingly human life is not spent chasing a goal systematically beyond our reach. If we cannot know what God is, perfection consists in understanding why we cannot and in giving up the desire to find out. If, as Maimonides tells us, reason has a place where it stops, then the search for perfection has a place where it stops as well. In short, "*ought* implies *can*" remains true even at the highest levels of human excellence.[45]

From the Medieval Argument to the Modern

By the eighteenth century the medieval position crumbled in two important respects. The theory of cognition that regarded knowledge as union or conjunction between knower and object known was abandoned in favor of one that emphasizes the way in which the mind organizes and interprets the information at its disposal. Physics ceased to concern itself with matter and form and took up the question of how microscopic particles or fluids interact with one another. More important for my purpose, the idea of a metaphysical realm from which we receive emanations was replaced with a natural realm governed by the same scientific laws that apply on earth. With the rejection of heavenly intelligences came the rejection of the last vestige of intermediaries.

But there is still an important point of similarity: Both Maimonides and the quintessential modern thinker Immanuel Kant believe in a transcendent God. If transcendence cannot be interpreted in terms of matter and form, or spheres and intelligences, there has to be another way to account for it. According to Kant, the solution is to shift the focus of theology from the theoretical realm to the practical. While reason in its theoretical capacity cannot prove the existence of God, in its practical capacity it cannot help but assume it. In fact, Kant argues that even if the traditional arguments for God's existence were valid, they would prove too little because what the religious believer wants is not a necessary being or first cause but a moral exemplar. He therefore concludes that the only content we can ascribe to our idea of God is moral (*CPR*, A818/B846): "It was the moral ideas that gave rise to that concept of the divine Being which we now hold to be correct—and we so regard it not because speculative reason convinces us of its correctness, but because it completely harmonizes with the moral principles of reason."

We saw that in its practical capacity, reason seeks not to determine an object but to realize an end. But it is important to note that the ends that reason establishes are not generalizations from experience. In its present form, human behavior is depressing and disappointing. If all we could strive for were success as measured by human standards, we would set our sights too low and capitulate to evil.[46] The crux of Kant's position is that reason establishes norms of behavior independent of existing conditions. Thus Kant's philosophy is based on a fundamental distinction between *is* and *ought*. According to *Foundations of the Metaphysics of Morals* (pp. 407–8), "The question at issue is not whether this or that happened but that reason of itself and independently of all experience commands that it ought to happen."

Once we make the shift from a metaphysical conception of God to a moral conception, we do not confront a heavenly order and an earthly one, but the world with all its problems and the ideals to which it falls short.[47] In this way, reason presents us with a task: not only to know the world but to improve it. The task would make no sense unless we were outraged by the injustices we see and able to conceive of better alternatives. Without indignation we would compromise our principles; without a vision of something better, we would be lulled into a false sense of complacency. The upshot is that human perfection is no longer the gaining of knowledge but the transformation of the will from a pleasure-seeking life to a life based on principles with universal application.

In keeping with this approach, Cohen is highly critical of any attempt to argue, with Hegel, that the real *is* the rational or that the gap between reality and ideality has been closed.[48] According to classical Jewish teaching, the messiah has not come and therefore the world, though redeem*able*, is not yet redeemed.[49] Not surprisingly, Cohen argues that morality is future oriented: Because present conditions fall short of the ideal, morality requires a time when injustices can be corrected and sins atoned for. Cohen finds the origin of the idea of futurity in the prophets, who taught that history does not have to repeat itself, because a sinful Israel can repent and alter its ways. Thus Ezekiel (18:31) implores us to cast away our sins and get a new heart and a new spirit.

The gap between reality and ideality allows Kant and Cohen to put as much distance between God and humans as Maimonides did. Like Maimonides, they stress the imperfect nature of human existence and the importance of awe, humility, and reverence. God, whose will is completely rational, is the ideal against which every person is judged and from which every person must seek forgiveness. In an important passage in the *Critique of Pratical Reason* (p. 123), Kant argues that the ideal established by the moral law is not only distant but "infinitely remote." As for mystical union, he terms it a monstrosity (*CPrR*, pp. 120–21).

Unless moral perfection is infinitely remote, in Kant's terms, it would be "completely degraded from its holiness, by being made out as lenient (indulgent) and thus compliant to our convenience, or its call and its demands are strained to an unattainable destination . . . and are lost in fanatical theosophical dreams which completely contradict our knowledge of ourselves."[50] In other words, if perfection became too accessible, then either (1) it would be too easy and no longer worthy of respect, or (2) we would flatter ourselves to suppose that we had achieved it.

The problem is that while Maimonides can say that holiness *is* the recognition of God's infinite distance and the awe and humility that result from it, Kant and Cohen cannot say the same thing about the moral law. For if *ought* implies *can*, then by saying that the moral law is obligatory, Kant and Cohen are committed to saying that it can be fulfilled. If it is capable of being fulfilled, then we must be capable of closing the gap that separates reality from ideality. It may be that it has not been closed before and that we are a long way from closing it now. Nevertheless, it cannot be unbridgeable in principle or else we will be back to Sisyphus. In sum, the shift from metaphysical to moral separation carries with it a very different assessment of human capacity. That assessment raises important questions for how we interpret the commandment to be holy.

The Modern Argument: Kant and
Cohen on Self-Sanctification

Following Maimonides, Cohen connects the commandment to be holy at Leviticus 19:2 with a similar command expressed at Leviticus 11:44: "Sanctify yourselves therefore, and be holy; for I am holy."[51] Although he was the product of a different tradition, Kant too interprets sanctification as a process of becoming like God (*RWL*, pp. 60–61):[52]

> The law says: "Be ye holy (in the conduct of your lives) even as your Father in Heaven is holy." This is the ideal of the Son of God which is set up before us as our model. But the distance separating the good which we ought to effect in ourselves from the evil when we advance is infinite, and the act itself, of conforming our course of life to the holiness of the law, is impossible of execution in any given time.

In the *Critique of Pratical Reason* (p. 122) he claims that sanctification is "the supreme condition of the highest good." Needless to say, Kant and Cohen both assume that the ground and final end of religious law is the moral law, which can be expressed as obedience to the idea of law as such. According to Kant, holiness is therefore complete fitness of the will to the moral law: in short, doing the law for its own sake with no taint of selfishness.

For Kant, too, holiness is connected with purity. In God, the will always acts for the sake of principle and is not tempted by sensuous motives. Thus God's good will is completely a priori. But in beings made up of a sensuous and an intellectual component, even the most noble motives are corrupted by the presence of self-love. Though Maimonides does not envision a reduction of all commandments to one imperative, he does insist that obedience to commandments be disinterested and that rulers try to show justice or mercy without responding to feelings or dispositions. All three thinkers agree that it is not just the performance of commandments that makes one holy but the performance of commandments in a principled or impartial way. They also agree that selfless behavior is not accidental but requires cultivation of the rational part of our nature, what Kant (*RWL*, p. 43) calls a transformation of a person's "cast of mind." Finally all agree that people need rituals and religious institutions to make this transformation possible.

The problem is that according to Kant, purity of purpose cannot be achieved by a rational agent in the world of sense, so that on any

given occasion it is impossible to bring the *is* into complete conformity with the *ought.* In *Religion within the Limits* (p. 32) he argues
that the reason a sensuous being cannot achieve holiness is not, as
Maimonides thought, that matter is inherently corrupting, but that
there is in all people a propensity to evil that Kant terms "a perversity of the heart."[53] In other words, the culprit is not the fact that we
have a body, or that we are constantly exposed to evil in the world
around us, or even that we are predisposed by nature to act one way
rather than another. Kant's point is that since we are responsible for
the evil we do, the source of that evil cannot lie in something over
which we have no control. Rather the source is that our will
(*Willkür*) chooses of its own to subordinate noble motives to ignoble
ones (*RWL*, p. 17): "When we say, then, Man is by nature good, or,
Man is by nature evil, this means only that there is in him an ultimate ground . . . of the adoption of good maxims or of evil maxims."
Although this ground is universal in the sense that "evil can be predicated of man as a species," Kant still wants to hold that the problem
is the way we choose to act rather than something we inherit (*RWL*,
p. 36): "In the search for the rational origin of evil actions, every such
action must be regarded as though the individual had fallen into it directly from a state of innocence."[54] So humanity constantly falls
short of the goals it sets for itself even though there is no external
force compelling it to do so.

The problem is that the failure to adopt good maxims runs so
deep that it is "rooted in humanity itself" and therefore cannot be
corrected by human powers.[55] If it cannot be corrected by human
powers, then, Kant reasons, it cannot be corrected in finite time. But
if purity of purpose is an obligation, it must be attainable; and if it
is attainable, the perversity of the human heart must be correctable
in some way. The only way out of the dilemma is to conclude that
purity of purpose is not attainable *in this life,* from which it follows
that the soul must be able to survive the death of the body. Simply
put, one life is not enough to fulfill the commandment to be holy.
And if one life is not enough, neither is a finite number of lives. If
Kant is right, complete moral improvement requires infinite time,
which means that the soul must be immortal. Yet even infinite time
may not be enough. Maimonides believed in immortality but claimed
that when the soul gets to the next world, it will remain in one and
the same state. By contrast, Kant says not only that the soul will
live forever but that it must be capable of making endless progress
toward its goal.

Like Kant, Cohen (*RR*, p. 204) agrees that God presents humanity with the task of self-sanctification and that this task makes sense only if it is infinite: "Like ethics, religion too must always be concerned only with tasks which, as such, are infinite and therefore require infinite solutions." Thus the commandment to be holy can have no time limit. In Cohen's words (*RR*, p. 305): "Self-purification remains an infinite task for the individual; it cannot have its termination in death."

Behind the thought of Kant and Cohen is the belief that we cannot degrade the moral law by putting it within the reach of finite agents. Kant therefore insists on obedience to a command that is "stern, unindulgent, truly commanding, and really not just ideally possible." To think that one has achieved it is surely presumptuous. As Allen Wood points out, Kant thinks morality is defined by reason prior to any resolve on our part so that it is characteristic of our nature never to be satisfied with what is temporal.[56] Along these lines, Kant quotes Romans 3:9: "They are all under sin—there is none righteous (in the spirit of the law), no, not one," while Cohen quotes Ecclesiastes 7:20: "Surely there is not a righteous person on earth who does good and never sins."

The problem arises from the fact that our intuitions are pulled in two directions. The first direction is moral radicalism, the view that we should not compromise in defining perfection. The commandment that asks us to sanctify ourselves and be holy was not meant as a justification for lowered standards but just the opposite: to have no standard except God. The second direction is Platonism, the view that the world of sense is a crude imitation of the ideal world. Surely we would be skeptical of anyone who claimed that she had in fact fulfilled the commandment and succeeded in becoming holy. When we put the two together with the "*ought* implies *can*" principle, we get the conclusion that the process of becoming holy requires infinite time and infinite progress in that time.

There is, of course, an illicit move in this argument. From the fact that I cannot become holy in this life, it does not follow that I need infinite time in another one. This point is complicated by the fact that Kant does not—indeed cannot—tell us what moral progress in a disembodied state is like. Why, for example, can I not achieve holiness the moment I shed my sensuous nature and become a spiritual being? If I have become a purely spiritual being, why do I need infinite time to rid myself of the contamination that arises from physical desire and self-love? Worse, if time is a form of intuition that characterizes our experience of phenomena, how can it apply to life in the next world at all?[57] A standard reply is that Kant is not claiming that we have theoretical knowledge of the next life, only that the idea of immortality is possible and morality requires it.[58] Although it is natural for us to conceive of this progression in a temporal fashion, it is no more temporal than the expansion of a mathematical function. But even if this response is right, the same question arises: What meaning can we give to moral progress that does not involve time? Ultimately Kant would have to fall back on the claim that our existence in the next life is mysterious so that all we can do is suppose that some form of moral improvement could occur. In Kant's words (*RWL*, p. 149): "We know nothing of the future, and we ought not to seek to know more than what is rationally bound up with the incentives of morality and their end."

Note, however, that as Kant presents it, the "*ought* implies *can*" principle appears to have two forms. According to the strong form, if moral purity is commanded, it must be attainable. If I ought to act for the sake of duty, it must be possible for me to so act without any taint of self-love. According to the weak form, if moral purity is commanded, then all that is possible are successive approximations to it. In other words, the weak form says that all I can be obliged to do is strive for the ideal, not reach it. The ambiguity arises from the fact that Kant conceives of possibility in two ways: what is possible in itself and what is possible as a historical reality. While there is nothing in the moral law that renders it impossible in the first sense, the perversity of the heart renders it impossible in the second. "The act," Kant tells us (*RWL*, p. 60), "is *always* (not eternally, but at each instant of time) defective." Therefore complete conformity with the holiness of the law is "impossible of execution in any given time." So no matter how hard we try to achieve moral purity, there will always be more progress to make. If so, then progress toward the ideal is all that can be commanded.

In the *Critique of Practical Reason* (pp. 32–33), Kant puts the point this way:

> This holiness of will is, however, a practical ideal which must necessarily serve as a model which all finite rational beings must strive toward even though they cannot reach it. The pure moral law, which is itself for this reason called holy, constantly and rightly holds it before their eyes. The utmost that finite practical reason can accomplish is to make sure of the unending progress of its maxims toward this model and of the constancy of the finite rational being in making continuous progress.

This is virtue, and, as a naturally acquired faculty, it can never be perfect, because assurance in such a case never becomes apodictic certainty, and as a mere opinion it is very dangerous.

The question of *how we can know* if we have acted for a completely noble motive is another issue. In the *Metaphysics of Morals* (p. 446) Kant enlarges on the issue of moral striving by invoking the distinction between perfect and imperfect obligation:

> It is man's duty to *strive* for this perfection, but not to *reach* it (in this life), and his compliance with this duty can, accordingly, consist only in continual progress. Hence, while this duty is indeed narrow and perfect *with regard to* its object . . . *with regard to* the subject it is only a wide and imperfect duty to himself.

It follows that all I can be expected to have is the disposition to moral perfection, not perfection itself. Cohen too (*RR*, p. 212) remarks that "I remain man, and therefore I remain a sinner, I therefore am in constant need of God, as the One who forgives sin."

In view of the persistence of sin, the weak or imperfect form of the *"ought* implies *can"* principle is the only one Kant and Cohen can accept. As Lewis White Beck argues, "We are told to seek the Kingdom of God, not to settle in it."[59] Let us suppose, then, that I have made the decision to seek God's Kingdom but, because of the perversity of my heart, I continue to sin. Kant goes on to say that God will see in my pursuit of holiness a firm disposition (*Gesinnung*) to achieve it, and this disposition is all that is needed to fulfill the commandment to be holy. Kant therefore takes refuge in the hope that divine grace will close the gap between disposition and deed (*RWL*, p. 70): "What in our earthly life . . . is ever only a *becoming* . . . should be credited to us exactly as if we were already in full possession of it." In other words, God will see that while in my earthly life I remain a sinner, my change of heart has made me into a new person "in the eyes of a divine judge for whom this disposition takes the place of action" (*RWL*, p. 68). So God will credit me for the moral self I have decided to become rather than the empirical and imperfect self I still am.

Along similar lines, Cohen (*RR*, pp. 204–5) argues that since the commandment to be holy is directed to us rather than to God, anything we achieve must be "the lot of man." But it cannot be the lot of man to overcome finitude and establish union with God. Nor, as we saw, can God assign a task that amounts to a labor of Sisyphus. Cohen rejects the idea that salvation can be understood as a gift in

which God miraculously takes away our sin. It is instead the outcome of a process that we must initiate by confessing sin and asking
for God's forgiveness. Accordingly (*RR*, p. 206): "Man himself must
cast off his sin." As with Kant, sin can be cast off only if we have a
complete change of heart; unfortunately it is impossible to know
when or if such a change has occurred. Thus Cohen's claim that man
himself must cast off sin continues: "but whether his deed succeeds,
whether it leads to the goal, this he cannot know."

Still, Cohen continues, we can hardly be indifferent to the question of our success. Unless we had reason to believe that redemption
is possible, there would be no reason to repent. This means that we
must look to God as the one who guarantees the success of repentance, who looks upon our sin as inadvertent and grants expiation.[60]
If so, repentance is the key to self-sanctification, or as Cohen puts it
(*RR*, p. 205), repentance "is" self-sanctification. With each act of repentance, God grants us a new lease on life and therefore "a new way
of life." To be sure, the need for repentance never ends. In Cohen's
words (*RR*, pp. 230–31): "Redemption is to be thought of only for one
moment's duration. Only for one moment, which may be followed
by moments of sin." But unlike Sisyphus, we can hope that God responds to our confession so that our efforts are not in vain. In sum,
acceptance of the task of self-sanctification is the goal; to *try* to
change one's heart in an honest and sincere way is to succeed in becoming holy.

Here too we have a weak form of "*ought* implies *can*." The goal is
not to achieve perfection in the sense of actually fulfilling the moral
law (with all that implies) but to pursue it, confess one's failure, and
try a second time. Again from Cohen (*RR*, p. 207), "Self-sanctification
must arrive at its infinite conclusion in the *forgiveness* of sin by God."
So Kant and Cohen invoke grace or forgiveness to do what endless
progress cannot. While the ultimate goal is still infinite, it is an
infinity we can reach *with God's help*.[61] Either we are credited with
success or we are allowed to succeed by admitting that we have fallen
short and will make a good-faith effort to rededicate ourselves.

According to Henry Allison, the difficulty is that the need for
infinite time arose in the first place because our disposition to pursue
holiness falls short of holiness itself: Motives generated by self-love
contaminate motives based on principle.[62] Therefore any attempt to
identify holiness with the pursuit of holiness begs the question. If all
that is required to achieve holiness is either (1) a firm disposition and
the grace of God, or (2) sincere repentance and continual forgiveness
by God, there is no need for infinite time. Assuming God is respon-

sive, either can be achieved by a person here and now. By contrast, if infinite time is needed, then our pursuit of holiness must fall short of its goal, in which case it cannot be identical with the goal.

Aside from the issue of infinite time, there is the more troubling issue of responsibility. Suppose I decide to renounce my evil ways and embark on the task of self-sanctification. Repentance is genuine only if I have a real change of heart. Since I can be deceived about my motives, only God can know whether my heart is pure. But now we face a problem.[63] If I am really sincere, then the process is complete and there is nothing God can add to what I have accomplished on my own. All God can do is provide encouragement and be certain that my heart is in the right place. If, on the other hand, I am not sincere, then grace or forgiveness would give me something I do not deserve. If I do not deserve them, then my newly found status as a saved soul is not something for which I can take credit and does not constitute progress in the task of sanctifying myself. In Kant's words (*RWL*, p. 179): "That which is to be accredited to us as morally good conduct must take place not through foreign influence but solely through the best possible use of our own power." Or again (*RWL*, p. 40): "Man *himself* must make or have made himself into whatever, in a moral sense . . . he is or is to become." How, then, can God's grace affect my standing? Near the end of *Religion* (p. 134), Kant calls atonement a mystery.

Not surprisingly, Cohen (*RR*, p. 207) raises the same question: "Is not the entire element of forgiveness through God external to the idea of self-sanctification?" Eliminating God as redeemer, as Cohen recognizes, would cause "the main scaffolding of religious knowledge" to collapse. Thus whether we can succeed by our own efforts or not, it must be the case that only God can forgive sin, for without forgiveness "God's being could not be conceived as understandable." Perhaps so, but this does not really answer the question. If I am worthy of being forgiven, God is only responding to what I have accomplished on my own; if I am not worthy, God cannot credit me with *self*-sanctification.

Holiness and Human Capacity

Having looked at a medieval and a modern account of *imitatio Dei*, I want to argue that for all its shortcomings, the medieval one is closer to the truth. In the first place, it is not saddled with the idea of moral improvement in a disembodied state. From Maimonides' perspective, there is no unfinished business to be completed in the next life. In the second place, it is not saddled with the idea that the goal of human life is always beyond our reach. For Maimonides God remains infinitely remote and incomprehensible. For that reason, it is fruitless to imagine ourselves uniting with God or sharing an attribute.[64] According to a rabbinic commentary on Leviticus 11:44, the commandment "Sanctify yourselves and be holy, for I am holy" means that God's holiness is higher than anything we can achieve.[65] Maimonides' point is that if we cannot achieve it, we should not set it up as a goal: If an admission of ignorance followed by awe and humility are all we can achieve, then they are all that can be commanded.[66]

To return to Deuteronomy 30, the commandments are not too difficult for us nor too far away. They were given not to angels but to ordinary human beings. As Maimonides stresses, the commandments are not a timeless abstraction; they were given with the details of the human situation in mind, including the fact that people cannot loosen the ties of matter overnight. While it may require effort to fulfill the commandments, it cannot require effort that is in principle beyond us. By *fulfillment* I do not mean merely doing the required action but doing it with the proper intention or for the proper motive. In other words, everything that is needed to satisfy the commandments is within our capacity. This means that it is within our capacity to get ourselves to the point where we worship God in a completely disinterested fashion. If this understanding is right, then sin, though pervasive, is not inevitable. According to a famous rabbinic text (*Berakhot* 60b), the soul God has breathed into us is pure. Even if we put special emphasis on the commandment to repent, it must still be true that genuine repentance is possible in this life. If the commandments can be fulfilled, there is no need to rely on an external source to close the gap between disposition and deed.

Kant's conception of an infinitely remote goal requiring endless progress is based on an effort to explicate the doctrine of original sin. The perversity of the heart is therefore his response to the claim (Romans 5:12) that "in Adam all have sinned." Kant does not take the phrase literally as signifying that one person's transgression is passed to another, because doing so would imply that we are not responsible for what we do. Nor does he take it to mean that evil is present in us by nature. As we saw, every evil act must be viewed as if we had just fallen from a state of innocence. But in his opinion, each of us keeps falling and will continue to fall for the rest of our lives. So while we are responsible for our moral failings, it remains true that failure is inevitable. It could be said therefore that Kant agrees with the doctrine of original sin to the extent that he does not think we can overcome the propensity to evil by our own power.[67] Eventually we need the grace of God to do what human striving cannot.

Cohen repudiates the doctrine of original sin on the grounds that guilt cannot be inherited and that it is monstrous to suppose that God, who is sanctified by righteousness, would put a predisposition to evil in the human heart.[68] For Cohen the human heart is pure, but because of the weakness of the human condition, we will continue to sin and therefore will continue to need God's forgiveness.[69] "*The forgiveness of sins,*" as Cohen (*RR*, p. 209) insists, "*becomes the special and most appropriate function of God's goodness.*" If we did not seek forgiveness, and were not assured that God would grant it, we would never be able to relieve the burden of guilt and would be left with a life of despair. Thus Cohen concludes, "The entire monotheistic worship is based on forgiveness of sin." The reason for this conclusion is that like Kant, Cohen thinks that while we are responsible for our failings, it is inevitable that we will fail.

From a Jewish perspective, Adam's sin brought death, toil, and fatigue into the world, but death, as Urbach points out, is typically seen as part of the natural order, not a punishment or evil decree.[70] On the basis of Genesis 8:21 ("for the *yetzer* [impulse] of man's heart is evil from his youth"), it could be said that Judaism does recognize an evil impulse or inclination that presents obstacles to human progress. Certainly the accounts of lust, murder, incest, and rape in the Bible dispel any notion that Judaism has an overly optimistic assessment of human behavior. Along the same lines, Genesis 4:7 maintains that like a wild animal, sin crouches at the door, and its urge is for us.

But an evil impulse is a long way from Kant's perversity of the heart. In the first place, the evil impulse, though formidable, *can* be overcome by human power. After saying that sin crouches at the door, the text of Genesis goes on to say, "Yet you can be its master." Second, the evil impulse is not radically or irredeemably evil. According to one rabbinic text, without the evil impulse, no one would build a house, marry, have children, or engage in commerce.[71] According to another, a group of rabbis set out to destroy the evil impulse but learned that if they did so completely, the world would die.[72] The idea seems to be that while the evil impulse can create havoc if left unchecked, it is within our power to control it or redirect its energy to worthwhile ends. This does not mean that everyone will succeed in controlling it, only that in principle nothing prevents us from doing so. As Saadia (*BBO*, pp. 217–18) claims, the probability of a person's achieving perfection may be quite low, but it must be possible or else God would not have prescribed it.[73]

There are also rabbinic texts that express pessimism about human behavior or suggest that for all intents and purposes everyone is a sinner.[74] But these texts can be matched by others that imply that it is possible to die in as pure a state as one had at birth.[75] Whichever set one wishes to emphasize, the fact remains that there is no *official* doctrine of inherited sin or of the need for supernatural power to overcome it. It is true that the prayer book for the Day of Atonement constantly speaks as if we are throwing ourselves on God's mercy and begging for forgiveness, but we saw that this kind of language does not have to be taken literally.

For Maimonides the crux of monotheism is not forgiveness of sin but the overcoming of idolatry. As any student of Jewish philosophy knows, Book 1 of the *Mishneh Torah* contains a long section on repentance. But aside from issues pertaining to the place and proper manner of repentance, the main purpose of this section is to stress that we are responsible for our actions and that the ultimate goal of human life is disinterested love of God. In keeping with Jewish tradition, he claims that the level attained by penitents is higher than that of those who have never sinned, because the former require greater effort to subdue their passions.[76] He also claims that Israel must repent in order to be redeemed. But there is nothing to suggest that repentance is the primary way we relate to God or that it requires infinite time or superhuman effort to complete. In fact, he argues that while not every sage achieved the highest level of perfection, at least one person—Abraham—did achieve it.[77]

With the rabbinic tradition in mind, Maimonides does say that God answers our requests for forgiveness immediately and goes from hating us to loving us.[78] I will argue in the last chapter that while there is a kernel of truth to this claim, it should not be taken literally either. In both the *Mishneh Torah* and the *Guide* he emphasizes that God is outside of time and that neither humans nor anything else have it in their power to change God. So God's mercy or graciousness is not a response to us as much as a permanent feature of God's governance of the world. The reason God is called merciful or gracious is the original act of creation in which "He . . . brings into existence and governs beings that have no claim upon Him with respect to being brought into existence and being governed."[79] In this scheme, every benefit we receive from God, including the gift of reason and the giving of the Torah, is an instance of graciousness.[80] Graciousness, then, is directed to all of creation or to human beings in general, not to me personally. Beyond creation and the giving of Law, there are no emotions, special gifts, or guarantees of success that we can call on or benefit from. If Israel is redeemed, it will be because Israel changes its ways and decides to seek God.

We do not have to accept all the details of Maimonides' intellectualism to see what he is getting at. Holiness involves gaining a perspective broad enough to recognize God's mercy and graciousness in the world around us and to realize that even they do not fully capture God's perfection. The problem is not that the persistence of sin puts holiness out of reach, but that even if we manage to achieve holiness and feel awe and humility before God, because of our nature as sensuous beings we cannot help but become fatigued or distracted.[81] Like love, intense conversation, or Sabbath observance, contemplation cannot go on forever. Though it may give us a taste of the world to come, it cannot be a permanent feature of human existence in this world. Put otherwise, the problem is not whether anyone has or ever will go through life without violating a commandment—something we will never be in a position to know—but whether the pervasive nature of sin puts us in a position from which we cannot liberate ourselves. Kant's answer is yes (*RWL*, p. 66): "SIN . . . brings with it endless violations of the law and so *infinite* guilt."[82] But Kant's position rests on a peculiar feature: Despite the fact that there is nothing to interfere with our will, and no predisposition to evil, it is nonetheless assured that even the best person will continue to subvert the moral law and fall from innocence. From Maimonides' perspective, there is no such difficulty: Liberation from sin, though difficult, is always possible.

It will be objected that if the disposition does not fall short of the deed, we run the risk that people will come forward, proclaim themselves holy, and start to gloat. Throughout his writings Kant warns of the danger of having people flatter themselves about the nobility of their behavior. Aside from the fact that holiness is impossible without humility, this objection can be answered by pointing out that nothing requires us to understand human striving in an all-or-nothing fashion. In other words, there is nothing that says that once a commandment is fulfilled, it can be forgotten. Answering the call of God is not like being elected to the Hall of Fame. In general the fact that you fulfill a commandment today does not mean you are relieved of the obligation to fulfill it tomorrow. As Kant says, virtue can never settle down in peace and quiet.[83] That is why no matter how much perfection we achieve, as long as we are in this life, there is always more work to be done.

So the task is infinite not in the sense that it is too difficult for us to achieve, but in the sense that there is no point at which we are justified in relaxing our efforts. In this vein Kant claims that virtue is always in progress yet always starts from the beginning.[84] But it is not true, as Kant goes on to say, that in this life virtue is unattainable so that all we can hope for are finite approximations to it. It is always beginning, because whether we have achieved our goal or failed, we still have to strive to become holy in the days ahead.

Holiness as Rationality

What, then, is holiness? I have already remarked that the meaning of the Hebrew word *kadosh* is separation. As Gerhard von Rad pointed out, the holy may be understood as "the great stranger in the human world."[85] So the most obvious way to interpret Leviticus 19:2 is in terms of separation or even isolation. But *separation* is a vague term. For much of Jewish history, it meant that Israel should separate itself from the other nations of the earth and from actions that bring defilement. Thus Abraham is commanded to leave the home of his father and set out for a new land. But again one must ask: What kind of separation is intended? Should Abraham's journey be taken literally or metaphorically? Does Judaism see itself as standing outside of culture, as Hegel thought, or as playing an important role within it?

To philosophers in the rationalist tradition, separation is not a matter of geography or genetics but of intellectual vision. Reason is needed to reject ignorance and superstition and accept the first two commandments, which Maimonides considers the essence of the religion. Maimonides emphasizes, however, that the human tendency to think in material terms and therefore violate the first two commandments is universal and can be overcome only by a lifetime of study and practice. While Jews may inherit a body of knowledge that reveals the folly of this material thinking, in Maimonides' opinion they do not constitute a separate species and do not acquire a leg up on the rest of humanity by virtue of their birth. By the same token, physics and metaphysics are available to the people of every nation, a fact Maimonides could scarcely deny given the enormous debt he owed to Aristotle, Ptolemy, Alfarabi, and Avicenna.[86] There is even some evidence that he recognizes the possibility of gentile prophets.[87] Recall that the differences between things in the created order pale into insignificance compared with the overwhelming difference between the created order and God. Since God does not have a race, gender, or social function, we are encouraged to see that these divisions are not ultimate and to hope for the day when all people are able to look beyond them. Just as Israel is asked to love a God who is separate, it is asked to love the stranger or non-Israelite, who is separate as well.[88] Note that when Maimonides describes human perfection at the end of the *Guide* (3.54, p. 635), he does so in a way that avoids any hint of parochialism: "Through it [true opinions concerning divine things] man is man."

Whether we think of intellectual vision in terms of Job repenting before God or of Kant's transformation of a person's cast of mind (*RWL*, p. 43) is not important at this point; the issue is whether we can separate that part of ourselves that is time-bound and pleasure-seeking from that part that is capable of looking at the world from a higher, broader perspective. It is this sense of separation that is captured in Bahya's claim that because the intellect is a spiritual entity, it is a stranger to the material realm.[89] In the present context, being rational does not mean being cool or apathetic. Though it may involve disengagement from material concerns, rationality does not lead to withdrawal into oneself but rather to greater involvement with spiritual matters. Looked at another way, rationality implies that one can achieve enough objectivity to approach God in selfless fashion, forsaking personal demands or any hope of material reward. It is true that Kant and Cohen speak of holiness as the sanctification of the self, but it is well to remember that they are talking about the noumenal self, the one free from sensuous input and capable of acting for the sake of duty.

It could be said, therefore, that reason in the sense here intended is not satisfied with anything partial or particular, which is to say anything finite. Rather than a faculty that comes to the aid of desire by calculating the most efficient means for realizing an end, these thinkers conceive of it as a motivating force of its own, what they characterize as a love or longing for perfection.[90] Maimonides is hardly alone in comparing the knowledge of God to romantic attachment.[91] All agree that nothing perfect is ever given to sense, which is why it is dangerous to rely on the imagination in thinking about God. Along these lines, Kant, following Plato and mimicking Bahya, speaks of reason's "spiritual flight" from the material world.[92] This is, I suggest, an appropriate way to interpret Abraham's spiritual flight from Ur and the Israelites' spiritual flight from Egypt.

In the last analysis, the thinkers I have examined all believe that *imitatio Dei* requires a rational awakening. We can quarrel over the superiority of theoretical to practical reason, but if my interpretation of Maimonides is right, the differences between them become harder to identify as we approach the highest levels of human awareness. By the same token, we can reject Maimonides' belief in a heavenly intelligence that serves as a bond between God and humans and we can question his conception of a spiritual leader who begrudges time spent with other people. His description of prophecy is not only extreme but speculative. At *Guide* 3.51, p. 624, he says that he cannot provide guidance for how to achieve it.[93] Perhaps he is thinking of the prisoner who escapes from Plato's cave or the forty days and nights Moses was on the mountain. In either case, we know that his own life was divided among community leadership, a prolific literary career, and a demanding medical practice.[94] In fact, he claims in a famous letter to Samuel ibn Tibbon that he often pushed himself to the point of exhaustion.

In view of these difficulties, it would be better to say that human perfection is reached when a person sees God's mercy extending over all of creation so that it is impossible to deal with anything without being reminded of God.[95] It may be true that such a person renounces everything other than God, but in this context renouncing something does not mean holding it in contempt. Maimonides was well aware that Jewish Law asks one to honor parents, love the stranger, heal the sick, and comfort mourners. And he was also aware that God looked over the entire created order and saw that it was good. Though he sometimes speaks of bodily functions in a contemptuous manner, his real point is that the prophet will view everything other than God not as a self-subsistent entity but as further evidence of the beauty of God's governance of nature (*GP* 3.51, p. 620). In other words, everything other than God exists by the grace of God and thus cannot satisfy reason's quest for perfection. That is why the prophets are in God's presence even when they are involved in day-to-day activities.

If Maimonides is right, the prophet will be exceedingly humble and treat every recipient of God's grace with tenderness and compassion. What she will not do is look upon a recipient of God's grace as worthy of worship. When it comes to worship, she will follow Isaiah in viewing the nations of the earth, the cedars of Lebanon, and the beasts of the field as nothing *compared with God*. But that does not mean that they have no value in their own right. Such is Maimonides' understanding of holiness.

That what passes for reason can be arrogant, cruel, chauvinistic, and dogmatic no one will deny. But the same can be said of holiness or religious commitment in general: Efforts that begin as an attempt to sanctify life have resulted in torture, bigotry, and fanaticism. It does not follow, however, that the goal of sanctifying life has to be given up. The claim that the rationalist thinkers have on our attention is that if holiness is possible, and the commandment expressed at Leviticus 19:2 can be fulfilled, then rationality in their sense must be possible as well. This means that it must be possible for reason not only to establish the truth of propositions but to motivate and give meaning to worship of the heart. It is hardly surprising, therefore, that Maimonides says early in *Guide* (1.2, p. 23) that reason is the image of God in us. Given the context, this remark can mean only that we become holy to the degree that we embody rationality with all the consequences that follow from it, including the fact that reason must recognize its own limits. In this way, rationality is not just a virtue but a sacred obligation.

6

Monotheism and Freedom

The conclusion of the previous chapter was that for thinkers in the rationalist tradition, the possibility of holiness implies the possibility that we can perfect our nature as rational beings. In this connection, both Maimonides and Cohen cite Deuteronomy 4:6: "[F]or this is your wisdom and your understanding in the sight of all the people, that, when they hear all these statutes, shall say: 'Surely this great nation is a wise and understanding people.'" Thus Israel is supposed to be a source of wisdom for all peoples. We saw that according to Maimonides, the crux of that wisdom is the existence and unity of God as summed up in the first and second commandments.[1]

Even if one is sympathetic to this tradition, there is something odd about saying that the first and second commandments constitute the crux of a body of wisdom, since as Mendelssohn pointed out, no commandment in the Torah says in so many words, "Thou shalt believe . . . ." Nor is there anything in Judaism that corresponds to grace in the sense of a divine gift that enables one to assent to a proposition without evidence.[2] While there have been attempts to introduce articles of faith to Judaism—the most obvious one being that of Maimonides—they have generally met with resistance both in principle and in specifics.[3]

This situation has led some people to say that Judaism is best described as an ortho*praxy* rather than an ortho*doxy*. But rationalists like Maimonides point out that unless one accepts the existence and unity of God, all the other practices, rituals, and benedictions are pointless. "Dogma," as David Bleich put it, "does not stand apart from the normative demands of Judaism but is the *sine qua non* without which other values and practices are bereft of meaning."[4] According to this view, the existence and unity of God are required beliefs. That is why Maimonides does not hesitate to say that belief in them was commanded at Sinai. There is even a tradition that maintains that the people needed Moses to relate all the commandments except the first two; for those two alone, all Israel became a prophet and heard the voice of God directly.

Uplifting as this tradition may be, it raises a serious question: Can belief be commanded? If people are free agents, it is possible to command actions like truth-telling, fasting, Sabbath worship, and daily prayer. But how is it possible to tell someone what to think? If a person is convinced that God exists, the commandment is superfluous; if, on the other hand, someone is not convinced, the commandment will have no force. We can view the problem in another way by turning to Deuteronomy 6:5, which commands love of God. Again, if a person already loves God, there is no need for such a commandment; but if a person does not love God, it is hard to see how a commandment can produce the required feeling.[5] Clearly the problem strikes at the heart of the rationalist position, for if belief cannot be commanded, the whole strategy of approaching Judaism as a worldview rather than a nationality or set of rituals is in jeopardy.

Baḥya on Duties of the Heart

The classic defense of the need for mandatory beliefs can be found in the introduction to Baḥya's *Duties of the Heart*. His first argument is that contrary to what its critics may say, Judaism is not behavioristic: It distinguishes between outward observance in the form of prayer, fasting, resting, and so on and inward observance in the form of fear and love of God. In Baḥya's opinion, though, the former presupposes the latter. We cannot rest unless the heart (*lev*) chooses to do so. But if we choose something and choose it for the right reasons, we must have adequate knowledge of the Law and the principles on which it is based. Thus Baḥya concludes that the commandments cannot be fulfilled without knowledge and practice. Since knowledge implies belief, I take him to mean that what a person believes has a direct bearing on the quality of the action he or she performs. To take his example, a person who asserts that "God is one" while reciting the *Shema* but who has no idea what this means cannot serve a God who is one in a unique and completely immaterial way.

Bahya's second argument is that it is absurd to think that God would issue commandments dealing with our arms, legs, or mouths and neglect the noblest part of our existence—the heart. To see his point, we must understand that in biblical and rabbinic Hebrew, *lev* and its derivatives do not have the same connotation that *heart* does in English. For us the heart is often the seat of emotion or affection and therefore separate from the mind. People can suffer from heartache, wear their heart on their sleeve, or have their heart in their mouth. By contrast *lev* is often the seat of reason or considered judgment. Thus Deuteronomy 29:3: "The Lord has not given you a heart to know and eyes to see"; or Proverbs 16:23: "The heart of the wise teaches his mouth"; or Ecclesiastes 10:2: "A wise man's heart is at his right hand." When God hardens Pharaoh's heart (Exodus 4:21), the meaning is that Pharaoh's mind is set against letting the Israelites leave Egypt. In other contexts, *lev* implies will or resolution. According to Jeremiah 3:15, "I will give you shepherds according to my heart."[6] While there are occasions in which the Bible uses it in connection with emotions, in general *lev* refers to the inner and therefore truest side of a person's character. Not surprisingly, the Bible often speaks of "the heart" as distinct from the eyes, ears, mouth, or other bodily organs.[7] Finally there is the ideal of worship of the heart, which clearly means more than an outpouring of emotion.

Seen in this light, Bahya's point is quite reasonable: If our bodies can serve God, surely our hearts can too. The title of the book, *Duties of the Heart*, should therefore be taken in the sense of duties of the mind, or more generally, duties of thought. As Bahya makes clear (*DH* 1, p. 19), all of what are called "duties of the heart" are based on rational principles. In support of his argument, he cites Deuteronomy 6:5: "You shall love the Lord your God with all your heart, with all your soul, and with all your might." Simply put: God wants more than outward shows of behavior. If so, there have to be internal as well as external obligations. If there are internal obligations, eventually they impinge on what we believe. Thus Deuteronomy 4:39: "Know this day and lay it to your heart that the Lord, He is God." Bahya concludes it is a duty to believe in a Creator who brings the world into existence ex nihilo and does not resemble anything in it.

In one respect the idea of internal obligations is not new. As Bahya points out, it is forbidden to covet your neighbor's belongings or to hate your brother in your heart (Leviticus 19:17); by contrast,

you are required to love your neighbor as yourself (Leviticus 19:18).
Here we might add that repentance is a duty but impossible to fulfill
without honesty and sincerity. But Bahya takes the argument further.
If God is concerned with our heart, then God is concerned with what
we want, how we feel, and more important, what we believe. Yet it is
not enough to accept important claims on other people's authority or
to repeat them without taking the time to ask what they mean. For
Bahya, it is a duty for each person to pursue truth, inquire into meaning, and examine alternatives.

It bears repeating that Judaism did not always understand itself
in this fashion. While there are dozens of prooftexts supporting the
claim that the acquisition of knowledge is a divine command, it may
be questioned whether biblical authors had a consistent view of
monotheism or any inkling of theoretical subjects like physics and
metaphysics. A defender of Bahya could reply, however, that if we are
commanded to seek truth, that commandment extends to all subjects needed to understand and accept the principles on which the religion is based. To take a modern example, it is a duty to heal the
sick. The fact that fulfillment of this duty requires one to master
bodies of knowledge beyond anything that could be imagined by the
biblical or rabbinic authors does not mean that such knowledge can
now be neglected. Maimonides would insist that what is true of med-
icine is also true of physics and metaphysics: If secular learning is
needed to understand what we are doing and why, then secular learning is obligatory even if it takes us into new realms of inquiry.[8]

It is clear that Bahya makes one very big assumption in arguing
for an intellectualized version of Judaism. A duty implies the freedom to obey or disobey. This principle is compelling when applied to
external duties like fasting. But if Bahya is right about duties of
thought, the principle must also apply to what we believe. In other
words, we must be free to believe what we want if it makes sense to
say that God commands belief. The problem is that I cannot be convinced about God and creation as easily as I decide whether to pray or
fast. So anyone who accepts an intellectualized form of religion must
answer the question of how or in what sense belief is voluntary.[9]

Maimonides on Representation and Affirmation

There is little doubt that Maimonides' position is an extension of
Bahya's. The purpose of the law is twofold: to promote the welfare of
the body and the welfare of the soul. Of the two, the latter is primary
and consists in rational activity based on the acquisition of true opin-

ions (*GP* 3.27, pp. 510–11). We saw that in the Parable of the Palace this view is strengthened by the claim that true opinion is not enough: To achieve the highest levels of piety, one must know the causes and principles that make them true. The subject matter of the *Guide* is said to be the science of the Law in its true sense, by which Maimonides means that it will deal primarily with beliefs rather than actions. In keeping with the distinction between belief and action, he also distinguishes between love of God, which is achieved by apprehension of God's existence and unity, and fear of God, which is achieved by performing all the other commandments (*GP* 3.53, p. 630). Accordingly the commandment to love God "becomes valid only through apprehension of the whole of being as it is and through the consideration of His wisdom as it is manifested in us" (*GP* 3.28, p. 513).[10]

In abbreviated form, the beliefs Maimonides considers mandatory are: (1) the existence of God, (2) the unity of God, (3) the incorporeality of God, (4) the eternity of God, (5) that God alone is worthy of worship, (6) prophecy, (7) that Moses is the greatest of the prophets, (8) that the Torah is of divine origin, (9) that the Torah is valid for all times, (10) that God knows everything we do, (11) that God rewards and punishes people for their actions, (12) the coming of the messiah, and (13) eternal life. Recall that those who reject any of these beliefs are cut off from Israel and have no share in the world to come. Since the soul is more important than the body, mental error is the worst fate that can befall someone. Aware that his position is controversial, Maimonides still holds that people can be praised or blamed for what they believe:[11]

> As regards the rational faculty, uncertainty prevails (among philosophers), but I maintain that observance and transgression may also originate in this faculty, in so far as one believes a true or false doctrine.

If we are responsible for what we believe, we must exercise some degree of choice in believing it.[12]

We can better appreciate Maimonides' position by turning to his analysis of belief at *Guide* 1.50. Maimonides begins by setting forth the essentials of the internalist position: "Belief is not the notion that is uttered, but the notion that is represented in the soul." A few lines later he claims that belief involves two factors:

> For there is no belief except after a representation [*taṣawwur*]; belief is the affirmation [*taṣdīq*] that what has been represented is outside the mind just as it has been represented in the mind.

As Wolfson points out, the Arabic *taṣawwur* is derived from Aristotle's *noesis*, while *taṣdīq* is derived from *apophantikos logos*.[13] To have a belief is therefore to represent something to oneself *and* affirm that the representation is faithful to an external reality. The distinction is essentially that between apprehension and judgment. I can apprehend the concept *unicorn* with perfect clarity, but I do not believe in unicorns until I judge that the world contains at least one creature fitting that description. According to this account, belief is an active process; not only does the mind receive information about the world, it makes a decision about the accuracy of that information.

I bring in the notion of judgment because Maimonides' view of belief is part of a long tradition best known to philosophers from Descartes' *Fourth Meditation*:[14]

> Regarding myself more closely, and considering what are my errors (for they alone testify to there being any imperfection in me), I answer that they depend on a combination of two causes, to wit, on the faculty of knowledge that rests in me, and on the power of choice or free will — that is to say, of the understanding and at the same time of the will. For by the understanding alone I [neither assert nor deny anything, but] apprehend the ideas of things as to which I can form a judgment.

Descartes goes on to say that error arises because behind every judgment there is an act of will consisting in the affirmation or denial of what the understanding presents to us:

> . . . for the faculty of will consists alone in our having the power of choosing to do a thing or choosing not to do it (that is, to affirm or deny, to pursue or to shun it), or rather it consists alone in the fact that in order to affirm or deny, pursue or shun those things placed before us by the understanding, we act so that we are unconscious that any outside force constrains us in doing so.

Another way to grasp this point is to distinguish between meaning and truth. The understanding can tell us what the content of an idea is or how a group of ideas are related; but it takes an act of judgment and therefore will to determine whether it is true.

If Descartes is right, error arises when the will is not properly restrained. As long as I restrict affirmation to things I understand clearly and distinctly, then, he thinks, error is impossible. The problem is that I often allow myself to affirm or deny things about which I am still confused. The implication is that error is something for which I have responsibility. According to Descartes, this is true not only when I have difficulty determining the truth or falsity of an idea but when I am absolutely certain of it. Faced with a demonstration of the Pythagorean Theorem, I cannot get myself to withhold consent. Still, Descartes insists that even in this case, I consent freely:

> For in order that I should be free it is not necessary that I should be in-different as to the choice of one or the other of two contraries; but con-trariwise the more I lean to the one—whether I recognize clearly that the reasons of the good and true are to be found in it, or whether God so disposes my inward thought—the more freely do I choose and embrace it. And undoubtedly both divine grace and natural knowledge, far from diminishing my liberty, rather increase it and strengthen it.

Maimonides would be sympathetic with this analysis for several reasons. Like Descartes, he defines volition as the power to will or not will. And there is no reason to think Maimonides would restrict volition to situations of indifference. On the contrary, there is every reason to think that if I affirm God's existence and unity on the basis of demonstration, I affirm it of my own accord and accept responsibility for it. For if I were not free to accept it, I could not fulfill a commandment by doing so.

Enlarging on the previously cited passage from *Eight Chapters*, Maimonides goes on to say in Section 8: "The commands and prohibitions of the Law refer only to those actions that man has absolute free choice to perform or not to perform." Interestingly enough, the example he uses to illustrate this point is not an outward action like praying or fasting but an inward one: fear of God. Maimonides argues that fear of God is a consequence of free will and thus not predetermined by God. I take this to mean that behind any feeling, attitude, or belief commanded by the Law is the will. If so, all these feelings, attitudes, or beliefs must be within our power in the sense that it is possible for us to have them or not have them.

The Case for Involuntariness

The most serious challenge to Maimonides comes not from an anti-dogmatist like Mendelssohn but from a dogmatist of a different variety: Crescas. Crescas admits that in order for something to be commanded, we must be able to choose whether to obey or disobey.[15] Although we seem to have a choice in regard to actions, Crescas insists we do not have one in regard to belief, so unlike action, belief cannot be commanded.

Consider an example. I can decide to raise or lower my arm any time I want. When I do, the action follows immediately. But beliefs cannot be formed at will, and in some cases cannot be formed at all. No amount of effort can get me to believe that Michael Jordan is president of the United States or that Chicago is south of New Orleans. Rather than an act of will, beliefs arise from experience or the evaluation of evidence. This is not to say that I always evaluate evidence correctly or wait for all the evidence to come in before making up my mind. Obviously some beliefs are prejudiced, foolish, or self-serving. But whether my beliefs are true or false, other regarding or self regarding, there is no faculty capable of turning them on or off. Since beliefs and actions are so different, how can both be governed by commandments?

We can enlarge on Crescas' insight by recognizing that not only can I not form a belief at will, but *it is a good thing that I cannot*. Imagine what would happen if I could change my beliefs as readily as I raise my arm. Each time I read a newspaper editorial or listened to an advertisement, I would run the risk of believing everything I hear. It is precisely the fact that I cannot change my beliefs at will that gives rise to pangs of conscience or attempts at critical thinking. If I tell a lie to extricate myself from a difficult social situation, no amount of will power can convince me that I have acted properly. So if my beliefs were subject to the vagaries of will, my life would be very different from what it now is. If an analogue to Maimonides' position can be found in the works of Descartes, a partial analogue to Crescas' can be found in Hume's contention that forming beliefs is mainly an involuntary process, since "belief consists merely in a certain feeling or sentiment, in something that depends not on the will, but must arise from certain determinate causes or principles, of which we are not masters."[16] In other words, beliefs are not formed as much as caused.

The problem is that the term *belief* covers a wide range of attitudes or mental states. After a day at the office, I drive home almost by instinct. While an external observer could say that I believe there is a 35-mile-an-hour speed limit on a particular stretch of road or that Central Park is seven blocks east of Crawford, these truths may be the furthest thing from my mind. So it would hardly make sense to call these beliefs free, if indeed they are beliefs at all. Nor does it make sense to say that sensory beliefs like accepting the reality of the table in front of me are free—unless, like Descartes, I take the time to stop and think about them. In this sense Hume is right: Most of what philosophers put in the category of belief is the result of causes over which I have no control. But Baḥya and Maimonides are not talking about sensory beliefs; they are talking about religious and philosophic attitudes, where people have the time to consider alternatives and examine their commitments in detail. While we may be inclined by what Hume calls "an absolute and uncontrollable necessity" to believe what our senses tell us, this sort of belief is very different from that involved when a person maintains that he believes in a supreme being.

Even if we move beyond sensory beliefs and consider those that are singled out for discussion and debate, it is still not clear that beliefs depend on the will. A person may really want to believe that a friend is telling the truth but find it impossible to do so. Or a person may believe that the members of a minority group are lazy or dishonest and feel shame as a result. The question is whether beliefs about God and creation work the same way. Do they result from causes over which we have no control or does the will play an active part in their formation?

Indirect Influences on the Will

The standard to deal with this problem is to argue that while I may not be directly responsible for my beliefs in the sense that I can form them at will, I can be indirectly responsible in a variety of ways. A person who holds racist beliefs can be held responsible for acquainting himself with evidence that shows that such beliefs are groundless; a person who believes that a close friend is lying can be held responsible for getting all relevant information and hearing the friend's side of the story. And there are any number of situations, ranging from legal to moral to hygienic, where we expect people to be responsible for bodies of information and to hold beliefs based on them. To cite an example from Halbertal and Margalit, it would be reasonable to praise or blame a person with a heart condition for adopting living habits that decrease or increase the risk of greater disease.[17] Though a person cannot simply will his heart to become healthy, he can certainly will things that help it or hinder it. So while beliefs may be involuntary, given certain conditions what I do with my beliefs is not.

In the Middle Ages the indirect argument was advanced by Abravanel, and in the modern period by Pascal.[18] Though it may be impossible to command belief per se, it is possible to command activities that typically give rise to belief. Is this what Maimonides had in mind when he set forth the principles every Jew must accept? Although Maimonides is not completely clear on this point, I submit that there is every reason to think he adopted the indirect view. Certainly it would have been unrealistic for him to think that we could pick a person at random, command her to believe all thirteen principles, and expect her to agree immediately. And it is equally unrealistic to think a person will come to accept them through repetition. Recall that for Maimonides belief is not what is uttered but what is represented in the soul.

A more sympathetic reading of Maimonides is that the principles of religion are conclusions we are expected to reach *if* we observe the precepts, study the sacred texts, say the prayers, and examine the alternatives. Observance, in other words, begins at a rudimentary level — like a child pounding keys on a piano. It would be just as foolish to insist on true belief at the start as it would be to insist that a six-year-old enjoy Beethoven. But if you cannot ask a six-year-old to enjoy the classics, you can provide lessons so that after years of study and practice, enjoyment will come naturally.

Evidence for this interpretation can be found in the opening pages of *Perek Helek*, where Maimonides presents one of the most familiar themes in all his work: Learning is a slow process that requires constant attention to the needs and capabilities of the student. To present the student with finished material right from the start only invites confusion. In the *Guide* (1.33, p. 71) Maimonides compares it with giving wheat bread, meat, and wine to an infant. Although there is nothing wrong with these foods in normal circumstances, they would be lethal if swallowed by a baby. At various places in his writing, he allows the teacher the liberty to offer material rewards, speak in parables or metaphors, and say something that will have to be retracted at a later stage. Even his frequent asides to the reader (or Joseph)—"be careful that you understand this," "be sure to remember that," "do not be too hasty in concluding something else"—reflect patience and thoughtfulness. It was after all a desire to move too quickly that got Joseph into trouble in the first place (*GP* 1, Epistle, p. 3).

In regard to commandments, Maimonides follows the traditional view in arguing that obedience has a cumulative effect because doing one makes it easier to do others. In *Perek Helek* he claims that it is as if God were to say, "If you do some of these commandments out of love and with genuine effort, I will help you do all of them." Though he often justifies his position by claiming one cannot study if one is constantly sick, hungry, or under siege, clearly he has more in mind: Observing the commandments is a developmental process that purifies the soul and gets it in the habit of dealing with nonmaterial reality.

Recall that to apprehend mercy and graciousness, one must first acquire a merciful and gracious disposition. It could be said, therefore, that just as Aristotle claims we become just by performing just acts and courageous by performing courageous ones,[19] so Maimonides seems to think we become holy by performing holy acts over a period of time and with increased awareness of what we are doing. In the *Mishneh Torah*, he writes:[20]

> How shall a man train himself in these dispositions? Let him practice again and again the actions prompted by those dispositions that are the mean between the extremes, and repeat them continually till they become easy and are no longer irksome for him, and so the corresponding dispositions will become a fixed part of his character.

If this interpretation is right, it is a mistake to regard Maimonides' principles as articles of faith dropped into the laps of unsuspecting people. Rather they represent a minimum standard of awareness for a community already committed to worship.[21] By *already committed* I mean that acceptance of these principles is the *aim* of the commandments dealing with behavior, not the starting place. Reduced to simplest terms, the principles require the community to bow and pray to something other than an image of a man on a throne. This assumes, of course, that if commandments dealing with behavior do what they are supposed to, the principles will not seem forced or foreign but an elementary statement of what the religion is all about.

It follows that while there is no commandment that says "thou shalt believe . . ." in so many words, Maimonides can hold that Judaism mandates the actions and moral habits that make belief possible. Commenting on *Pirkei Avot* 3.9 ("He in whom the fear of sin comes before wisdom, his wisdom shall endure . . ."), he points out that when sound moral habits precede the acquisition of wisdom, the delight and love of wisdom grow as well as the determination to add to it.[22]

Perhaps Maimonides was too optimistic. Perhaps many people cannot help but look upon ritual as an end in itself rather than an inducement to study and silent reflection. Still, two claims can be made on Maimonides' behalf: (1) his position is coherent in the sense that beliefs can be commanded indirectly, and (2) he is not so naive as to think that people will become convinced of something by repeating isolated statements with no psychological preparation. Accordingly (*GP* 2.31, p. 359): "You know from what I have said that opinions do not last unless they are accompanied by actions that strengthen them." In saying that we are commanded to love God and believe in the existence and unity of God, all he is asking is that people embark on a way of life that makes love of God its final end. He cannot, of course, guarantee that the end will be reached—any more than a parent can guarantee that a child will appreciate Beethoven after years of piano lessons. But he insists that it is impossible to love God thinking that God is corporeal or admits multiplicity. Unless certain beliefs are adopted, the end can never be reached at all.

Evidence and Conviction

Although the indirect approach fits well with Maimonides' understanding of Judaism, it solves one problem only to create another. According to Maimonides, Judaism mandates the actions and moral habits that make it possible to hold true beliefs. His position would be easy to assess if Judaism were a seamless web of belief all resting on a logically secure foundation. If a person were not convinced by the evidence and argument for an important principle, Maimonides could say that he should study harder and look at the matter again. Unfortunately things are not that simple. We saw that Maimonides never tires of pointing out that once we get beyond basic truths like the existence and unity of God, demonstration is impossible, and whether we rely on the prophetic tradition or the philosophic, all we can do is tip the scales in one direction. Thus even among the enlightened few, perplexity on religious issues is widespread; if it were not, there would be no need for him to write a guide to the perplexed. Without a demonstration, Maimonides cannot simply say, "Go back and think again." While he has no doubt that creation, providence, and prophecy are real, and argues that belief in them is required of all Jews, he has no way to prove which account of them is the correct one.

One way to handle this situation would be to fall back on the Kantian dictum that knowledge must be limited to make room for faith. If this means that even a bewildered soul must obey the Law, Maimonides would certainly agree. But if it means, as it often does, that faith can take over where knowledge fails—that it is a virtue to believe something for which there is no evidence—he would strongly disagree. His normal view seems to be the opposite: that belief should be proportioned to the evidence. Again using Akiva as his model, he claims (*GP* 1.32, p. 68):

> For if you stay your progress because of a dubious point; if you do not deceive yourself into believing that there is a demonstration with regard to matters that have not been demonstrated; if you do not hasten to reject and categorically to pronounce false any assertions whose contra-

dictories have not been demonstrated; if, finally, you do not aspire to apprehend that which you are unable to apprehend—you will have
achieved human perfection and attained the rank of *Rabbi Akiva*.

Note that even though Maimonides rejects the eternity of the world
and maintains that it destroys the foundation of the Law, he never
doubts that eternity is a possible alternative, that prominent people
in his own religion have held it, and that it would be possible to interpret the opening lines of Genesis in accord with it.[23] We saw that
he even allows for the possibility that new developments in astronomy might undermine some of his conclusions. Though he does
not think that this outcome is likely, he cannot rule it out. In view
of this quotation, it appears that Maimonides does not want us to
have more conviction than what his own admittedly provisional arguments allow.

The problem is that creation is not just *a* claim about God and
the world, by his own admission; it is a pillar of the Law, second in
importance only to God's existence and unity. Aquinas' solution to
the problem of creation is a direct appeal to faith (*ST* 1.46.2): "That
the world did not always exist we hold by faith alone: It cannot be
proved demonstratively; which is what we said above of the mystery
of the Trinity." For Aquinas, faith is not a second-class form of apprehension but a perfection in its own right; faith "presupposes natural knowledge, even as grace presupposes nature and perfection the
perfectible" (*ST* 1.2.2). Faith, then, is the perfection of natural reason
as grace is the perfection of nature (*ST* 1.1.8).

By contrast, Maimonides (*GP* 3.53, p. 631) quotes Genesis 15:6 to
show that faith (*emunah*) is a virtue, but the context indicates that for
him it is a moral virtue akin to justice (giving every person her due)
rather than the vision of an unseen reality. We saw, for example, that
those who accept beliefs on traditional authority are further from God
than those who accept them on the basis of argument. Even the reference to "traditional authority" is misleading, because Jewish tradition
on this issue is anything but unanimous. Recall that Maimonides
himself admitted that the Platonic view is an acceptable alternative.

What, then, does he recommend? To answer this question, we
have to go back to the idea that creation is one of the issues that is
not supposed to be discussed in public. On the basis of Maimonides'
arguments, the problem is not that the true position is heretical or
contains potentially dangerous information but that we cannot be
certain what the true position is. Note, for example, that the difference between the *Guide*, which is an esoteric book, and the *Mishneh*

Torah, which is not, is not that the former puts forward an intellectualized view of Judaism while the other confines itself to prayer, holidays, and other rituals. Rather it is that the *Mishneh Torah* presents
astronomy and metaphysics as firmly established while the *Guide*
expresses considerable skepticism.

So the problem is that a person whose commitment to Judaism is
already shaky will see that creation cannot be demonstrated, conclude that the foundation of the Law is insecure, and decide that the
commandments do not have to be obeyed. That is why the *Guide* is
written to an advanced student whose commitment to Judaism is beyond question. The hope is that for someone who has achieved the
requisite degree of maturity, lack of certainty on this issue will not
cause him to reject the Law. Such a person will recognize that we are
often called upon to make decisions with less than perfect knowledge. In this case, the problem is not only that we lack relevant information but that we will probably always lack it. Maimonides assumes that someone can come to this recognition and not be destroyed
by it, that someone can accept intellectual limits and remain faithful to the tradition.

In keeping with his rationalistic orientation, Maimonides does
not ask us to generate conviction where none is warranted. If educated guesses are all we can have, then educated guesses are all we
should claim to have. Rather than a propositional attitude that provides an inner source of vision, Maimonides is talking about a quality like moral steadfastness. Let us grant that such steadfastness is
not only possible but desirable. Recall that Plato did not want the
guardians exposed to philosophy until they were at least 35 years old
and had completed rigorous moral and physical training. Still, Maimonides cannot rule out a situation where rational people committed to monotheism reach different conclusions about issues not susceptible to demonstration.

One conclusion we can draw is that intellectual freedom is more
than the ability to accept or reject specific pieces of dogma. Using the
Guide as an example, it is also the ability to assess arguments, revise
opinions, make room for alternatives, and remain open to new sug-
gestions. It seems, then, that Maimonides is a philosopher whose intuitions push him in two directions. On the one hand, there is the desire to get beyond popular religion and strive for a truth that is totally
independent of human wants or needs; rationality is then defined by
the amount of that truth we obtain. On the other hand, there is the
recognition that in religious matters, truth is difficult and in some

cases impossible to achieve; thus all rationality can do is present us with a range of options and indicate certain preferences. A modern philosopher sympathetic with Maimonides therefore has two choices: (1) emphasize that monotheism is indubitable even if not every detail can be worked out, or (2) admit that one's commitment to monotheism has less to do with demonstration than with a series of insights, choices, and aspirations loosely classified under the term *religion*.

A person who recognizes a distinction between the sacred and the profane, who refuses to admit that humans are the measure of all things, and who lives for a day when justice will triumph over cruelty and oppression will see in monotheism a worldview that has the authority of tradition behind it and ties together many of the things she stands for. This person will put a great deal of stock in Maimonides' warning "do not deceive yourself into thinking that there is a demonstration" and will conclude that what Maimonides says about creation is true of religion in general: that all we can do is tip the scales in one direction. As David Hartman put it: "Sinai teaches the power of the beginning and not the certainty of the end."[24] But if this is true, then, as Hartman goes on to say, we can no more look upon people with different views—including atheists—as being affected by hubris or malice than Maimonides could look upon medieval Aristotelians as being stupid or stubborn.[25]

The difference between Maimonides and Hartman has to do with the fact that Maimonides did not confront a range of sources as diverse as the one we face. For him the choices ranged from the extreme voluntarism of the Asherites to the determinism of the Aristotelians. He did not have to concern himself with the *Zohar*, feminism, existentialism, or modern Bible scholarship, let alone the scientific revolution or the skepticism of Nietzsche or Foucault. Given Maimonides' conviction that truth must be taken from wherever it may emerge, the proliferation of sources and disciplines that have arisen since the twelfth century cannot help but make us ask whether we have found truth at all—or more radically, whether Maimonides' understanding of truth is valid even as an ideal.

It follows that while Maimonides views the lack of certainty on religious matters with regret, modern thinkers typically do not. For Maimonides, there is *a* true theory about the world, and human perfection is measured by the amount of that theory we accept. Both in *Perek Ḥelek* and the *Guide* (3.51, p. 619) he advocates the death penalty for heretics. Even if we drop the question of the death penalty, Kant (*RWL*, p. 152) protests that salvation should not be reserved for the educated few and that "recognition and respect must be accorded . . . to universal human reason." Like Mendelssohn, Kant thinks it would be an outrage if salvation were based on anything not accessible to humanity at large.

It is noteworthy that of the thirteen principles Maimonides regards as binding on Jews, a Christian like Aquinas would have no hesitation accepting ten of them.[26] In regard to gentiles, Maimonides thinks the requirements for salvation are less demanding than they are for Jews: rejection of blasphemy and idolatry and commitment to five basic rules of behavior such as the prohibitions against murder, theft, and impermissible sexual unions.[27] Since unlike Kant, Maimonides is convinced that God's existence and unity can be demonstrated, he would no doubt reply that he is not asking for anything more than what a rational person could accept. The main sticking point concerns belief in the prophecy of Moses, which Maimonides considers binding on Jews and gentiles alike.[28] But overall Hartman is right to say that Maimonides has more tolerance for levels of worship than for worship directed to a false conception of God.[29] To believe in a material God is to forgo salvation no matter how humble or obedient one has become.

The fact remains, however, that few modern philosophers believe there is *a* true theory of God and that salvation depends on its acceptance. For a modern philosopher like Hartman, human finitude is not a condition we have to put up with but an opportunity we should celebrate. In a similar way, Hilary Putnam argues that it would be a bad thing if the truths of religion could be deduced by reason and therefore it is a good thing that they are problematic.[30] It is important to see what Putnam is *not* saying: He is not taking the old line that it is a good thing the truths of religion cannot be deduced by reason because we therefore have no choice but to rely on faith. Rather he is saying that it is a good thing we will never know the truths of religion with certainty because that knowledge would take us down the road to fanaticism. In other words, Hartman and Putnam agree with Maimonides that we are called upon to use reason "in a situation which is in certain important respects dark."[31] But they view darkness as a justification for tolerance while Maimonides' opinion is much more complicated.[32] For them lack of certainty goes hand in hand with freedom of choice, and within appropriate boundaries freedom of choice is something that should be cultivated rather than discouraged.

In defense of Maimonides, it is worth remembering that no one in the twelfth century could foresee the massive paradigm shifts that would come in science or anticipate people like Galileo, Kepler, Newton, and Darwin. As Josef Stern put it, the changes in knowledge that Maimonides recognizes are mainly examples of progress in "normal science," not revolutionary changes of paradigm.[33] We saw that in the *Guide* Maimonides talks as if the physics of the sublunar realm were perfected by Aristotle and that while astronomy had not been perfected, because of the limits of our knowledge, it is unlikely that it ever will.[34] So it is not surprising that he views deviation from the paradigms of sublunar physics with disdain. The fact that astronomy had not been perfected forced him to admit the possibility of scientific change and acknowledge disagreement on how to account for observable facts, but that is as far as he is willing to go. Needless to say, Hartman and Putnam are willing to go much further.

To be sure, neither Hartman nor Putnam proposes that we throw out vast chunks of tradition or think of God as corporeal. By emphasizing finitude, Hartman too is committed to a radical separation between God and humans.[35] But where Maimonides stresses the freedom to accept or reject particular beliefs, Hartman and Putnam open the door to a wider conception: the freedom to accept a range of beliefs or what Putnam terms a *moral image of the world*.[36] And even if one image can be supported by good arguments, even if it can be given a precise logical formulation, Hartman and Putnam insist it is still a matter of choice rather than demonstration. If they are right, we should not imagine the human race on a simple trajectory that begins with ignorance and approaches certainty in an asymptotic fashion. Rather we should imagine a trajectory in which bad theories are rejected but the choice among good ones is still significant. In other words, we should picture a messianic age in which critical thinking, conceptual revision, and intellectual conversation are still very much alive. It could be argued that this view of knowledge is consistent with Maimonides' outlook. We saw that even prophets do not get answers to every question and will experience moments of doubt. The difference is that by fallibility Maimonides means that all we can get are momentary glimpses of a metaphysical order much of whose nature and purpose are beyond our grasp; for modern thinkers it means that there are competing accounts of the nature and purpose of this world as well.

It is worth repeating that the modern view agrees with Maimonides on one point: the degree to which even the wisest among us are in the dark when it comes to God. Tolerance would disappear if we were to accept personal experiences that shed so much "light" on God that all doubt and perplexity were lost. Again from Goodman (cited in chapter 1, note 48), God is not a subject about which we can have experts, unless it is the "expertise" that comes with learned ignorance. We can have people who are grateful to God or feel awe and reverence in the presence of God. We can have people who see the ways and works of God in nature. But if in the end our knowledge of God does not lead to humility, we must question whether it is knowledge at all. The issue, then, is how one can have humility without tolerance—if not on every issue, then at least on speculative matters like creation, prophecy, and providence.

From a historical perspective, monotheism has often produced fanaticism of its own. It is well known that Israel is commanded to destroy the pagan nations around it and show them no pity (Deuteronomy 7:1–16; 20:16). Maimonides, too, thought it was a duty to despise and destroy heretics. We should keep in mind, however, that monotheism did not come down to us as a theory that could be examined in isolation from social factors and historical change. I remarked earlier that at one point it was tied to national liberation and the establishment of a priestly cult, at other times to a geocentric cosmology and questionable conceptions of male superiority. Yet through it all, the logic of monotheism continues to assert itself: uniqueness, separation, learned ignorance, humility. Even Maimonides would have to admit that substantial portions of his worldview derive from gentiles, many of whose beliefs he would regard as heretical if espoused by a Jew. Akiva exemplified humility and retained his composure in the face of esoteric matters beyond his comprehension; in the modern world we are asked to do the same thing in the face of equally humble people who have arrived at different conclusions from ours or maybe even no conclusions at all.

In one sense, it may seem that Maimonides has lost the war, for once we emphasize diversity and conceptual change, then the attempt to formulate timeless articles of faith or to connect religion to a particular scientific theory is bound to seem objectionable. But in another sense he has won the war, for once we emphasize diversity and conceptual change, it becomes ever more reasonable to say that we exercise some control over and therefore are responsible for the beliefs we hold. Put otherwise, our religious and philosophic commitments are not just thrust upon us, not just "given" as sense data theorists once used that term. They are the result of a lifetime of gathering, sorting, and evaluating information drawn from a wide range of sources. To return to the conversation metaphor, they are the result of years of dialogue with living figures and imaginary dialogues with dead ones. If it is fair to say that we exercise choice over the commitments we hold, the tradition that derives from Bahya and includes Maimonides is importantly right.

7

Popular Religion and a Personal God

Having come this far, we would do well to take stock. I have argued that monotheism is central to Judaism and have defined monotheism in a way that emphasizes the uniqueness of God and the primacy of the distinction between God and creation. We saw that while prayer may not be the highest form of spiritual achievement, Maimonides not only permits it but regards it as mandatory. His point is that we should rid ourselves of the temptation to think that the function of prayer is to assert literal truth. It can lead us to God or inform us about God without telling us what God is or exactly how God acts.

We also saw that Maimonides' view of creation, though provisional, upholds divine freedom and with it the idea that existence is a gift. Once we view existence as a gift, we can view commandment and revelation in the same way, which means that we are in a position to uphold the foundation of the Law. And while Maimonides' negative theology requires us to interpret the principle of *imitatio Dei* in an intellectual fashion, stressing the need for silent reflection, it does allow us to make sense of it.

The obvious conclusion is that Maimonides' strategy is not to reject popular religion as much as to educate it. Behind that strategy is the conviction that whether we are talking about the population in general or the wisest people in it, a religion that mandates the worship of something other than God, that directs all human energy and aspiration to a fantasy image, is an abomination. According to *Guide*

1.35, the minimal criteria for worshipping God are that the object of such worship is not corporeal, not subject to affections, and not comparable to anything in the created order. For present purposes, the issue of affections is critical. If Maimonides has established anything, it is that God is not a temporal being who endures throughout all time but a being who stands outside of time altogether.

But it is widely held that any attempt to raise the standards of popular religion is impossible. "Maimonides," Yirmiahu Yovel tells us, "upholds a view of God that makes the bulk of popular, historical religion either spurious or downright idolatrous. Yet most of his active life as a rabbi and thinker has been spent in consolidating that same religion which his pure philosophy seems to undermine."[1] How could a thinker of genius and a man with deep religious sensibilities have devoted so much of his life to something he considered idolatrous? How could the philosopher have been so out of touch with the rabbi? Having taken up issues relating to corporeality and comparability, I want to focus on the affections, in particular the question of whether it makes sense to ascribe personality to God.

God as Person

Although it may seem that Maimonides is opposed to any suggestion of personality in God, the issue is more complicated than it appears. The thrust of his opposition to Aristotle's view on the eternity of the world is that while it may not be idolatrous to think of God as a causal force ruled by necessity, there are good reasons not to. He would be overstepping his bounds if he claimed to know for certain that God manifests purpose and intention. We saw, however, that he points out on numerous occasions that he is dealing with possibility rather than necessity and claims only that a conception of God that includes purpose and intention is defensible. According to that conception, God is both self-aware and free, neither of which is true of a causal force, a Platonic form, or a metaphysical abstraction.

Here we must be careful not to make more of freedom than Maimonides' arguments allow. Recall that the sort of freedom Maimonides has in mind is that of a self-contained or autonomous will. Unlike the Mutakallimun, he does not think that God has a separate act of will for every event in the world's history. In keeping with Ecclesiastes 1:9 ("There is nothing new under the sun"), he maintains that "[We] believe that the Divine Will ordained everything at creation and that all things, at all times, are regulated by the laws of nature and run their natural course."[2] If my reading of Maimonides is correct, God can will change and does so in creating the world, but it does not follow that God can change the divine will in response to new situations. According to *Guide* 3.13, p. 454: "We are obliged to believe that all that exists was intended by Him . . . according to His volition." If the world was created according to divine volition, it is reasonable to believe that God approves of some actions and disapproves of others.[3]

But the idea of divine volition raises a number of questions. Maimonides begins *Guide* 3.13 by claiming it is an established fact that something that exists for a purpose must have been created "in time after not having existed." Since God is not part of the created order and exists necessarily, it makes no sense to ask about the final end of God. The world, on the other hand, was created by a free act of will, "making it indispensable for us to say that what exists, its causes, and its effects, could be different from what they are"; again existence is a gift. Not surprisingly, he quotes Genesis 1:31, which says that God saw all of existence and that it was very good. But what does that mean?

Since Maimonides (*GP* 3.13, p. 453) defines *good* as "an expression applied by us to what conforms to our purpose," one might think that he takes Genesis 1:31 to mean that the whole world was made to promote human interests. The fact is, however, that he goes to some length to show that this impression is wrong because (1) it is presumptuous to think that everything in the world was created for our sake, and (2) if we contemplate all of existence, including the stars and spheres, we cannot tell what things were intended for the sake of something else and what things were intended for their own sakes. For all we know, it may be that everything was intended for its own sake.[4] So just as we cannot ask about the purpose of God's existence, it is futile to ask about the purpose of the world as a whole—except to say that because it was created by God, it must conform to God's intention.

One way to account for the goodness of the world is to return to *Guide* 1.54 and God's attributes of action. There Maimonides cites Genesis 1:31 to explain what God meant in saying to Moses (Exodus 33:19), "I will make all my goodness pass before you." Maimonides takes "all my goodness" to mean "all existing things" and goes on to say that Moses saw how all of existence fits together and is governed by God. It is certainly possible to see how everything fits together without knowing what purpose it serves. A person might observe that everything in nature is well suited to its environment, that animals have organs or faculties to protect themselves and acquire food, and that there is a general balance between life, death, and regeneration; but it does not follow that she will be able to answer, or even understand, the question "What is all this for?" Though she might come away with the impression that nature does not exist for nothing, this is a long way from knowing what it is designed to accomplish.

If what exists could be different, it would be possible for God to create a world in which species are not well provided for and do not live in harmony with each other. But this does not appear to be the case. According to *Guide* 3.25, p. 505:

> this was explicitly stated by our prophets: namely that the particulars of natural acts are all well arranged and ordered and bound up with one another, all of them being causes and effects; and none of them is futile or frivolous or vain. . . . Philosophic wisdom similarly requires that there should not be anything futile, frivolous, or vain in all the acts of nature.

So the world God created is orderly even if we do not know what purpose the order serves.

Elsewhere (*GP* 3.10, p. 440) Maimonides cites Genesis 1:31 in defense of the view that evil is a privation and "all being is a good." If this is true, *any* world God created would be good merely because existence is positive rather than negative. Quite possibly he believed both, so that creation is good in itself and the particular world we inhabit is good because it is more harmonious than the alternatives and allows us to view God as just and merciful. In fact the previous chapter of the *Guide*, 3.12, p. 448, ends by making each of these points: "His bringing us into existence is absolutely the great good, as we have made clear, and the creation of the governing faculty in the living beings is an indication of His mercifulness with regard to them." Whatever option we pick, Maimonides tries to emphasize both the contingency of the world and the smallness of our place in it.

Note, however, that none of Maimonides' warnings about finding a purpose for God or the world as a whole prevents us from asking about the purpose of human life, a subject on which he is very explicit. Since "the ultimate purpose consists in bringing about perfection," the ultimate purpose of being a human being consists in achieving the highest form of contemplation and the spiritual purity connected with it. It therefore makes perfect sense to say that God intends us to achieve as much perfection as our natures allow and that all the commandments were fashioned with that achievement as their goal. Just as Maimonides opposes the idea that God is ruled by necessity, he also opposes the idea that God issues commandments in an arbitrary or capricious fashion.⁵ Thus every commandment accomplishes a function: to promote the welfare of the body or the welfare of the soul.⁶

Reward and Punishment

It is worth repeating that the "reward" for performing the commandments is not fame and fortune, only the possibility that we may experience awe and humility in contemplating God and the vastness of the universe. But accepting divine volition does not mean that we can sway God with entreaties or cause God to feel angry at one moment and merciful at another.

The question is: What happens to popular religion when the possibility of swaying God is removed? In a famous passage, Maimonides claims that certain beliefs must be adopted not because they are true but because they are useful to society (*GP* 3.28, pp. 513–14):

> In some cases a *commandment* communicates a correct belief, which is the one and only thing aimed at—as, for instance, the belief in the unity and eternity of the deity and in His not being a body. In other cases the belief is necessary for the abolition of reciprocal wrongdoing or for the acquisition of a noble moral quality—as, for instance, the belief that He ... has a violent anger against those who do injustice, according to what is said: *And My wrath shall wax hot, and I will kill, and so on* [Exodus 22:23], and as the belief that He ... responds instantaneously to the prayer of someone wronged or deceived: *And it shall come to pass, when he crieth unto Me, that I shall hear; for I am gracious* [Exodus 22:26].

This passage not only ascribes violent emotions to God but suggests that God acts like a cosmic police officer, responding to every call that comes in. A bit later (*GP* 3.36, p. 539–40) he again invokes utility to justify the belief that God improves our situation if we obey the commandments and makes it ruinous if we do not. Finally it is worth noting that belief in divine retribution is one of the thirteen principles that Maimonides considers binding on every Jew.

What are we to make of these claims? In a passage that has caused considerable controversy (*GP* 3.32), Maimonides goes so far as to say that God sometimes plays tricks on us by mandating practices that may not be necessary when viewed in isolation but are perfectly justifiable when viewed in light of historical circumstances. We saw, for example, that the ancient Israelites would have rejected a religion that did not contain animal sacrifice or priestly vestments because it would have been too radical a departure from the practices they were used to.

Although Maimonides sometimes talks as if requiring animal sacrifice or belief in divine retribution amounts to a noble lie on the part of God, his point is not that God is dishonest but that any law must take into account the historical circumstances of the people for whom it is intended. To use a word that came up in regard to prayer, the Law of Moses contains numerous concessions to human fallibility. The fact that they are concessions does not mean that there is something wrong with them, only that the human propensity toward material things is so powerful that if religion did not involve concessions, the primary intention of the Law—that God and only God be worshipped—would never be fulfilled. Recall that according to Maimonides, Abraham tried to win people to monotheism on the basis of argument alone but failed. So Maimonides never doubts that something more than philosophy is needed if the principles established by philosophy are to be adhered to. The question is: What happens when the additional material is at odds with those principles—as it is in the claim that God becomes violently angry and can be swayed by prayer?

The simple answer is to fall back on the God of the philosophers versus the God of Abraham, Isaac, and Jacob, the first utterly lacking in personality, the second abounding in it, one asking for contemplation, the other for blind obedience. I hope it has become clear that this answer fails to address the real issue and constitutes an injustice to both traditions. In the first place, there are aspects of personality that Maimonides ascribes to God even in his most philosophic moments. In the second, we must be careful lest the God of Abraham, Isaac, and Jacob not only have *a* personality but one that is objectionable and brings out the worst qualities in human beings. Do we really want people to strive to be like a God who becomes violently angry? Maimonides does not think so, because in the *Mishneh Torah*, he writes: "Anger, too, is an exceedingly bad passion, and one should avoid it to the last extreme. One should train oneself not to be angry even for something that would justify anger."[7] He goes on to point out that according to the sages, anger is comparable to idol worship and that once a person becomes angry, her wisdom leaves her.[8]

Why, then, does Maimonides say that belief in a God who becomes violently angry is necessary? The answer is that such a belief, though highly misleading if interpreted to mean that God has passions or moral dispositions, not only has social utility but contains a kernel of truth. There is a sense in which God does exhibit anger, and people who violate the commandments are worse off as a result; but that sense has nothing to do with anthropomorphism. Anger, it will be recalled, is an attribute of action (*GP* 1.54, pp. 126–27). When the Bible talks about natural disasters, political upheavals, and other calamities, "these actions would proceed from one of us in reference to another only because of a violent anger or a great hatred or a desire for vengeance." Thus God is *called* jealous or angry or wrathful. But, Maimonides insists, it does not follow that God *is* hardhearted or manifests a desire for vengeance. In the same way, a ruler who must inflict punishment for a crime should not be hardhearted or desire vengeance either. And overall (*GP* 1.54, p. 127), "acts of mercy, forgiveness, pity, and commiseration should proceed from the governor of a city to a much greater extent than acts of retaliation."

By classifying anger and mercy as attributes of action, Maimonides avoids having to say that God makes a separate judgment on everything we do. Attributes of action are permanent features of the created order. Graciousness has to do with God's decision to create beings who have no claim on God; mercy with the fact that nature provides for living creatures by endowing them with faculties needed to protect themselves; anger with the fact that nature is unkind to creatures who abuse or fail to develop their faculties. In either case, reward and punishment do not flow from momentary decisions on the part of God but from permanent factors of which God is the underlying source. Problems occur when we in our ignorance personalize features of the world that have nothing to do with the happiness or misery of particular people.

Maimonides' view is couched in general terms and does not deal with the issue of what to say about intelligent, God-fearing people who are stricken with cancer or are hit crossing a street. Even if we accept his view as a fair statement of how things work *overall*, there is still the question of what divine reward and punishment consist in. In *Perek Ḥelek* he points out that Judaism is anything but monolithic on this issue. One group holds that the reward for fulfilling the commandments is the Garden of Eden, another the coming of the messiah, another resurrection of the dead, another bodily peace and worldly success, yet another all of the above. Not surprisingly, his solution is to accuse all of them of literalism and argue that passages that promise reward or threaten punishment have to be interpreted metaphorically. Just as it is necessary for the sacred books to describe God in physical terms in order for people to believe that God exists, so it is necessary to warn people that justice pays and wrongdoing does not.[9] If a religion were to begin by saying that justice does not bring a material reward, people would conclude that there is no reason to obey its precepts. But the same tradition that contains dire warnings about good and evil *also* contains the wherewithal to realize that material rewards are beside the point so that it is a mistake to conceive of God rewarding and punishing people like a politician dispensing favors. But how do you get someone to see this?

Maimonides asks us to imagine a small child studying the Torah for the first time. In such a situation, the teacher will have to bribe the student to ensure progress. The result is that while the child "thinks of study as work and effort, he is willing to do it in order to get what he wants, a nut or piece of candy." As the student matures, the bribes become more sophisticated: from candy to clothing, from clothing to money, from money to honor and social status. Yet, Maimonides concludes, "all this is deplorable"—deplorable but unavoidable "because of man's limited insight." Citing *Pirkei Avot* (4:7: "Do not make the Torah a crown for self-glorification nor a spade with which to dig"), he argues that according to the sages, the Torah must be studied for its own sake and commandments obeyed for their own sake: "Our sages have already warned us about this. They said that one should not make the goal of one's service of God or of doing the commandments anything in the world of things." In the *Mishneh Torah* (1, Laws of Repentance, 10.1) Maimonides writes:

> Let not a man say, "I will observe the precepts of the Torah and occupy myself with its wisdom in order that I may obtain all the blessings written in the Torah, or to attain life in the world to come; I will abstain from transgressions against which the Torah warns, so that I may be saved from the curses written in the Torah, or that I may not be cut off from life in the world to come." It is not right to serve God after this fashion, for whoever does so serves Him out of fear. This is not the standard set by the prophets and sages.

In the last analysis, all commandments must be performed out of love for God and "only a disturbed fool whose mind is deranged by folly and by fantasy will refuse to recognize this truth."

Despite the intemperance of Maimonides' rhetoric, his point is clear: Judaism does not condone performing the commandments in order to achieve a material reward or avoid a material punishment; hence we are obliged to get ourselves to the point where material factors are irrelevant. Allowances have to be made for children or people unable to comprehend the true meaning of the commandments: "The masses, after all, lose nothing when they do the commandments out of fear of punishment and out of hope for reward, since they are not perfect." But the reason for these allowances is not that the true message must be diluted so that even the uneducated will have a chance to accept it but exactly the opposite: If a person performs the commandments not for their own sake, there is some hope that in the future he *will* perform them for their own sake. As we saw, the purpose of the commandments is to quell the impulses of matter and redirect the soul's energy from a preoccupation with earthly matters to a preoccupation with eternal.

It follows that the purpose of the commandments is to get us to the point where we change our outlook on what constitutes benefit and harm. To a person hoping to improve his social standing in return for obedience, taunts or insults may be devastating; to a person engaged in theoretical study, the same insults may seem trivial. We saw, for example, that Maimonides' ideal is that of a person who deals with everyday matters but only because inwardly her heart is turned toward God.

Further evidence for this interpretation can be found in Maimonides' reading of the book of Job. At first Job offers his suffering as evidence that divine providence does not extend to individuals, for it is clear that he has committed no sin to justify his torment. Maimonides points out, however, that while Job was blameless, at the beginning of the story he knew God only by report. As Job's knowledge increases, his view of providence undergoes a significant change so that (*GP* 3.23, pp. 492–93):

> When he knew God with a certain knowledge, he admitted that true happiness, which is the knowledge of the deity, is guaranteed to all who know Him and that a human being cannot be troubled in it by any of the misfortunes in question. While he had known God only through the traditional stories and not by the way of speculation, Job had imagined that the things thought to be happiness, such as health, wealth, and children, are the ultimate goal. For this reason he fell into such perplexity and said such things as he did.

As Howard Kreisel points out, a person whose life is focused on intellectual apprehension will not be immune from pain or physical misfortune, but from the resultant suffering they cause.[10] In other words, such a person might experience pain but would not regard it as the worst thing that could happen and therefore would not be tempted to see it as a punishment handed down by an angry God. Neither would such a person be tempted to see wealth and social standing as rewards handed down by a merciful God. Such a person would be concerned with only one thing—apprehension of God—and would measure all good and evil on the basis of whether they promote it or interfere with it. To be sure, pain interferes with one's ability to think, but then so do money and social standing. In this respect, Maimonides' teaching is clearly influenced by Stoicism.

Maimonides' other example of a person who came to the realization that reward and punishment do not matter is Abraham (*GP* 3.24, p. 501). Clearly Abraham did not agree to sacrifice Isaac because he thought that disobedience would result in poverty or his own death. In Maimonides' opinion, the only motive was fear and love of God. Thus Genesis 22:12: "Now I know that you fear God."

At a more general level, Maimonides tells us that God's providence does not watch over everyone equally (*GP* 3.18, p. 475). Rather providence "of necessity" watches over individuals more carefully to the degree that they share in the divine overflow. This means that providence extends to people to the degree that they achieve holiness or human perfection.[11] It follows that "His providence that watches over excellent and righteous men is proportionate to their excellence and righteousness." This would be a hard position to defend if we took Maimonides to mean that excellent and righteous people receive material rewards for their virtue. If, however, we take him to mean that excellent and righteous people are closer to apprehending the infinite transcendence of God, then, while controversial, his position is at least defensible. In many ways Maimonides' position is a restatement of Socrates' claim that "no evil can befall a good person either in life or in death, and God does not neglect his or her affairs."[12] Again, this view is hard to accept unless we ask ourselves what Socrates means by *evil*.[13]

In what do divine reward and punishment consist? To return to *Perek Ḥelek*, spiritual delights are eternal, indivisible, and nothing like their earthly counterparts. More to the point: "They come to us only after great searching." While Maimonides sometimes talks as if the distinction he has in mind is analogous to Mill's distinction between higher and lower pleasures, it would be more accurate to say that spiritual delights are not pleasurable moments that result from performing commandments but the act of performance itself. Thus Maimonides quotes Rabbi Eliezer to the effect that the true servant desires God's commandments, not the reward of God's commandments, and quotes *Pirkei Avot* (4:2): "The reward of a commandment is the commandment itself, and the reward of a sin is sin." A commandment done out of love is its own reward because there is no higher value or greater achievement than love of God. If love is genuine, the worst evil that can befall the lover is removal from the object of love, which in this case is another name for ignorance. To tell such a person that unless he performs the commandments he risks retaliation by an angry God is to miss the point entirely.

According to Maimonides, the commandments reach their fulfillment in contemplation of God. We saw that once a person reaches this state "there is no external power to deny his soul eternal life." Eternal life, then, is nothing more nor less than disinterested contemplation. "Life in the world to come," as Kellner notes, "is not a *reward* in the sense that if a person does X, God *responds* by granting that person a share in the world to come. For [Maimonides], one *achieves* a share in the world to come by learning about God."[14] Nor, as we have seen, is eternal life a motive for obeying God in the sense that one puts up with restrictions in this life in order to be blessed in the next, for all eternal life "offers" is more of the contemplation the soul has acquired on its own.

The key point is that the process by which a perfected soul enters the next life is a natural one. Having achieved a degree of union with the Agent Intellect, the soul becomes eternal.[15] From our perspective, the idea of an embodied soul achieving partial union with an eternal object is much too vague to do the work Maimonides asks of it. How much union is needed and how do we know when we get it? Maimonides creates any number of problems by trying to answer these questions in terms of acceptance of a fixed set of propositions. Some propositions are tied to outdated systems of thought like the idea of the Agent Intellect. Some are vague and require considerable exposition before it is clear what Maimonides has in mind.

To take one example, the second principle has to do with God's unity. Maimonides does a remarkable job of expressing himself succinctly. But as any reader of the *Guide* knows, unity is a difficult concept that requires much more than a paragraph to explain. To take another, several principles deal with prophecy. To most of Maimonides' readers, prophecy would be seen as a miracle in which God speaks to Moses in a literal fashion. Though Maimonides is honest enough to say that this is not what he means and that a full explanation would require more time, scholars of medieval philosophy are still not sure what he has in mind.[16] As he himself admits (*GP* 2.35, p. 367), *prophecy* is an equivocal term. So even though Maimonides has only thirteen principles, he has really committed himself—and us—to much more.

Beyond these difficulties, there is the general question of how Maimonides or anyone can presume to know exactly what is required to achieve salvation. The important point is that whatever is required, Maimonides asks us to think of it not as a sudden change in fortune but as the inevitable result of what we have achieved in this life. In the words of Hannah Kasher, Maimonides replaces "the principle of just recompense with a rational doctrine of natural consequence."[17] It is therefore a mistake to think of God sitting behind the bar of justice passing sentence on the souls who come before it. Special pleas will not work, and unexpected verdicts are out of the question. In Maimonides' words:[18]

> Whoever fulfills what is written therein [the Law] and knows it with a complete and correct knowledge will attain thereby life in the world to come. According to the greatness of his deeds and abundance of his knowledge will be the measure in which he will attain that life.

The only respect in which we have anger and mercy is the limited one in which it is true to say that in the world we occupy, people who perform the commandments out of love reach the highest form of human perfection and experience it forever; by contrast people who perform the commandments but not out of love cannot reach this goal, while people who do not perform them at all take their chances with uncontrolled desire for material satisfaction.

While there is some truth to the claim that God becomes violently angry with sinners and rewards obedience, it is not literal. These expressions are only colorful ways of saying that one form of behavior is incompatible with human perfection while another form is required by it. Just as Maimonides seeks to transform our understanding of phrases like "God spoke," "God descended," or "God saw," he tries to reinterpret the reward and punishment scheme so that it has no trace of hedonism or anthropomorphism. This does not mean that he wants to throw out traditional language altogether. After setting forth his view of human perfection, he maintains that it is mandatory for all Jews to believe (*Perek Helek*):

> God rewards those who perform the commandments of the Torah and punishes those who transgress its admonitions. The greatest reward is the world to come; the worst is extinction.

All he wants is to get people to the point where they can understand what the traditional language really means—or at least that the traditional language cannot be interpreted in a literal fashion.

Does God have a personality? Not in the sense that is usually thought. One cannot bargain with God or delve into the psychology of God. But if Maimonides is right, it makes sense to think that the world was created for a purpose, part of which is that we can fulfill our nature as rational beings. It bears repeating that Maimonides' theory does not address "the problem of evil" as it relates to abused children, natural disasters, or victims of genocide. He does not have a general answer to the question "Why do innocent people suffer?" except to say, again with the Stoics, that there are cases where a person can rise above pain and sorrow by reflecting on a higher order of existence. It should be understood, however, that people who believe that God has a personality in a stronger sense, that God does get angry and responds to special pleading, have no better explanation. Worse, they have the added burden of having to explain what provoked the anger and why the special pleading failed. Apart from metaphysical issues, the danger of such explanations is that they take some of the meanest and most arbitrary of human motives and project them into heaven; hence the ugly suggestion that victims of tragedy would have been saved if they had said an additional prayer or been more vocal in asserting their faith.

Love of God: Modern Approaches

To love God is not only a commandment but the commandment par excellence. As such, it puts the question of personality in sharp relief. Is it possible to love something wholly other or is it true, as Buber claims, that God loves as a personality and wants to *be* loved as a personality?[19] On this issue, Buber follows the lead of Rosenzweig, who argues that God must not be lost "behind the infinity of creation" but must burst forth in an act of love that reaches the heart of a particular person. In Rosenzweig's words (*SR*, p. 164):

> Thus love is not an attribute but an event, and no attribute has any place in it. "God loves" does not mean that love befits him like an attribute, as does, say, the power to create. Love is not the basic form of his countenance, fixed and immutable. It is not the rigid mask which the sculptor lifts off the face of the dead. Rather it is the fleeting, indefatigable alternation of mien, the ever youthful radiance which plays on the eternal features. . . . "God loves" is present, pure, and simple.

This view is the result of making existence prior to essence or adopting what Rosenzweig calls "radical empiricism."

The first thing to see in trying to think about these issues is that for Maimonides, as for most religious thinkers, love is more than attraction or obsession. Obviously it involves attraction and obsession, but it also involves knowledge. In the sense in which Maimonides uses the term, it is impossible to love a fantasy image. You can become infatuated with it or, like Ponce de Leon, spend your whole life searching for it; but insofar as the object is an illusion, it is not really an object of love. Nor is there love in a relationship that is dominated by expectation of reward or fear of punishment. A despot who becomes violently angry and demands total obedience may be treated with care or respect, but again one hesitates to call these responses love. Love in the sense intended by Deuteronomy 6:5 is a virtue; the fact that someone wants it does not necessarily mean he has a right to claim it.

It may be doubted, then, whether popular religion gives one the opportunity to love God at all. Certainly it does not give one the opportunity to love God unless it motivates her to study the sources from which its view of God derives and encourages her to get beyond the constraints imposed by literal interpretation. It could be said, therefore, that Maimonides' critique of popular religion is not that it ignores Plato and Aristotle but that unless it gets past the idea of a God who becomes violently angry, it cannot inspire the kind of devotion required by "the standard set by the prophets and sages." According to the rabbinic interpretation, "with all your heart" means that the heart should not be divided; "with all your soul" means even at the cost of your life; and "with all your might" means even at the cost of your property.[20] This does not mean that every martyr went to his death with mastery of Jewish teaching in hand, but that whatever causes a person to accept death in order to sanctify the name of God, it cannot be an assessment of present and future risks.[21] Thus far Maimonides and the existentialists would agree.

Where they disagree is on the issue of personality. Buber, for example, clearly sides with Pascal:[22]

> The God of Abraham, the God in whom Abraham had believed and whom Abraham had loved ("The entire religion of the Jews," remarks Pascal, "consisted only of the love of God"), is not susceptible of introduction into a system of thought precisely because He is God. He is beyond each and every one of those systems, absolutely and by virtue of His nature. What the philosophers describe by the name of God cannot be more than an idea. But God, "the God of Abraham," is not an idea.

Buber's immediate opponent in this passage is Cohen, and his criticism of idealism is that only persons can love or be loved. So unless God is a person in the strong sense intended by Pascal, the commandment expressed at Deuteronomy 6:5 is empty.

For Rosenzweig the situation is more radical. It is not that I love God because God returns my love but the opposite: God's love for me is prior to my love for other things.[23] As we saw, God's love for us is needed to awaken the dead self. According to Rosenzweig (*SR*, p. 169): "It is only . . . in the love of God that the flower of the soul begins to grow out of the rock of the self," or, as he puts it elsewhere (*SR*, p. 215): "Ere man can turn himself over to God's will, God must first have turned to man." That is why God can command love in Deuteronomy 6:5: God's love is not an eternal attribute but a voice that reaches out to us with the words "Love me!" As Rosenzweig emphasizes time and again, God's love is distinguished by its immediacy.

While much has been made of the debate between Cohen and Buber, there is a respect in which the terms used to discuss it miss the mark. Cohen, too, found God in the sphere of the personal. For Cohen sin is both personal and nontransferable. In fact, Cohen argues, it is from Ezekiel's recognition that I must take responsibility for my own sin that the idea of the self or person is born.[24] By taking responsibility, I have the possibility of renouncing sin and, again following Ezekiel (18:31), getting a new heart and new spirit. "This possibility of self-transformation," Cohen (*RR*, p. 193) argues, "makes the individual an I." In philosophic terms, it is the individual's ability to take responsibility for past mistakes and set herself on a new course that establishes her as an autonomous agent.

Aside from the formation of the self as an autonomous agent, it is in the infinite willingness to forgive sin that divine goodness manifests itself. While it is true that repentance often takes place in the public sphere, it is also true that repentance before God is one of our most personal and private moments because it demands total honesty. As Cohen (*RR*, p. 168) reminds us, "Only God looks into the heart." So Cohen, too, believes that we come to God as a person seeking something personal: forgiveness for our sins. Again, the person Cohen is talking about is the moral subject who takes responsibility for her actions, but a person nonetheless.

In a nutshell, Buber retained the idea of personal involvement with God but sought to make it concrete. His chief objection to Cohen is that only a person, not a moral construction, can grant forgiveness.[25] Put otherwise, repentance makes sense only if I am the recipient of the *act* of forgiveness, not the transcendental possibility of it. Cohen, in short, treats the I as a noumenon and God or Thou as an ideal (*RR*, p. 161): "The love of man for God is the love of the moral ideal. Only the ideal can I love, and I can grasp the ideal in no other way than by loving it." By contrast, Buber wants to treat the I as a living, breathing person and God as a concrete presence: "Even the idealized person remains a person and has not been transformed into an idea." That is why Buber sides with Pascal over Cohen and much of the philosophic tradition.

Whatever their differences, Buber and Cohen agree on one point: that however we conceive of them, humans and God are, to use Cohen's expression, correlates. It is through repentance that the individual establishes herself as an autonomous agent, and by guaranteeing the success of repentance that God manifests perfection. Although Cohen insists that the individual and God cannot coalesce in mystical union, they do exist together in a spiritual "community."[26] From a philosophic perspective, this means that we cannot understand the idea of one without explicating the idea of the other. "Thus God," in Cohen's view, "*is* for the sake of the holiness of man."[27] We saw that Buber too maintains that God loves *as* a personality and wants to be loved *like* a personality.

Though all three thinkers—Cohen, Rosenzweig, and Buber—oppose the idea that God and humans are causally related, all think of God from the standpoint of God's relation to humanity. "God becomes alive not simply by virtue of having his nature," Rosenzweig (*SR*, p. 18) tells us, but by virtue of having that nature augmented by "divine freedom," the ability to "burst forth" or reach out to humans. It is involvement with humanity (for Cohen) or with individual people (for Rosenzweig and Buber) that constitutes God's perfection—in a word, that makes God God. The reason they conceive of God this way is that they are all characteristically modern: Rather than begin with proofs for the existence of God, they approach God from the standpoint of the experiencing subject. The problem is that the experiencing subject remains primary and therefore God, as Yovel remarks, becomes "explicitly transformed into the assistant of man" rather than man remaining the assistant of God.[28] God, in other words, is called upon to guarantee the success of our projects, to tame nature, forgive sin, or provide lasting companionship. For Rosenzweig, God is called on as an antidote to fear of death, the fundamental fact of all human existence. Again from *The Star* (p. 164):

> God loves everything, only not yet. His love roams the world with an ever fresh drive. It is always and wholly of today, but all the dead past and future will one day be devoured in this victorious day. This love is the eternal victory over death.[29]

While God is not anthropomorphic, the manner in which we reach God is unmistakably anthropocentric. It is almost as if we write a job description for God to fulfill: Imbue me with life, grant me atonement, and help me to deal with the prospect of dying.

Love of God: Maimonides' Approach

Maimonides, on the other hand, approaches God from the standpoint of the subject's place in a larger order. Unlike other premodern thinkers, he admits that vast portions of that order are and may always be incomprehensible. That is why it is easier for us to appropriate his thought than the thought of many of his contemporaries: He is willing to call attention to the limits of scholasticism. It is also why he resists any temptation to humanize divinity. While some of the differences between Maimonides and modern thinkers can be explained by the fact that no one in the twelfth century would have understood the modern stress on self, self-identity, and self-sanctification, not all can. Charles Taylor has done an excellent job of showing how the idea of the self came to dominate Western culture. Still, the real issue has more to do with theology than intellectual history: Maimonides firmly believes that monotheism is incompatible with any approach that puts human wants and aspirations at the center of things and that tries to characterize God in terms of them.

Though love of God is the supreme commandment, according to the view put forward in the *Guide*, it must be preceded by the fear of God, which is commanded at Deuteronomy 6:13.[30] It is true that Maimonides sometimes uses fear (*yirah*) to mean that one suspects immanent danger, but we saw that ultimately "it is not right to serve God after this fashion."[31] Thus fear in the proper sense can only mean awe. In Maimonides' opinion, it is a passion that arises when one obeys the commandments that regulate behavior.[32] So praying, fasting, eating the proper foods, and living in a responsible fashion can make one feel awe in the presence of God but cannot induce love of God. Love represents a higher state that one must come to after one has obeyed all these commandments and is ready to take the next step: to contemplate God's great and wondrous works and ponder how lowly we stand by comparison.[33] In the *Mishneh Torah*, he writes:[34]

> One only loves God with the knowledge with which one knows Him. According to the knowledge will be the love. If the former be little or much, so will the latter be little or much. A person ought therefore to devote himself to the understanding and comprehension of those sciences and studies that will inform him concerning his Master, as far as it lies in human faculties to understand and comprehend.

Later, at *Guide* 3.28, pp. 512–13, he claims that "*love* becomes valid only through the apprehension of the whole of being as it is and through the consideration of His wisdom as it is manifested in it," a remark that can only refer to the study of physics and metaphysics.

Such love is not based on a reciprocal relation where God's love either awakens ours or returns it; on the contrary, it is based on the recognition of a radical asymmetry, of God's uniqueness and our relative obscurity. There is, then, nothing like what Levinas calls "a spiritual friendship."[35] Physics and metaphysics are necessary if one is to get beyond mythology and contemplate God in a manner compatible with the first and second commandments. Though modern physics does not present us with a finite cosmic order like the one the medievals accepted, it does fulfill a Maimonidean function by relieving us of the conceit of thinking that there is something special about our location in the universe or the way we experience space and time. Whether we are talking about the medieval period or our own, Maimonides would insist that like the language of prayer, the categories of physics and metaphysics eventually break down: God is not in space and time, has no essence, and does not enter into causal relations.

In sum God does not exist for our sake and cannot be invoked to guarantee our success. The best way to approach God is to put personal considerations aside and try to comprehend "the whole of being." The challenge involved in loving God is primarily negative: We must love something that does not cater to our needs and cannot be subsumed under our categories. That is why Maimonides' conception of love has so many prerequisites: One must first obey the commandments, then obey them for their own sake, then feel awe in the presence of God, then study physics and metaphysics to have a love pure enough to involve God rather than a fantasy image.

But there is still the question of whether such love is possible. Can we love something whose only aspect of personality is creation of a universe for a purpose too great for us to comprehend? Obviously Maimonides thinks the answer is yes. To see why, let us return to the issues posed by monotheism. Behind Maimonides' account of love is the assumption that once reason's desire to seek perfection is stimulated, it will not be satisfied with anything less. The study of physics and metaphysics brings us in contact with forces and objects much larger than what we encounter in everyday experience. This is even truer today, when astronomers deal with whole galaxies or clusters of galaxies. Maimonides' point is that our study will reveal only that, great as they are, these objects or forces owe their existence to something else, and once that realization is made, reason is led to ask, "What else?"

From Maimonides' perspective, the study of physics and metaphysics is not just a theoretical exercise but a lesson in continual dissatisfaction: Each time a new subject is broached, it shows itself as a contingent being subject to the existence of another contingent being. If Maimonides is right, it is possible to love or admire contingent beings, to feed them, house them, clothe them, and mourn their loss; but if we reflect on the nature of contingency, eventually we will be motivated to seek something whose existence is unconditional.

One way to approach the search for perfection is to say that it is not complete until it settles on a general description like "necessary being" or "source of all being" or even "ground of being." It is important to see, however, that Maimonides' approach is more radical. Though it is true to say that God exists necessarily or is the ground of being, there is a sense in which this too is false: false to the degree that it puts God under a description or attempts to locate God in logical space. In the last analysis, Maimonides' approach is to say that reason will not be satisfied until it recognizes that anything that falls under a description is conditioned no matter how general the description may be. Cohen took Maimonides' rejection of metaphysical descriptions as evidence that he wanted to assert the priority of ethics. But whether we take metaphysical ideas like being and essence or ethical ones like love and forgiveness, the conclusion is the same: All such descriptions particularize God.

It follows that in one respect the existentialist criticism of Cohen is correct: God is more than an idea in a philosophic system. In Buber's terms: "When man learns to love God, he senses an actuality which rises above the idea."[36] It is not that God falls short of the moral ideal but that even the moral ideal restricts God to a set of conceptual boundaries. Worse, it gives us the mistaken impression that if we only think hard enough, we can get God in our intellectual grasp. Again from Buber:

> He who answered Job out of the tempest is more exalted even than the ideal sphere. He is not the archetype of the ideal, but he contains the archetype. He issues forth the ideal but does not exhaust himself in the issuing.

In the last analysis, all the thinkers we are considering would admit that God is not exhausted by conceptual boundaries that we impose. Recall that according to Buber, God is beyond the reach of any system of thought. Thus far Maimonides would agree. The problem is that Buber still prefers "the God of Abraham" and insists on a "living" or "concrete" presence. What are we to make of this? Does the mention of Abraham do anything more than emphasize the intensity of religious experience, or does Buber mean to suggest that we should try to restore the innocence of a pre-philosophic age? Maimonides regarded the patriarchs as philosophers, but clearly that is not the message Buber wants to impart. Buber's point is that once we get beyond systems of thought, we encounter something that loves as a personality and wants to be loved like a personality. To be sure, Buber refrains from saying God "is" a personality for fear of compromising God's uniqueness. Still, *personality* is a loaded term. If all Buber means is that God is self-aware and free, Maimonides would concur. But surely Buber means more than this; he means that God lives and loves in a way we can relate to and reciprocate. From Maimonides' perspective, God can never be present in the way Buber's rhetoric requires. Once we get beyond systems of thought, we do not get a personality but something that is utterly devoid of emotions and dispositions, something that is characterized more by distance and transcendence than by immediacy.

The point is not that descriptions like "ground of being," "moral ideal," or "living presence" are invalid. Nor, for that matter, are parent, spouse, monarch, or employer. All convey something true about God, or, to use Maimonides' expression, point the mind in the direction of God. The point is rather that they are ways in which the idea of divinity is presented to us, not ways in which it is circumscribed by our attempts at classification. In sum all these descriptions present divinity and distort it at the same time: present it by making us think about perfection, distort it by giving the impression that God has been identified with a particular virtue or function.

What Maimonides wants us to see is that we cannot love a distortion, which means that reason can never be satisfied with God under a description. The only way it can be satisfied is to come up against something it cannot define or contain. It could be said, therefore, that reason cannot love God until it admits its own inadequacy before God. To put the point another way, it cannot be satisfied as long as it regards itself as totally successful. Like a lover surrendering himself to his loved one, and giving up everything in the world for her, reason must surrender itself to God. It is hardly surprising, then, that both in the *Mishneh Torah* and the *Guide*, Maimonides finds it natural to quote the erotic poetry of Song of Songs to explain himself.[37]

At one point Rosenzweig comes close to the same insight. Recognizing that God is always beyond our attempts at description, he writes (*SR*, p. 381):

> We learn that God loves but not that he is love. He draws too nigh to
> us in love for us to be yet able to say: He is this or that. In this love we
> learn only that he is God, not what he is. The What, the essence, re-
> mains concealed.

Still, the Maimonidean tone of this passage should not blind us to the
vast difference between the two thinkers. In keeping with his radical
empiricism, Rosenzweig considers the commandment to love God as
primary in the sense of being simple, immediate, and entirely of the
moment. The imperative "Love me!" is therefore "God's first word to
the soul."[38] While all the other commandments deal with past, present, and future, this one is the highest of all because it remains in the
immediate present, "which is ever kindled anew" and "makes no
provision for the future."

By contrast Maimonides sees the commandment to love God as
the highest and therefore the last, the one whose fulfillment presupposes all others. For Maimonides we cannot begin with love of God
because we have no idea what our love is directed to and might join
the legions of well-intentioned people who bowed to and served a
figment of their imagination. That is why we must first understand
and then renounce everything other than God before we can love
God in the proper way. As always, the problem for Maimonides is
not trying to instill enthusiasm but trying to ensure that the search
for knowledge is fulfilled. Once again his philosophy has a sobering
effect: Love is neither simple nor momentary—even in Rosenzweig's extended sense of *moment*. Rather than an experience that
awakens and empowers the soul, it is an experience that humbles it;
rather than God's "bursting forth" to meet us, it is our recognition
of the radical otherness of God. Where Rosenzweig emphasizes the
voice of love (*SR*, p. 202: "For love is—speech, wholly active, wholly
personal, wholly living, wholly—speaking"), Maimonides emphasizes silence. It is not that God is being coy and trying to conceal
something but rather that even if everything were laid out before us,
we would be incapable of understanding it and have no choice but to
remain within our limits. So there is no possibility of dialogue—unless one means prophecy and the prayers derived from it. Even then,
we must keep in mind that prayer is a concession that introduces a
host of difficulties.

We saw that renouncing everything other than God does not
mean holding it in contempt, only that we are not satisfied with substitutes for perfection. We can think of substitutes as physical objects or natural forces; but if Maimonides is right, we can also think
of them as verbal descriptions. In short, love must get beyond the

mode of presentation to the thing presented; it must see that the object of love is never exhausted by theories, narratives, prayers, or anything else we can devise. To the question "Is God personal?" Maimonides' answer would be negative in the sense specified earlier: God does not lack personality in the way that a natural force like gravity does, but neither does God possess a personality analogous to that of a human being. Is it possible to love such a thing? Maimonides' position is that if love means a desire for perfection, for something whose appeal can never be exhausted, something to which we will always feel inadequate, then God is the only thing we can love absolutely.[39] Here it is worth noting that while the Torah commands love for things other than God, it does not add the phrase "with all your heart, with all your soul, and with all your might." As we saw, love of God is another name for worship of the heart, which is why God alone can be the recipient.

This exposition still leaves open the question of how or if God loves us. If existence is a good, and God gave existence to things by a free act of will, then everything that exists is a manifestation of God's grace (*hesed*).[40] With respect to human beings, Maimonides typically speaks of God's grace or love not as an attitude directed to a particular person but as the giving of the Torah. When Abraham's arguments for monotheism no longer convinced people, and the Israelites adopted the idolatrous practices of the Egyptians, God gave the Torah to Israel out of love and loyalty to the oath made to Abraham (*MT* 1, Laws Concerning Idolatry, 1.2).[41] Likewise the decision to wean the Israelites from idolatry rather than present them with a radical change is credited to an act of divine grace (*GP* 3.32, p. 528).

The fact that Abraham's monotheism proved inadequate is yet another reason to be suspicious of people who want to go back to the God of Abraham, Isaac, and Jacob, for in Maimonides' opinion doing this is tantamount to rejecting the Law. Though God's grace confers a gift we have no right to claim, we should keep in mind that Maimonides is not Paul: The gift involves the imposition of Law rather than relief from the obligation to fulfill it. We saw that according to Maimonides' understanding of the "*ought* implies *can*" principle, nothing in the Law is beyond human capacity. What grace means is that having endowed humans with reason, God also provides guidance on how to develop it. Whether they succeed is up to them.

It follows that neither love nor grace is a miracle in the sense that it disrupts the normal course of things. Though Maimonides is convinced that God could alter human nature by an act of will, he is also convinced that such an act would render the Torah useless (*GP* 3.32,

p. 529). Even in the days of the messiah, Maimonides argues, human nature will remain as it is, and the laws and precepts of the Torah will still be valid. Like mercy and anger, God's love is a permanent feature of the world. If so, God's love is directed not to me in my individuality but to me insofar as I strive to fulfill my nature as a human being.

Similar remarks apply to Maimonides' understanding of repentance. Repentance is a way that human beings restructure their lives and make a new attempt to seek perfection. Since the laws of repentance come from God, they are a clear manifestation of God's love for humans and hold out the eternal hope of redemption. But Maimonides' understanding of redemption does not imply acts of God that are independent of human action.[42] In other words, God does not erase guilt or overlook it by sheer force of will. Since there are no actions directed to specific individuals, there is nothing miraculous. Rather than a gift that comes to us from an external source, redemption is something we must strive for and be worthy of. Maimonides would therefore agree with Kant that man himself must make himself into what he is or is to become.

Obviously repentance must be more than a request for forgiveness; in particular it must include a firm conviction not to repeat the offense. In the *Mishneh Torah* Maimonides compares a person who verbalizes his confession but does not resolve to turn away from sin to someone who immerses himself in a ritual bath while holding a dead lizard.[43] We saw that Maimonides sometimes talks about repentance as if God went from hating someone to loving him overnight.[44] But this is clearly a case where he is speaking loosely. In the *Guide* (3.36, p. 540) he puts the laws of repentance in the same class as those that ask us to call upon God in times of duress and justifies both on the grounds of social utility. This does not mean there is no truth to the view that God listens to our pleas and grants expiation, only that the truth is not literal. We can say that God disapproves of sin and looks with favor upon those who try to overcome it as long as we keep in mind that God does not experience emotion or undergo change. Nor can we persuade God to manifest mercy rather than justice.

Rather than a ticket to heaven, Maimonides conceives of repentance as part of the pathway to heaven. We may stumble along the path, but as long as we are willing to move forward, the way before us remains open. What God's love does not do is shorten the path or confer upon one individual a blessing not available to all. In this connection, Maimonides (*GP* 3.12, p. 448) cites Psalm 145:9: "The Lord is good to all; and His tender mercies are over all his works."

Popular Religion and Its Teleology

Maimonides upholds a view of God that makes the bulk of popular religion either spurious or idolatrous *if* we take popular religion at face value rather than as a stepping-stone to something higher. If we insist on worshipping a God who threatens people with bodily harm and succumbs to flattery, who works miracles and promises ecstasy, then Maimonides would regard popular religion as no better than the pagan religions it was supposed to replace. In fact, this is exactly the kind of religion he ascribes to the Sabians when he says that the sum and substance of Jewish Law is "the effacement of these opinions" from our minds.[45] But why do we have to take popular religion at face value? Why can we not see it as the beginning of a spiritual search rather than the end?

Mention of a spiritual search calls to mind the Parable of the Palace. The Parable begins with people outside the city who have no doctrinal beliefs at all and whom Maimonides, in a passage dripping with racism, considers less than human. Of those in the city, he leaves no doubt that the worst group are people who engage in speculation but have reached the wrong conclusions. In fact, he suggests they are really worse than people with no religious beliefs at all. The next group, which Maimonides identifies with the majority of adherents of the Law, consists of people who seek the ruler's palace but never get a glimpse of it. In view of the harshness of Maimonides' description—"ignoramuses who observe the commandments"—we may interpret him as saying that simple obedience is not enough. Those who come up to the palace and walk around it are jurists who have studied the Law and accept true opinions on the basis of traditional authority. Since they do not enter the Palace, Maimonides' point is that even true opinions are not sufficient if our approach to them is passive. Once again he wants opinions that are accepted on the basis of argument and evidence.

The next group consists of several stages and amounts to people who have studied the fundamental principles of the religion and decided to press on: those who also study logic and mathematics, those who study physics, those who study metaphysics. They correspond to people who walk around the palace looking for the gate, who enter the palace and walk into the antechambers, and who enter the inner court. Since God's grace and mercy are reflected in the natural order, we cannot understand them, let alone imitate them, unless the principles on which the natural order is founded become clear to us. Next comes the study of the heavenly order, which, in Maimonides' opinion, cannot help but acquaint us with the limitations of our knowledge. The final group, those in the ruler's council, are prophets, whose minds are turned toward God at all times and who experience the intense love described above. One always has to be careful with the term *prophet*, because Maimonides holds that Moses' prophecy was unlike that of anyone else. But the differences need not concern us here. The important point, as Kellner argues, is that the study of the sciences is in addition to, not in replacement of, the study of the Law.[46] People who study the sciences are a subset of those who study the fundamental principles of the religion, and prophets of any description are a subset of philosophers. Not only does worship not cease as one moves closer to the inner court, we saw that in Maimonides' opinion it increases.

No doubt the parable is based on an outdated conception of physics and metaphysics according to which both are established sciences with little room for change. From our perspective, the important point is that Maimonides conceives of religion as a way of taking people from a passive state, in which they either do not think about principles or are unwilling to consider alternatives, to an active one in which the reasons for believing something come from one's own study and reflection. An obvious case in point is Maimonides' opinion about astrology and superstition. It is not enough, he tells us, to reject these practices because they are forbidden by the Torah but believe in one's heart that there is some basis for them.[47] A sensible person should see that they have no scientific support and are "chimerical and inane." Though contemplation of God is at the end of this process, it is still true that we must complete it for ourselves. To recall a point made earlier, there is no such thing as specifically religious cognition, no form of learning that sidesteps the normal philosophic problems or overturns the normal obstacles.

The problem with taking popular religion at face value is that it offers both too much and too little: too much by holding out the promise of miraculous solutions to human problems, too little by holding us in a state of moral and intellectual passivity. Still, popular religion is based on a body of law that reflects God's love for humanity and cannot be rejected out of hand. The fact that God provides for everyone means that the majority of worshippers and the educated few can read the same prayers and perform the same rituals.

They will, of course, have a very different understanding of what they are doing. The majority will insist on literal interpretation, while the educated few will see that literal interpretation leads to absurdity and search for a deeper meaning. But both will find something of value in the sacred books and be able to regard them as sacred.

If that were all there were to say, we would be stuck with spiritual schizophrenia. The fact is, however, that Maimonides takes another step. The distinction between divine law and human or nomic law (*sharī'a nāmūsiyya*) is that the latter provides for a well-ordered city by abolishing injustice and oppression but pays no attention to speculative matters or the perfection of the rational faculty; by contrast divine law provides for a well-ordered city but also takes into consideration people's opinions about God and tries to awaken their desire to learn (*GP* 2.40, pp. 383–84). If nomic law aims at happiness, divine law aims at happiness and wisdom together. It follows that the law on which popular religion is based has more than one dimension. In addition to inculcating beliefs that promote respect for authority, it will encourage people to gain as much understanding of God as their natures allow.[48] It will, in short, put them on a course that has love of God as its final end. To the degree that it promotes happiness alone, it fails—at least as divine Law.

This is all a way of saying that even from a traditional standpoint, popular religion cannot be taken at face value; it cannot justify itself by saying that even though it appeals to the imagination rather than the intellect, at least it keeps people out of trouble. For if that is all it does, we might just as well fashion our own laws and forget about Sinai. Maimonides' point is that correctly understood, popular religion must also encourage people to seek something more. Like religious language, it must point the mind in the right direction even if it exhausts itself in the process. It is for this reason that popular religion is not spurious or idolatrous. At whatever level it may begin, it offers a systematic way to get to higher levels. As we saw, the performance of one commandment makes it easier to perform others.

The problem is with people who think that popular religion represents the sum and substance of Judaism—that any attempt to move to something higher by showing that God cannot have a body or experience emotion is an attempt to introduce foreign elements, to "hellenize" the religion. Nothing could be further from the truth. In Maimonides' opinion, to hellenize the religion would be to rob the Law of its sacred character by making it nothing but a set of rules designed to keep people in line. Once the Law failed to provide for spiritual needs, it would no longer reflect God's love and become what he terms a body of *nomoi*. Once again, Maimonides does not think he is changing Judaism as much as rediscovering truths that allow it to reach its full potential.

Judaism and Enslavement: Hegel Revisited

Is a rigorous definition of monotheism compatible with a religion people can practice? The answer is yes in the sense that the prayers, rituals, and sacred books lose none of their depth or beauty when interpreted along the lines Maimonides suggests. We may have to approach them in a new way, but if Maimonides is right, rather than hellenizing the religion, we will be rediscovering its true meaning: that all the commandments are ways of getting us to love God, taking an active part in the evaluation of our beliefs, and coming as close as we can to an honest assessment of what we know and what we do not. In Maimonides' defense, it could be said that part of the vitality of a sacred tradition is that the process of rediscovery is always possible; one can always push beyond the surface meaning of texts or rituals to a deeper one.

One way to think about this point is to compare monotheism with a secular idea like that of a perfect democracy. Suppose someone were to ask whether equality and respect for human dignity are compatible with the day-to-day operations at city hall. It is true that many people at city hall are more interested in dispensing favors than in upholding human rights. The point is that there is nothing in principle to stop city hall from reforming itself and living up to the ideals to which it is supposed to be committed. The fact that individual people would have to adopt a new understanding of their functions is hardly an argument for tolerating inequity. By the same token, we do not have to accept the argument that since people cannot pray to an impersonal God, they have no choice but to make peace with anthropomorphism. If this chapter has proved anything, it is that religion has to look beyond human behavior in its present form and articulate a vision of something better, what Levinas, somewhat optimistically, calls "a religion for adults."

The real question, then, is not whether a monotheistic religion is possible in principle but what kind of vision it offers. Recall Hegel's contention that an unmediated relationship between humans and God cannot help but lead to estrangement. As long as we insist on the absoluteness of finitude, we cannot see our image or even our categories reflected in God. If Maimonides is right, neither can we fathom

God's purpose in creating the universe. So the vision Maimonides articulates does not foster "man's confidence in man" but exactly the opposite: man's acceptance of the limits in man.

Hegel's criticism of Judaism is that God becomes so awesome that everything else in the universe is "negated" or trivialized by comparison. In Hegel's words (*LPR* 2, p. 172):

> This unity of God contains itself One Power, a Power which consequently is absolute, and within this all externality, and consequently all that belongs to the world of sense, that takes on the form of sense, or is a picture, disappears.

Faced with a God who is infinite and incomprehensible, the only legitimate response is in (*LPR* 2, p. 207) "not allowing the particular . . . to have a valid existence as something independent." In human terms, this means that those who worship God must honor, recognize, and show absolute faith in what is completely beyond them: the one God who, unlike the Greek gods, is limited by nothing and embodies all of wisdom and holiness. "The people of God," as Hegel puts it, "is accordingly a people adopted by covenant and contract on the conditions of fear and service."[49]

Although Hegel's analysis of Judaism displays ignorance of rabbinic and medieval sources, not to mention important biblical ones, there are many respects in which it is accurate. I have remarked several times that Isaiah (40:15–17) claims the mighty nations of the earth and the cedars of Lebanon are as nothing before God and have stressed that the differences between things in the created order are overwhelmed by the enormous difference between the created order and God. Nothing in the created order resembles God or exists except for the grace of God. According to Maimonides, the prophet is supposed to see this, fear God, and eventually come to love God. But the prophet is not supposed to see his image reflected *in* God. The prophet's fear, as Hegel sees, is not the fear of anything finite, because before God everything finite ceases to matter. Rather the fear spoken of is (*LPR* 2, p. 207) "pure surrender of the self to the absolute Self, in contrast to which and into which the particular self melts away and disappears."

Why is this bad? Because, Hegel (*LPR* 2, p. 206) answers, it is inevitable that God will be conceived as "a Power above me, which negates my value as a person."[50] Thus "only God Himself can be His end," which is to say that God is the only thing in the universe worth thinking about or glorifying.[51] Worse, God is totally unconcerned with humans and exists entirely for the sake of God. Since we have no claim on existence except through God, our lot becomes that of a humble servant who must submit to an alien will he can neither question nor comprehend. In this connection, Hegel cites Leviticus 26 to show that God's power is exemplified by a long series of curses threatening the people with reprisals for any act of disobedience. The conclusion is that Judaism robs humanity of its dignity and fails to account for the inner life: The Law is absolute, disobedience angers God, obedience pleases God and makes one holy. The only thing approaching an inner life is the sorrow one feels in violating the Law.[52] Therefore it is not until it sees itself as manifesting the glory of Zeus or Athena in Greek religion that humanity can assert an independent right to exist and begin to experience freedom. In this context, freedom demands reconciliation (*Versöhnung*) with God (*LPR* 2, pp. 346–47):

> Reconciliation starts from the fact that there are different forms of existence which stand to each other in a relation of opposition, namely, God, who has opposed to Him an estranged world, and a world which is estranged from its own essential Being. Reconciliation is the negation of this separation, of this division; it means that each recognizes itself, finds itself and its essential nature, in the other. Reconciliation is thus freedom.

In Hegel's opinion it is not until the arrival of Christianity that such reconciliation is really achieved.

In Hegel's view, then, the history of religion is but one manifestation of the general history of the struggle for recognition. The problem with Judaism is that all recognition goes to God. Is this true? Is the Hebrew Bible a record of a subjugated people trying desperately to please a vengeful God? From a literary standpoint, it is exactly the opposite: a heroic landscape in which characters take bold actions, bring down an empire, lead a nation out of slavery, and raise any number of questions about divine justice. Contrary to the notion that "the God of the Old Testament" demands blind obedience, there is a tradition, beginning with Abraham, where characters do question God or demand that God back down.[53] The idea is that God is not a tyrant who stands above the Law but a partner who has pledged to obey it. There is no question that Abraham, Joseph, Moses, David, and Job occupy as prominent a place in Western literature as Achilles or Odysseus. Their lives do much to inform us about the limits and creative possibilities of the human condition, and their stories are anything but simple morality plays. So the suggestion that all efforts to assert human freedom are an act of rebellion against God is ridiculous.

It is true, as Hegel claims, that the main event in the Bible is God's giving the Law to Moses, but it is well to remember that the Law is not presented as an edict. God is not Pharaoh. The typical way to describe the Law is as a covenant or agreement (*brit*), which implies freedom and recognition of both parties. Rather than insisting on arbitrary forms of behavior, God is portrayed as both needing and asking for human consent. The prophets typically compare the giving of the Law to the taking of a marriage vow, which is why our term *revelation* can be misleading. In this respect, the idea of *choosing* Israel is a better description than that of *commanding* it. The rabbis went so far as to say that while God is the author of the Law, the job of interpreting it is given over entirely to humans—so much so that humans do not have to consult God or even listen to God in deciding what the Law requires.[54] But as Fackenheim points out, Hegel cannot make anything of the idea of a covenantal relationship.[55]

All this raises the question of how finite beings can relate to an infinite one. At bottom, monotheism comes down to the fact that there can be only one necessary being, and as Descartes points out, when I examine myself, I cannot help but see that I am not it. Why should I assume that because I am not the source of my own existence, I am locked in a struggle for recognition with the one who is? To worship God I must accept the fact of finitude and contemplate the universe *sub specie aeternitatis*. Why does this mean I have to give up my dignity as a human being? Even if we think of this issue in terms most favorable to Hegel, and imagine a prophet turning wholly to God, is it clear that God and humans are pitted against each other?

One way to approach this question is to ask what it means for a finite being to pay tribute to an infinite one. In paganism paying tribute is an easy matter: Since the gods eat, drink, fight wars, and enjoy sexual encounters with mortals, it does not take much imagination to figure out how to make them happy. But sooner or later one is faced with a question like the one Socrates puts to Euthyphro: How does our tribute improve the lot of God? How does slaughtering animals, pouring out anointing oil, wearing special clothes, immersing oneself in a pool of water, or using epithets like Great, Mighty, Terrible, or Exalted make God better? Much the same question was raised by Rav: "What can it matter to God whether a beast is slain at the throat or at the neck?"[56] The answer is that it cannot matter, at least not directly. The ritual may purify the people who perform it, or help them minimize the pain they inflict on the animal, but strictly speaking the idea of improving the lot of a necessary being is incoherent—just as it is incoherent to suppose that we can confer additional glory on God or ease God's burden.[57]

What does God want? Maimonides' answer is that while we should not tackle this question for the universe as a whole, we have every reason to think that God wants us to achieve the highest level of perfection available to us. In this respect, the Law is comprehensible, and it is our duty to try to comprehend it. To obey the Law in a mindless, repetitive fashion is, to use Maimonides' word, to behave like an ignoramus. For Maimonides even the statutory commandments have a rational purpose. As Twersky puts it, they are "messages which must be deciphered and decoded; they appear undecipherable only for lack of knowledge, insight, and sensitivity."[58] Maimonides goes so far as to say that anyone who believes that God would issue a commandment for which there is no rational justification is sick (*GP* 3.31, pp. 523–24).

Maimonides therefore goes to great length to show that the Law never commands obedience for its own sake. With three exceptions, all commandments must be suspended the minute human life is in jeopardy.[59] The justification for this principle is that the commandments were given in order that people may live (Leviticus 18:5); therefore any commandment that threatens life should not be performed. In short, he tries to show that acceptance of the Law involves not submission to an alien will but the development of human reason. This does not mean that commandments can be justified in the way that scientific principles are; rather it means that if we take into account the problem of getting people to put personal considerations aside and worship God in a satisfactory way, we will see that there is no choice but to introduce prayers, festivals, symbols, and with them a body of ritual law. In his defense, it should be noted that clubs, corporations, universities, military regiments, and secular democracies have ceremonies, mascots, special clothing, special music, and a variety of other devices to represent or reinforce shared commitments. To suggest that these things are forced on people by an alien will is to ignore the fact that most people need ritual to arouse emotion and foster a sense of identity. Recall that according to Maimonides, there was nothing wrong with Abraham's monotheism as a philosophic theory; the problem is that it was only a theory and did not take hold in the minds of ordinary people. So far from making people's lives more difficult, in Maimonides' opinion the ritual law makes it easier by giving people something tangible to focus on.

From a historical perspective, the prophets rail against the people for violating the Law, but their point is usually not that the people failed to pay tribute to God by forgetting to perform a ritual or offer high enough praise. On the contrary, the prophets often acknowledge that the people have slaughtered herds of animals, poured out rivers of anointing oil, and sung hymn after hymn.[60] Thus Isaiah 1:11: "To what purpose is the multitude of your sacrifices to me? saith the Lord; I am full of the burnt-offerings of rams, and the fat of fed beasts." What bothers the prophets is that the people have resorted to paganism, practiced black magic, and taken advantage of the less fortunate. Even when God speaks to Job—the prooftext par excellence for the Hegelian interpretation—the issue is never obedience to ritual.

Where, then, is there a struggle for recognition? The answer is that there is a clear struggle if we regard the Law as a burden that humans either cannot or do not want to fulfill. If Paul is right and the Law brings sin into the world, and sin brings death, then the only way people will obey it is if a vengeful God forces them to. Since God, as one might say, holds all the cards, the interaction between humans and God cannot help but rob humans of their dignity. According to Hegel (*LPR* 2, p. 211):

> All law is given by the Lord, and is thus entirely positive commandment. There is in it a formal, absolute authority. The particular elements in the political system are not, speaking generally, developed out of the universal end, nor is it left to man to give it its special character, for the Unity does not permit human caprice, human reason, to exist alongside of it, and political change is in every instance called a falling away from God; but, on the other hand, particular laws, as being something given by God, are regarded as eternally established. And here the eternal laws of what is right, of morality, are placed in the same rank and stated in an equally positive form with the most trifling regulations.

In short, Hegel's approach is correct if, contrary to Maimonides, we assume that the Law was *not* given as an act of love—or that it was given as an act of love but presents too great a burden for humans to fulfill.[61]

To be sure, many of the laws, such as those pertaining to the sacrificial cult, would seem arbitrary to someone in the nineteenth century, but clearly Maimonides is right in saying that these laws should be viewed as concessions to the people for whom they were intended. What we may regard as arbitrary, they would have regarded as essential; what we see as forced, they were only too happy to obey. In fact, Maimonides' criticism is that the people found it much easier to obey the commandments dealing with things they could see and touch than to obey those dealing with the existence and unity of God.

The alternative to Hegel is to say that what distinguishes monotheism from paganism is that for the former, the Law is given for our sake, not God's. According to a rabbinic commentary on Leviticus 19:1, the commandment "You shall be holy" should be taken as meaning, "If you sanctify yourselves, I shall account it to you as if you had sanctified Me."[62] So there is no hint of a struggle for recognition. From Maimonides' standpoint, the problem is not with the Law per se but in getting people to see the rationality inherent in it. The problem, in other words, is getting people to see that the Law is exactly what its name *(torah)* implies: a body of instruction designed to raise people up from ignorance and lawlessness. So there is every hope and expectation that rationality *can* exist alongside God, that God asks for rationality above everything else.

It is true that once the Law is embodied, it culminates in humility, while the Greek worldview (with the clear exception of Socrates) is sometimes said to culminate in Aristotle's great-souled man. But again: Why is this bad? Once I recognize that I am not the source of my own existence and cannot begin to compete for recognition with God, why is humility not an appropriate response? Humility, after all, is not self-denial; it is rather a denial that my image is reflected in or comparable to God. The fact that I did not bring myself into being means that I have to respect the one who did.

Monotheism, then, is a lesson in how to deal with an other infinitely greater than ourselves. The hope is that by learning to respect something greater than ourselves, we will be better than if we restrict our attention to things in which we see ourselves reflected. In other words, we will be better if we accept the wholly other for what it is and resist the temptation to think that history has brought us to the point where we have overcome our finitude. The fact that it is other does not mean that it is threatening or that all attempts at reconciliation are bound to fail; in this context, reconciliation means living *with* the other rather than seeing ourselves *in* it. Recall Maimonides' claim that by acquiring knowledge "man is man"—man and not God. Thus reconciliation simply means that humans see their well-being bound up with God and agree to live in harmony with God. Rather than sameness, this understanding of reconciliation implies respect for—nay, insistence on—difference. It is no accident, then, that God, whose holiness is comparable to that of the stranger, loves the stranger and asks us to do the same (Deuteronomy 10:18–19). In the last analysis, the logic of monotheism is either/or and no purpose is served by trying to overcome it.

Conclusion

I began this study by suggesting that philosophy is not a monologue and that the best way to understand the issues at stake is to have an imaginary conversation in which Maimonides confronts the arguments of other thinkers. Since many of the arguments he uses are dialectical, it could be said that they too are the result of imaginary conversations. It should be clear, however, that once the conversation gets going, the terms in which it is phrased begin to change. At the outset, we have Platonism, Aristotelianism, prophecy, and unassisted human reason. But it does not take exceptional ability to see that after a while these categories begin to crisscross. By the twelfth century, Platonism became so heavily entwined with revealed religion that Maimonides found it natural to define prophecy in terms of emanation. In many instances the comparison between prophets and philosopher-kings is so obvious that it hardly needs to be pointed out. We saw that the Aristotelianism Maimonides discusses in the chapters on creation has a strong Neoplatonic flavor and is probably closer to Plotinus than to the historical Aristotle. And with the possible exception of proofs for God's existence, a topic we have not considered in detail, there is little Maimonides claims to establish by reason alone. That he is a rationalist no one will deny. But we must be careful not to oversimplify his position. Rationalism does not mean that appeals to Scripture, history, or human psychology are unwarranted. On the contrary, it means that any appeal is warranted as long as it helps the conversation move forward.

It should come as no surprise that terms can undergo a natural evolution during the course of a conversation. But unless we keep this point in mind, we will lose sight of Maimonides' contribution and the subtlety of the issues he addresses. More important, we will lose sight of Judaism's role in world culture. If reason is one thing and revelation another, if the God of Abraham, Isaac, and Jacob is out of place in the history of philosophy, then Judaism has only a marginal role to play in Western thought. Take philosophy out of Judaism—or, what amounts to the same thing, cut Judaism off from Plato, Aristotle, Plotinus, or Kant, Hegel, and Wittgenstein—and you will have a religion *manqué*. To many people, Jewish and gentile alike, this is an accurate assessment of the situation: Christianity is central to the development of Western thought, Judaism not.

The justification for making Maimonides the central figure of this book is that he had the courage to confront philosophic issues rather than claim that because Athens and Jerusalem are different, Judaism is exempt from them. His treatment of philosophic issues was not an attempt to respond to external influences as much as a need to articulate the true meaning of the religion. If he was not as tolerant of other faiths as we might like, at least he tried to make the world take his faith seriously. Where moderns look to religion for closeness and comfort, he looked to it for truth. Where we want to bring God into the sphere of our own subjectivity and experience what Buber calls "a living presence," he wanted to bring us out of this sphere by acquainting us with a vision the whole world can share. Thus his fondness for quoting Deuteronomy 4:6: "Surely this great nation is a wise and understanding people."

We have seen that parts of Maimonides' vision are no longer credible. But the idea of a God separate from creation surely is. More important, the idea that popular religion has a teleology and that even the wisest among us should not exceed the limits of human understanding gives needed structure to religious life. If the purpose of religion is to seek truth, then truth on matters of this sort is another name for honesty. What Maimonides asks is that we think about God in a critical fashion, getting beyond the mode of presentation to the thing presented, distrusting theories that make God serve us and putting more stock in theories that make us serve God. Structure is difficult to achieve in any age but even more difficult given the tenor of this one. Few people in our culture want to think of God as distant or other. Maybe it is time that we ask ourselves whether Maimonides' view is not closer to the truth.

Appendix

Esotericism and the Limits of Knowledge: A Critique of Strauss

The dichotomy between popular religion and the religion of the educated few raises the question of esotericism and takes us back to the thought of Leo Strauss.[1] As we saw, the *Guide* is not a formal treatise but a letter written to an advanced student whose commitment to Judaism is well established. The most immediate problem Maimonides faced in writing such a book was that no one could guarantee that everyone who read it would be as qualified and conscientious as Joseph. Whether we are talking about the twelfth century or the twentieth, the majority of Jews are, in Maimonides' opinion, those who *seek* to enter the ruler's habitation but never do. He was well aware that if the tenets of popular religion were challenged in too abrupt a fashion, the results could be disastrous. Informed that God does not look down on the world like a judge looking down on her court, people would conclude that there is no God—or at least none that they have to worry about.

Throughout the *Guide* Maimonides cites the talmudic dictum that prohibits discussion of the secrets of the Torah in public, and in several passages he indicates that even without the prohibition, it would be imprudent to present advanced material to a beginning student. As always, the issue of who learns what and when is critical. But we also saw that Maimonides is not content to let people believe in a corporeal God and perform commandments whose purpose is to facilitate belief in an incorporeal one. His response is to say that belief in incorporeality is mandatory but that when it comes to more difficult matters, the best course of action is to keep the secrets of the Torah out of the public domain. The question is how secret does he have to be to ac-

177

complish this end? At what point would he have so much esotericism that even the most sophisticated readers would be left in the dark?

A Book with Seven Seals?

According to Strauss, Maimonides' esotericism runs very deep. Confronted by an esoteric book, a responsible interpreter, in Strauss's opinion, must also be esoteric, lest the secrets of the original author fall into the wrong hands:[2]

> It may fairly be said that an interpreter who does not feel pangs of conscience when attempting to explain that secret teaching and perhaps when perceiving for the first time its existence and bearing lacks that closeness to the subject which is indispensable for the true understanding of any book.

Since the Torah is esoteric, and the *Guide*, by Maimonides' own admission, an explanation of obscure passages in the Torah, the *Guide* is an esoteric interpretation of an esoteric original. To use one of Strauss's images, it is a book with seven seals.

Yet Maimonides was not the only author to to face the problem of esotericism. According to Strauss, the interpreter of Maimonides is in the same boat as Maimonides himself. Unless the interpreter wants to reveal a doctrine Maimonides labored to keep secret, he must also write in an esoteric manner. The upshot is that a person who reads Strauss on Maimonides confronts an esoteric interpretation of an esoteric interpretation of a doctrine that is esoteric in its own right. It should come as no surprise, then, that Strauss's introduction to the Pines translation of the *Guide* never takes up the basic question of what Maimonides contributed to the history of philosophy.

Since Maimonides' goal was to speak to trained readers while keeping untrained ones at bay, Strauss argues that he had to become a master of the art of revealing by not revealing and of not revealing by revealing. What kind of art is this? According to Strauss, the need for esotericism is based on the "rigid division" of mankind into an inspired and intelligent minority and an uninspired and foolish majority.[3] While the majority lack the intellectual tools to understand religion at a sophisticated level, they often have the power to make life miserable for those who do. We saw, however, that for all the shortcomings of popular religion, Maimonides insists that it address spiritual needs and point the way to something higher. He himself tried to do as much in *Perek Ḥelek*. But even if we assume, contrary to Maimonides' explicit statements, that popular religion is one half of a rigid separation, we get the same problem over again. Do we need seven seals to keep an uninspired majority in the dark, and at what point does esotericism keep even the inspired majority guessing about the true meaning of the text?

To answer these questions, let us think about esotericism in two ways.[4] The first is what I will call *normal esotericism*. This applies to a book that deals with a demanding subject and requires intense concentration to be understood. Although the uninspired majority may not be able to follow it, the book contains no booby traps, blind alleys, or concealed doctrines—at least none that the author has put there intentionally. One could say that the *Critique of Pure Reason* is esoteric in this sense because it is inaccessible to all but a technically trained audience. While it challenges popular religion at a number of points, few people have been thrown into a spiritual crisis as a result of reading it.

By contrast, *deep esotericism* applies to a book in which the author hides the true meaning behind hints, clues, or cleverly constructed diversions. Maimonides alerts the reader that the *Guide* is a diffuse book in which one subject will be treated in a variety of places. And Strauss is certainly right to say that it is designed to reflect the give and take of oral instruction. But the same could be said of any number of works whose authors knew nothing of talmudic prohibitions against speaking in public.

As Strauss would have it, Maimonides' predicament in writing the *Guide* was this. The Torah is an esoteric book written in parables. If Maimonides were to write the same kind of book, he would be trading one parable for the other and not making any progress. Therefore he had to find a way simultaneously to reveal the truth and hide it, a way that would fool one audience but make good sense to the other. The solution to this dilemma can be found in Maimonides' famous admission that he intends to contradict himself (*GP* 1. Introduction, p. 20). After all, asks Strauss, what better way is there to hide the truth than to say "*a* is *b*" and then "*a* is not *b*"?[5] Since one of these must be true and the other false, the truth is revealed and then concealed at the same time. But which statement is the revelation and which the concealment? Strauss proposes that of two contradictory claims, the one that occurs *least* frequently is the one Maimonides regards as true.[6]

In the introduction to the *Guide*, Maimonides lists seven types of contradiction found in prophetic and philosophic writing. Of the seven, he says he will avail himself of two. The first type is unproblematic: A teacher speaking to introductory students may have to say something at the beginning of the inquiry that she intends to take back later. We saw, for example, that sometimes (e.g., *GP* 3.51, pp. 623–24) Maimonides talks about union with God when he really means partial union with the Agent Intellect. Or sometimes he talks about the essence of God when strictly speaking God has no essence.

The second type is more interesting, because it does involve a measure of concealment:

> In speaking about very obscure matters it is necessary to conceal some parts and to disclose others. Sometimes in the case of certain dicta this necessity requires that the discussion proceed on the basis of another premise contradicting the first one. In such cases the vulgar must in no way be aware of the contradiction; the author accordingly uses some device to conceal it by all means.

It is regrettable that Maimonides' description of this type of contradiction is not only vague but extremely short. He does not say how often he intends to use it, so that Strauss goes beyond the text by claiming that contradictions are the "axis" of the *Guide* or that Maimonides makes contradictory statements on all important matters.[7] In fact, Maimonides does not even say that he will *assert* P and then not-P. All he says is that some discussions will proceed on the basis of one assumption, while another discussion will proceed on the basis of an incompatible one.

It is also noteworthy that Maimonides limits the scope of this type of contradiction to "very obscure matters." I take this to mean that he will use contradictions in those areas where no demonstration is available and there is little hope of finding one.[8] The reason is simple: If you demonstrate *P*, you will not conceal anything by asserting not-*P*. What Maimonides appears to say, then, is that when a subject is obscure and no clear resolution of a problem is available, it is sometimes necessary for the discussion to proceed on the basis of contradictory premises. Why must there be concealment? To someone who thinks that religious matters are simple and straightforward, the suggestion that plausible arguments can be made on either side of an issue and that neither side can be demonstrated may be profoundly disturbing.

Though Maimonides does not connect this sort of contradiction with the philosophic tradition, it is nonetheless true that from a historical perspective there is nothing startling in what he proposes. As Aristotle claims, a dialectical premise begins with the choice between contradictory statements.[9] In the *Meno* and *Protagoras*, for example, Socrates presents reasonable arguments to show that virtue is teachable and reasonable arguments to show that it is not. But he is not attempting to conceal something; rather his point is that we have to ask more fundamental questions about virtue (e.g., what is it?) to resolve the puzzle. There is little doubt that Plato came to see how damaging this sort of argument can be to people who are not properly trained, which is one reason he restricted access to philosophy in the *Republic*.[10] But to people who are ready to think philosophically, it is a common mode of argument. Aristotle, too, uses it to introduce the subject of metaphysics in *Metaphysics* 2. I therefore follow Joel Kraemer in arguing that despite the use of demonstration in some contexts, the evidence strongly suggests that the *Guide* is primarily a dialectical work.[11]

Another way to look at the issue is to ask whether Maimonides has a doctrine that *could* be expressed in a simple, straightforward way or whether his view of philosophy and the limits of knowledge makes linear arguments and pithy conclusions all but impossible. In some passages Strauss suggests that direct and plain communication of the secrets of the Torah is impossible by nature.[12] Yet this view, as Strauss himself admits, runs into an immediate difficulty. The Talmud prohibits direct and plain communication of these secrets. Why would it try to prohibit something that is not within our power to do? Strauss therefore takes the Law to imply that direct and plain communication *is* possible and it is clear why. If Maimonides' way of communicating the secrets of the Torah is to contradict himself then of necessity one of the two contradictory statements must hit the nail on the head. As Strauss puts it, "While the other devices used by Maimonides compel the reader to guess the true meaning, the contradictions offer him the true teaching quite openly in either of the two contradictions."[13] Thus Strauss compares Maimonides' true teaching to an inscription in an unknown language that must be deciphered by an archeologist.

Against Strauss I want to argue that the *Guide* does not contain *a* true teaching that is hidden from the reader but a patchwork of doctrines, conjectures, and observations dealing with speculative matters. It is esoteric because it is difficult to achieve certainty in a field where all we have are brief glimpses of the truth; but there are no booby traps, and the *Guide* is not a book with seven seals.

The Need for Conceptual Flexibility

Let us consider some of the contradictions in the *Guide* and ask ourselves whether there is evidence of deep or normal esotericism. Strauss points out that Maimonides says that what distinguished Moses' prophecy from that of others is that Moses's apprehension was entirely intellectual and did not involve the imagination.[14] But, Strauss continues, it is the imagination that brings forth similes and metaphors, and the Torah, which is the record of Moses' prophecy, abounds in both. Why is this "a great difficulty"? Suppose Moses' apprehension were purely intellectual. If he had tried to communicate the truths he apprehended without using similes and metaphors, he would have seen that few, if any, people would have understood them. So the fact that Moses used similes and metaphors to make himself intelligible to large numbers of people does not mean that he himself needed them or that every one of his readers does.

To take another example from Strauss:[15]

> The nonidentity of the teaching of the philosophers as a whole and the thirteen roots of the Law as a whole is the first word and the last word of Maimonides. What he means by identifying the core of philosophy (natural science and divine science) with the highest secrets of the Law (the Account of the Beginning and the Account of the Chariot) and therewith by somehow identifying the subject matter of speculation with the subject matter of exegesis may be said to be the secret par excellence of the *Guide*.

It is not clear what Strauss means by "the teaching of the philosophers as a whole," but if we take the philosophy Maimonides himself puts forward in the *Guide*, the relation between philosophy and the thirteen principles is neither secret nor especially problematic. The principles were intended for a general audience and contain the conclusions of speculation rather than the arguments that support them. Certainly there is no incompatibility in regard to the existence, unity, incorporeality, and eternity of God. Nor is there an incompatibility in the claim that only God is worthy of worship.

It is true, of course, that philosophy cannot prove the existence of prophecy, but no philosophic conclusion derived by Maimonides undermines it. In fact, the general drift of Maimonides' account of prophecy is to deemphasize the miraculous dimension and insist that nothing in prophetic literature contradicts what reason can establish on its own. There is little question that in *Perek Ḥelek* Maimonides speaks very loosely and generally about Moses and the other prophets, but he says so and directs the reader to a more complete exposition elsewhere. Similar remarks apply to the claim that the Torah is from God: While it may seem as if Maimonides is asking the reader to accept it on faith, a more complete understanding reveals that he does in fact consider the Torah a perfect guide for the development of human excellence.

In regard to providence and reward and punishment, we saw that there is a kernel of truth in the idea of an angry God who punishes sin but that even in his popular writings, including *Perek Ḥelek*, Maimonides is anxious to take people to a higher level. Belief in a messiah does not contradict any philosophic conclusion, especially when one realizes that for Maimonides the messiah will be a teacher and political leader rather than a miracle worker. Thus Maimonides quotes a rabbinic text (*Sanhedrin* 91b) that says: "The sole difference between the present and the messianic is delivery from servitude to foreign powers."[16] As for the lion dwelling with the lamb, it is only a metaphor. There is a problem with resurrection of the soul if we take it to mean something beyond immortality, but discussion of that problem is well known and beyond the limits of this study. While the thirteen principles may not be identical with Maimonides' philosophy, they are exactly what he claims: an abbreviation. The influence of Aristotle is clear in those principles dealing with the unity and incorporeality of God. By the same token, the influence of tradition is clear in the principles dealing with prophecy and providence. Maimonides is quite open about the fact that he will take truth from wherever he can find it.

A supposed contradiction identified by Fox is that in the chapters dealing with negative theology, Maimonides claims that God bears no relation to the created order, thereby ruling out the possibility that God can be a cause; but in other chapters (e.g., *GP* 1.16, p. 42; 1.69, p. 167) Maimonides says quite clearly that God is the efficient cause of the world.[17] We saw, however, that Maimonides was not the only thinker to face this difficulty. Causality is a relation that holds between one thing in the created order and another. By contrast, creation is unique and cannot be understood on the analogy with cause and effect. In fact, we are better off not to ask ourselves about the "how?" of creation at all.

Even if creation is not a causal connection, it is still true that the created order depends on God and cannot exist without God.[18] One can describe God as the cause of the created order in a context where one wishes to speak loosely, and again, Maimonides is not the only thinker to do so. In his discussion of creation in the *Guide*, Maimonides goes to great length to show why this way of speaking is not strictly true. Fox also cites the principle of *imitatio Dei* as a source of contradiction, because it is impossible to imitate something you do not resemble. But we saw that Maimonides is well aware of the problem and attempts to explain *imitatio Dei* in a manner that preserves God's uniqueness.

Another source of perplexity in Maimonides is his attitude toward miracles. When criticizing the theory of eternal emanation, he says that it destroys the possibility of miracles and commits us to a God who cannot change the size of a fly's wing (*GP* 2.22, p. 319); but as any reader of Maimonides soon learns, he tries to take the miraculous dimension out of prophecy, providence, and repentance. I suggest that there is nothing contradictory here either. When criticizing the theory of eternal emanation, Maimonides wants to establish the *possibility* of miracles, which is to say the fact that God is not constrained by the laws of physics. But once this possibility is established, he turns skeptical, arguing that even if there are disruptions in the normal course of events, they are not permanent changes and were ordained by God during creation (*GP* 2.29, p. 345). Beyond that, Maimonides argues that while God could upset the normal course of the world, doing so would not help us achieve perfection and would render the Torah useless. As Aviezer Ravitzky argues, such action would be logically possible but physically, metaphysically, or theologically impossible.[19] As we might say, God could, but from everything we can tell, will not. Although this view is not without problems, it is hardly contradictory.

An additional problem dealing with will is Maimonides' reliance on the arguments of the Mutakallimun. Why would he turn to these arguments in book 2 of the *Guide* if he was so strong in his rejection of them in book 1? We saw, however, that his rejection of them as demonstrations does not preclude his use of them as arguments that help to tip the scale in the direction of volition.

Many scholars have pointed out that Maimonides is not always consistent in his discussion of volition. At *Guide* 3.13 he talks about the priority of will, whereas in *Guide* 3.25 he talks about the priority of wisdom. How can these statements be reconciled with the fact that strictly speaking, God's will and wisdom are identical? The answer is that he is trying to argue against different opponents, which is not uncommon in dialectical argument. At *Guide* 3.13 it is the Aristotelians, while in 3.25 it is people who think that God acts in a frivolous or arbitrary fashion—by "will and nothing else." Total consistency would require a restatement of divine simplicity each time the issue of volition came up; but under the circumstances, it is clear what Maimonides wants to say: There are arguments in favor of divine volition, but to say that God created the world by an act of will does not mean that God's will is arbitrary; hence the need to bring in wisdom as well. In humans, wisdom and will are separate, but in God they are identical.

I have remarked on several occasions that Maimonides views language as a heuristic device that must eventually be discarded. Therefore it is hardly surprising if he refuses to settle on a fixed, technical vocabulary. In some cases, such as his treatment of creation ex nihilo, the ease with which he shifts terminology can cause headaches for scholars. But the same could be said of Plato, Plotinus, and any number of other thinkers. Plato, who shared a similar view of language, used half a dozen words to describe forms and more than that to describe the relation between sensibles and forms.

Perhaps the most serious case of a contradiction occurs at *Guide* 1.68, where Maimonides puts forward a theory of intellection according to which God is simultaneously the intellect in action, the subject of intellection, and the object of intellection. The theory is not new, having been put forward in the *Mishneh Torah* as well.[20] But new or not, it raises two problems: (1) How can Maimonides know what intellection is like in God? (2) According to Maimonides, the theory applies not only to God but to us as well, the difference being that we pass from potentiality to actuality, while God is always in actuality; but even admitting this difference, the passage seems to imply an analogy between our cognition and God's, something Maimonides was at pains to deny in the preceding chapters on negative theology and in much of the rest of the book. At *Guide* 3.20, p. 482, for example, Maimonides continues to claim that "between our knowledge and His knowledge there is nothing in common."

According to *Guide* 3.20, the difference between our knowledge and God's is that ours proceeds from objects external to the mind, while God's does not. God, as it is often said, knows everything by virtue of being completely self-conscious. Thus Maimonides insists that no new knowledge can come to God. The question is whether this difference is enough to say that *knowledge* is completely equivocal when used of us and God or whether the equivocality is undermined by having a common theory of intellection. At *Guide* 1.68 Maimonides is not very explicit, leading some scholars to wonder whether the passage is anomalous.[21]

The context of this chapter indicates that Maimonides has nothing sinister in mind. Having argued that God does not admit plurality in any respect, he must now face the question of how God can have objects of thought. The answer is that if you understand the matter correctly, you will see that the knower, the act of knowing, and the object known are identical; hence no plurality. While the same theory is true of humans, the overwhelming difference between God and humans still holds. If it is asked how Maimonides knows that this is true of God, the answer is that it follows from the fact that God thinks and is one, two claims about which he has no doubt. It is significant that in the *Mishneh Torah*, where there is no suggestion of esotericism, Maimonides uses the unity of knower, knowledge, and object known as grounds for reaffirming negative theology, saying that God's unity is "beyond the power of speech to express, beyond the capacity of the ear to hear, and of the human mind to apprehend clearly." So it is by no means certain that Maimonides intended *Guide* 1.68 to stand out; in fact, the tone of the passage suggests that he regarded it as relatively unproblematic.

According to Barry Kogan, the discrepancy is a contradiction of the harmless variety. If God is knower, knowledge, and object known, and if God's knowledge is not caused by anything external, then an exhaustive study of nature and the heavenly intelligences will reveal that nothing other than God is a self-thinking form of forms. In other words, nothing else knows all things by virtue of knowing itself. This conclusion is perfectly consistent with the chapters dealing with negative theology and fits in well with Maimonides' overall position.

Obviously this is not a catalogue of every contradiction people have claimed to find. But it does contain several of the most notorious. The issue, as I see it, is not which booby trap we have run into but something much deeper: Most of the material Maimonides discusses cannot be given a rigorous formulation if the standard for rigor is set by Aristotle's *Posterior Analytics*. Rather than an exact science analogous to geometry, his presentation usually consists of a shifting set of insights and arguments designed to replace head-to-head conversation. Sometimes Maimonides draws his support from metaphysics, sometimes from biblical criticism, sometimes from astronomy, sometimes from moral psychology. As we saw, a person whose best hope is a glimpse of the truth is willing to get help from whatever quarter he can find it. Along the same lines, he often finds himself arguing with two opponents rather than one: for example, the extreme voluntarism of the Mutakallimun versus the determinism of Aristotle, or the view that God's actions are arbitrary versus the view that we can know exactly what God's intentions are.

This sort of approach requires enormous flexibility on the part of the reader. With few exceptions, Maimonides does not present his arguments in a linear fashion: As we saw with creation, contexts change, terminology changes, and standards of proof may change as well. Sometimes Maimonides is talking about demonstration, sometimes about what it is reasonable to believe. Sometimes he begins with premises, sometimes with generally accepted opinions. A case in point is his attitude toward the Platonic theory of creation. At the beginning of his discussion, Maimonides says that he does not believe the Platonic theory; but after weighing the evidence and considering the alternatives, he concludes that it is an acceptable, if not optimal, alternative. Such a result would be unthinkable in Euclid and has created no end of difficulties for interpreters who think that Euclid is the model to which Maimonides must aspire. But what is wrong with simply taking Maimonides at his word? There is a better alternative, but given the speculative nature of the subject, half a loaf is better than none.

Suppose the Talmud said nothing about discussing esoteric matters in public? And suppose Maimonides could be assured that none but the most qualified readers would have access to his book? Is there any reason to think that his treatment of these issues would be different? I suggest there is not. He would still have to proceed in a dialectical fashion, taking insights from whatever source was available to him. Note, in this connection, that he ex-

plicitly denies that his view on the limits of human knowledge has anything
to do with the need to please religious authorities (*GP* 1.31, p. 67). He would
still find that linguistic conventions present obstacles and that he must employ terms "not strictly applicable." In view of these difficulties, he might
well decide to use a variety of expressions to make his point. Most important, perhaps, he might still be committed to a view of philosophy that ab-
hors spoon-feeding and tries to awaken the student's own sense of discovery.

The talmudic prohibition cited by Maimonides does allow one to provide chapter headings to a student capable of learning on his or her own. Not
surprisingly, Maimonides says that we should not expect him to do anything
more than what the Law allows. What does *chapter headings* refer to? Strauss
appears to take it literally, poring over the opening words of Maimonides'
chapters for hidden clues. But in view of Maimonides' repeated warnings
about the dangers of literal interpretation, there is no reason why we have to
read it this way. In fact, *chapter headings* may simply be Maimonides' way
of repeating that he cannot resolve every issue with precision and will provide glimpses of truth.

In the Introduction to the *Guide* Maimonides says: "A sensible man thus
should not demand of me or hope that when we mention a subject, we shall
make a complete exposition of it, or that when we engage in the exposition
of the meaning of one of the parables, we shall set forth exhaustively all that
is expressed in that parable." In short, he assumes his readers can fill in many
of the details and see for themselves where an argument points and what it
presupposes. This is a long way from writing a book with seven seals. Given
Maimonides' mode of presentation, one can find contradictions galore if one
wishes to overlook issues like audience, context, or unavoidable linguistic
distortions. But these are exactly the sort of things Maimonides wants us to
attend to.

Glimpses of Truth

How, then, should we interpret Maimonides' claim that his purpose is to see
that the truth is glimpsed and then concealed? Although deep esotericism is
a possible reading, it is by no means compelling. We do not have to imagine
Maimonides to be like a poker player who shows his hand one card at a time
in an effort to keep his opponents at bay. In the Introduction to book 3 of the
Guide he repeats the talmudic dictum against speaking in public and adds
that it would be cowardly not to set down for others something he regards as
clear. He goes on to say that his understanding of these matters is not the result of a divine revelation but of following conjecture and supposition.

The intellectual modesty expressed in this passage is in keeping with
the passage that claims no one should expect him to remove every doubt.
The reason is that truth in these matters is not fully or completely known to
anyone (*GP* 1. Introduction, p. 7). I take this to mean that even the inspired
and intelligent minority has no choice but to rely on conjecture and suppo-

sition. So the reason truth is glimpsed and then concealed is not that Maimonides is being cagey but that once we appreciate the enormous difficulty of the subject, we will see that only a fool would claim to offer more than a partial vision.

In the same way, Maimonides' method for keeping the uninspired majority away from unsettling results is very simple: the book itself, which is to say a long, daunting, slow-moving exposition that presupposes a high degree of technical training and makes no concessions to popular taste. He claims that even a beginner ought to derive some benefit from reading his book, a statement that is probably a reference to the sections on incorporeality. But he also claims that a person who finds nothing of value in it should think of it as if it had never been written. As one who has taught the *Guide* for many years, I can say with assurance that many students have taken this advice to heart.

In short, normal esotericism is enough to ensure that untrained readers will have no access to Maimonides' views on obscure matters. The sections dealing with creation, prophesy, and providence do not occur until the issue of corporeality has been dealt with and several warnings about human limits put forward. In truth it is difficult for even an advanced student to work through the *Guide* without a profound sense of humility. Thus there is no need to think that Maimonides violated the talmudic injunction against speaking in public. On the general issue of putting pen to paper, it is well known that Maimonides took part in any number of public controversies. If his goal was to shield the public from views that might upset their faith, the publication of *Perek Helek* and Book 1 of the *Mishneh Torah* must be regarded as anomalous, since both challenge important features of popular religion as well. In fact, Maimonides accepts much more of the philosophy and science of the day in the *Mishneh Torah* than he does in the *Guide*. We must therefore ask what purpose would be served by adopting an esotericism as deep as the one Strauss proposes.

In my view, not only is no purpose served, but the literary integrity of the book is seriously compromised. It was, after all, Strauss who called attention to the fact that the *Guide* is not a treatise but a letter written to a student. While the text indicates that Joseph is a man of good character and intelligence, there is nothing to indicate that he is a budding genius. On the contrary, he has come to Maimonides because he is perplexed. What sort of book would put him on the right track? We can imagine a demanding one that would require close attention to every word and twist of argument. But if the book were more than demanding, if the truth were buried so deep that it is hard to see what philosophic contribution Maimonides has made, then the book would not relieve Joseph's perplexity or anyone else's. As Steven Harvey notes, Maimonides did not wish to be too explicit, but neither did he wish to be overly subtle.[22]

Even if we admit that the book is sometimes more subtle than we would like, Strauss's argument for deep esotericism goes well beyond anything required by the text. Maimonides says he wants to resolve Joseph's perplexity, to show how an observant Jew can obey the commandments without renouncing his intellect. Suppose, however, that no resolution is possible. Suppose that Strauss is right and the choice between Athens and Jerusalem is ultimate. If this view were right, or more important, if Maimonides regarded it as so, the *Guide* would have to be esoteric in the deepest possible way. Contrary to what Maimonides actually says, his purpose in writing the *Guide* would be to convince Joseph that faced with a legal system based on divine revelation and a philosophic system based on rational inquiry, he has to pick one or the other.

If the question is how to make the uninspired majority fear God and obey the Law, a traditional understanding of revelation is the only reasonable alternative; if, on the other hand, the question is how to formulate the most convincing arguments about God and the world, philosophy is. One is practical, the other theoretical; one is based on noble lies, the other on dangerous truths. If the choice between them is ultimate, then all the passages in the *Guide* saying that Judaism is not only compatible with philosophy but requires it must be diversions.[23]

But the uninspired majority is not the only problem. What about that part of the inspired minority who want a theory that unites moral and intellectual virtue, who honestly believe that a Jewish understanding of creation and God is superior to that of Aristotle? If Strauss is right, they too would have to be kept in the dark, lest someone call attention to the fact that Maimonides' attempt at a unified theory is a ruse. At bottom, Maimonides' esotericism would have to be clever enough to fool all but the tiniest band of followers.

What, then, is the true secret of the *Guide*? For medieval esotericists like Samuel ibn Tibbon, it was that the science of the Law in its true sense is identical to the teachings of Aristotle. For Strauss it is that the science of the Law in its true sense is incompatible with the teachings of Aristotle. For me it is that neither biblical scholarship nor the teachings of Aristotle can produce certain answers to every question, so the only option is to put together a patchwork of conjecture and supposition. But that is not the only difference, for unlike esotericists of any description, I do not think the secret of the *Guide* is buried beneath seven seals. In my view, it is there for anyone who wants to think about the issues and work through the problems. To some it may be upsetting to learn that all we can get is a patchwork of conjecture and supposition, but Maimonides is convinced that nothing will be gained by claiming more for an argument than what it shows. In the end, his hope is that we will leave the *Guide* as Akiva left *pardes*: without dying, going mad, or being tempted to abandon the religion.

Notes

1. The Urge to Philosophize

1. *PJ*, p. 3.
2. *BBO*, p. 4.
3. *Sifre Deuteronomy*, 28; cf. *GP* 3.28, p. 512; 3.32, p. 530; 3.37, p. 542.
4. *Megillah* 13a.
5. See, for example, Exodus 24:10; Numbers 12:8; Isaiah 6:1–3; Ezekiel 1:26–29. For an extended discussion of visual, tactile, and sexual references in Jewish mystical literature, see Elliot R. Wolfson, *Through a Speculum that Shines*, esp. chaps. 1–3. But note how the use of visual imagery to describe God quickly leads to sexual fantasies with God as partner.
6. Isadore Twersky, *Introduction to the Code of Maimonides*, pp. 501–2. On this theme, also see Herbert Davidson, "The Study of Philosophy as a Religious Obligation," in S. D. Goitein, ed., *Religion in a Religious Age*, pp. 53–68.
7. *GP* 3.51, p. 620.
8. *GP* 1.35, pp. 79–81. According to *Perek Ḥelek*, the principles are (1) the existence of God, (2) the unity of God, (3) the incorporeality of God, (4) the eternity of God, (5) that God alone is worthy of worship, (6) the existence of prophecy, (7) that Moses is the greatest prophet, (8) that the Torah is of divine origin, (9) that the Torah is valid for all times, (10) that God knows everything we do, (11) that God rewards and punishes people, (12) that the messiah will come, (13) resurrection. For further discussion, see Menachem Kellner, *Dogma in Medieval Jewish Thought*, chap. 1. The issue of Jewish dogmatics will be discussed in greater detail in chapter 6.

9. For a recent discussion and review of the available literature, see Idit Dobbs-Weinstein, "The Maimonidean Controversy," in *HJP*, pp. 331–49.

10. Guttmann, *PJ*, p. 138.

11. Moshe Halbertal and Avishai Margalit, *Idolatry*, esp. pp. 1–8.

12. Judith Plaskow, *Standing Again at Sinai*, p. 124. For a more general treatment, see Plaskow, "Jewish Feminist Thought," in *HJP*, pp. 885–94.

13. Plaskow, *Standing*, p. 128.

14. Rita M. Gross, "Steps Toward Feminine Imagery of Deity in Jewish Theology," in S. Heschel, ed., *On Being a Jewish Feminist*, p. 236.

15. Gross, "Steps," p. 237; cf. Plaskow, *Standing*, pp. 160–61.

16. Louis Jacobs, *A Jewish Theology*, p. 38.

17. On the issue of conceptual violence, see *DF*, pp. 21–23.

18. This passage will be discussed in greater detail in the chapters that follow; but note the traces of racism at *GP* 3.51, pp. 618–19.

19. See, for example, *GP* 1. Introduction, p. 13; 1.17, p. 43; 3.8, p. 431. For a recent discussion of this point, see Susan Shapiro, "A Matter of Discipline: Reading for Gender in Jewish Philosophy," in M. Peskowitz and L. Levitt, eds., *Judaism Since Gender*, pp. 158–73.

20. Leo Strauss, *Persecution and the Art of Writing*, p. 19.

21. Strauss, *Persecution*, p. 43. Cf. Strauss, "The Mutual Influence of Theology and Philosophy," in Peter Emberly and Barry Cooper, trans. and eds., *Faith and Political Philosophy*, p. 217: "No one can be both a philosopher and a theologian or, for that matter, a third which is beyond the conflict between philosophy and theology, or a synthesis of both."

22. Werner J. Dannhauser, "Athens and Jerusalem or Jerusalem and Athens," in David Novak, ed., *Leo Strauss and Judaism*," p. 167. Note that Dannhauser thinks that Strauss himself sided with Athens but goes on to admit (p. 168) that this conclusion is both "difficult" and "provisional." It is a short step from the incompatibility of Jerusalem and Athens to the need for people like Maimonides *and Strauss himself* to hide their loyalties and write in an esoteric fashion. For a more complete study of Strauss's view, see Kenneth H. Green, *Jew and Philosopher*, but note that the title of this excellent book begs the question: If Strauss was right, how could he have been both?

23. Strauss, *Natural Right and History*, p. 74.

24. Strauss, "The Mutual Influence," p. 221.

25. For more on Strauss's esotericism, see the appendix to this volume.

26. Aristotle, *Metaphysics* 982b12–20. Cf. Plato, *Meno* 84b and *Theaetetus* 155d. For an excellent treatment of the aporetic nature of Aristotelian first philosophy, see Joseph Owens, *The Doctrine of Being in the Aristotelian Metaphysics*, pp. 211–19.

27. Aristotle, *Topics* 145b17–20.

28. *Topics* 101a35–101b4 (my translation).

29. *Topics* 104b1–18.

30. *Topics* 104a3–5.

31. *Nicomachean Ethics* 1098b27–29. There is a long debate on the nature and scope of dialectic in Aristotle. Part of the problem has to do with the generally accepted opinions (*endoxa*) with which dialectic begins. According to *Topics* 104a7–10, the claims taken up by dialectic range from opinions that are probable at best to views of well-known thinkers and authoritative sources. This ambiguity raises the question of whether to interpret dialectic in a strong or weak sense: as establishing the first principles of a science or as indicating which of two opinions is more likely to be true. At *Metaphysics* 1004b22–26, Aristotle compares dialectic to sophistic and opposes both to philosophy. Since first philosophy cannot demonstrate its own first principles, it is easy to sympathize with those who think Aristotle has a strong sense of dialectic as well. For a single volume setting forth the main issues, see J. D. G. Evans, *Aristotle's Concept of Dialectic*. On how to understand *endoxa*, see J. M. Le Blond, *Logique et Methode chez Aristotle*, pp. 77–85. On the need for a strong sense of dialectic, see Terence Irwin, *Aristotle's First Principles*, pp. 37–39, 174–75.

32. Owens, *Doctrine*, p. 214, n. 13.

33. See *Metaphysics* 1026a19–23, 1064b1–6.

34. See, for example, *GP* 1.51, p. 113; 1.55, p. 129; 1.56, pp. 130–31; 1.59, p. 137; 2.1. p. 248.

35. *GP* 1.34, p. 75; 1.55, p. 129; 3.51, p. 619. Maimonides distinguishes strong proof or demonstration (*burhān*) from weak proof or persuasion (*dalīl*). See, for example, *GP* 2.18, p. 299, where he claims there is a demonstration that change in material things implies movement from potency to act but a persuasive argument that the Active Intellect can act at one time but not at another. For an excellent discussion of this aspect of Maimonides' logic, see Arthur Hyman, "Demonstrative, Dialectical, and Sophistic Arguments in the Philosophy of Moses Maimonides," in *MT*, pp. 35–51. Although I am generally sympathetic with Hyman's argument, I take issue with his interpretation of creation. According to Hyman, there are two types of dialectical argument in Maimonides: one in which either of two alternatives is accepted, the other in which the strongest position is a combination of insights taken from different alternatives. Hyman takes Maimonides' discussion of creation as an example of the first; in chapter 4, I will try to show it is an example of the second.

36. *GP* 2.15, pp. 289–93; 2.23, p. 322.

37. For a similar view and excellent discussion of dialectic in Alfarabi, see Joel Kraemer, "Maimonides on the Philosophic Sciences in His Treatise on the Art of Logic," in *PM*, pp. 102–4.

38. *GP* 2.11, p. 276.

39. For a different view, see Strauss, *Persecution*, pp. 43–46. For a view much closer to my own, see Steven Harvey, "Maimonides in the Sultan's Palace," in *PM*, pp. 56–57. The issue of Maimonides' use of contradiction will be discussed at greater length in the appendix.

40. Two recent examples are Marvin Fox, *Interpreting Maimonides*, p. 249, and Shlomo Pines, "The Limitations of Human Knowledge according to Alfarabi, ibn Bajja, and Maimonides," in *M*, p. 100.

41. Strauss, "How to Begin to Study *The Guide of the Perplexed*," in *GP*, p. xxxvii. There are passages where Maimonides suggests that prophetic understanding exceeds philosophic, e.g., *GP* 2.16, p. 294, but we must keep in mind that prophetic understanding is expressed in the form of parables and needs to be interpreted before we can be certain of its meaning.

42. For Maimonides' commentary, see *GP* 1.54, pp. 123–25.

43. Note the similarity between Maimonides' remark about the superiority of prophets to philosophers at 2.38 and his remark at 2.16, p. 294, that prophecy "explains things to which it is not in the power of speculation to accede."

44. See, for example, *Meno* 81a and *Symposium* 201d.

45. On this point, see Barry Kogan, "'What Can We Know and When Can We Know It?' Maimonides on the Active Intelligence and Human Cognition," *MT*, p. 129: "But the central point is that having this power of intuition does not make the prophet's knowledge different in kind from that of the philosopher because both grasp the middle terms and conclusions of syllogisms. The prophet does this instantaneously compared to others, and thus he can learn comparatively more. But there is no barrier or distinction of kind between him and other men."

46. *GP* 1.36, p. 85: "If, however, you should say that the external sense of the Biblical text causes men to fall into this doubt, you ought to know that *an idolator* is similarly impelled to his idolatry by imaginings and defective representations."

47. Note the qualification: imagination *alone*. According to this passage, the imagination can assist us if it is accompanied by reason.

48. Goodman, *God of Abraham*, p. 31.

49. Maimonides is not the only person to speak this way; see *DF*, p. 14.

50. For a recent discussion of why theology needs philosophy, see David Novak, "Philosophy and the Possibility of Revelation: A Theological Response to the Challenge of Leo Strauss," D. Novak, ed., *Leo Strauss and Judaism*, pp. 184–87.

51. See *Meno* 75d, where dialectic implies conversation carried on in a friendly and cooperative manner.

52. Novak, *The Election of Israel*, pp. 209–210.

53. For a modern defense of this view, see Novak, *Election*, p. 10. The claim that God chose Israel from all the other nations of the world and gave it the Torah is "irreducible to any other theological proposition." But note how little this claim tells us unless we answer certain basic questions: Chose Israel for what purpose? Gave the Torah in what manner? Expected the Torah to be interpreted in what fashion? In short, this claim, like most that single out Israel for special mention, presupposes a vast body of theological doctrine before its significance can be grasped, let alone accepted.

54. *SR*, pp. 16–19.

2. The Challenge of Monotheism

1. Maimonides comes close to this analogy at *GP* 1.56, p. 130, when he says that a mustard grain has more in common with the outermost sphere of the heavens than either of them has with God.

2. According to Marcia Falk, "Toward a Feminist Jewish Reconstruction of Monotheism," *Tikkun* 4 (1990): 53–56, viewing God as "other" inevitably leads to a situation where we view other people, other cultures, or other parts of the created order as "other." Thus monotheism in Maimonides' sense implies hierarchy and exploitation. But this is true only if God is on the same scale as humans. Once God is off the scale, the differences between people or creatures pale into insignificance compared with their difference with God. This issue will be taken up again in chapter 4 in regard to creation.

3. Alexander Altmann, "Essence and Existence in Maimonides," in *M*, p. 162.

4. *Genesis Rabbah* 1.3, cf. Saadia, *BO*, p. 121. For Maimonides' angelology, see *MT* 1. Basic Principles of the Torah, 2.3–9. For Maimonides' interpretation of biblical references to angels, see *GP* 2.6, pp. 263–65. The crux of Maimonides' argument is that angels should be understood as natural or psychic forces susceptible of rational explanation. Since angels are not bodies, they can be subjects of emanation. When emanation is applied to heavenly bodies like spheres and stars, however, the result is astrology (*GP* 2.12, p. 280). For Maimonides' attempt to "downgrade" angels, stars, and heavenly intelligences and deny that they are beings with one foot in the divine order and one foot in the created one, see Y. Tzvi Langermann, "Maimonides' Repudiation of Astrology," *Maimonidean Studies* 2 (1991): 149–51. For more on the naturalistic character of Maimonides' position, see Lenn Goodman, "Maimonidean Naturalism," in Goodman, ed., *Neoplatonism and Jewish Thought*, pp. 157–67.

5. See, for example, *Sanhedrin* 39b, *Genesis Rabbah* 8.4, and Rashi's commentary on Genesis 21:17.

6. See Philip Birnbaum, *Daily Prayer Book*, p. 784.

7. It may be objected that Moses is a messenger (*shaliah*). But it is well to remember that the rabbis chose not to mention Moses in the *Haggadah*, apparently in an effort to ensure that he does not lose his status as a human being and become a demigod.

8. *Sanhedrin* 59b, *Nedarim* 32a. For further discussion of this tradition, see Ephraim E. Urbach, *The Sages*, pp. 151–52.

9. According to one tradition, the people's need to have Moses intercede violates the commandment "You shall have no others gods before me." For discussion, see Solomon Schechter, *Aspects of Rabbinic Theology*, pp. 291–92.

10. Schechter, *Aspects*, pp. 291–92. Cf. Maimonides' fifth principle in *Perek Ḥelek*. Cf *RR*, p. 48: "Uniqueness excludes any *mediation* between God and natural existence."

11. According to Hermann Cohen (*RR*, p. 48), an entity like Philo's *Logos* would be a second God (*Nebengott*).

12. Cf. Maimonides, *Perek Ḥelek*, Principle 5. For further discussion, see Langermann, "Maimonides' Repudiation," pp. 149–51.

13. See *MT* 1, Basic Principles of the Torah, 2.8, cf. *GP* 1.59, p. 139: "None but He himself can apprehend what he is. . . ."

14. According to *GP* 3.9, the cloud may be a veil or barrier to knowledge. I owe this insight to Josef Stern.

15. See, for example, *Exodus Rabbah* 34.1; *Numbers Rabbah* 11.5; *Avot of Rabbi Nathan* 1.2.

16. See *Megillah* 29a; *Sotah* 5a, 17a; *Sanhedrin* 46a.

17. *Zohar* 1.22a. See Gershom Scholem, *Major Trends in Jewish Mysticism*, pp. 225–35, and Elliot Wolfson, *Through a Speculum that Shines*, chap. 7. Note that sometimes the mystic is described as the male partner and God the female one, but in other cases the roles are reversed. For attempts to divest the *Shekhinah* of sexual connotations, see Urbach, *The Sages*, pp. 64–65, and Steven S. Schwarzschild, *The Pursuit of the Ideal*, chap. 13.

18. Joshua Abelson, *The Immanence of God in Rabbinical Literature*; Urbach, *The Sages*, p. 63.

19. Urbach, *The Sages*, p. 44. Cf. E. Wolfson, *Speculum*, pp. 46–47, who is much closer to Abelson than to Urbach.

20. *GP* 1.19, p. 46; 1.21, p. 48; 1.21, p. 50; 3.7, p. 430. Cf. *ST* 1.12.6.

21. Schwarzschild, *Pursuit*, pp. 243–44.

22. Schwarzschild, *Pursuit*, pp. 239–40.

23. *MT* 1, Laws on Idolatry, 1.1–2.

24. *DH* 1, p. 117.

25. Cf. Rudolph Otto, *The Idea of the Holy*, p. 25. Also see Gerhard von Rad, *Old Testament Theology*, vol. 1, p. 205: "The concept of the holy cannot in any way be deduced from other human standards of value. It is not their elevation to the highest degree, nor is it associated with them by way of addition." Also note von Rad's criticism of Otto on p. 206: Otto's view makes the holy too closely related to the human soul. This issue will be taken up in chapter 7 in regard to love of God.

26. I will have more to say about religious language in the next chapter.

27. For discussion of the limits of negative predicates, see Josef Stern, "Maimonides in the Skeptical Tradition," unpublished manuscript, as well as "Logical Syntax as a Key to a Secret of the *Guide of the Perplexed* [Heb.]," *Iyyun* 38 (1989): 137–66. It was Stern who got me to see that negative predicates do not represent the last word in Maimonides' theology. The fact that they do not and are intended only to point the mind in the right direction answers the "logician's critique" raised by Steven Katz in "Utterance and Ineffability in Jewish Neoplatonism," in Lenn Goodman, ed. *Neoplatonism and Jewish Thought*, pp. 282–83. Note that Katz also repeats one of Aquinas' criticisms: If God has no positive attributes, why are some terms predicable of God but others not? I will address this criticism in the next chapter.

28. Aristotle, *Metaphysics* 1029b13, 1030a6–13.

29. For more on this point, see n. 33.

30. See, for example, *GP* 1.57, where Maimonides begins by saying that existence is superadded to the essence of what exists but then goes on to say that existence and essence are the same in God. On the other hand, Maimonides sometimes uses the stronger sense of essence to talk about contingent things, e.g., 1.51. This seems to be the distinction Altmann is drawing, "Essence and Existence," pp. 148–9. For the use of this terminology in Avicenna, see David Burrell, *Knowing the Unknowable God: Ibn-Sina, Maimonides, Aquinas*, pp. 16–27, as well as "Aquinas and Islamic and Jewish Thinkers," in Norman Kretzmann and Eleonore Stump, eds., *The Cambridge Companion to Aquinas*, pp. 66–67.

31. Although there is no evidence that Maimonides read Plotinus, he could have read any of a number of Arabic paraphrases that circulated in the Middle Ages. For more on the connection between the two thinkers, see Alfred Ivry, "Neoplatonic Currents in Maimonides," *PM*, pp. 115–40, and "Maimonides and Neoplatonism: Challenge and Response," in Goodman, *Neoplatonism and Jewish Thought*, pp. 137–56. There is, however, no conclusive evidence that Maimonides read the paraphrases either. In chapter 3 I will argue that Ivry is wrong to attribute a Neoplatonic theory of creation to Maimonides.

32. For discussion of metaphysical propositions like "God exists" or "God is pure intellect," see Herbert Davidson, "Maimonides on Metaphysical Knowledge," in *Maimonidean Studies* 3 (1992–93): 49–103. I agree in part with Davidson that Maimonides believed that humans can obtain nonempirical, metaphysical knowledge and that possession of this knowledge is the highest human perfection. But it should not be forgotten that the structure of this knowledge is not like earthly physics or mathematics, which deal with univocal terms and allow for a high degree of precision. By contrast metaphysics deals with equivocals and is largely negative. Thus a proposition like "God is pure intellect," though true and important, serves two functions: (1) it enables us to see that God is not material, and (2) it highlights the difference between God's intellect and ours. But even the category of intellect still presents God under under a description. So while it may be possible to demonstrate that God is pure intellect, the demonstration would culminate in a partial truth, and anyone who affirmed it would have to add that, strictly speaking, God has no attributes, no essence, and no resemblance to anything else. We can call this realization *knowledge* if we wish, but it is a form of knowledge that calls attention to its own inadequacy. Cf. Stern, "Maimonides on the Growth of Knowledge and the Limitations of the Intellect," unpublished manuscript, p. 7: "Thus the mode in which the intellect represents the demonstration, or demonstrated proposition, that the deity is one, contradicts or refutes the content of the demonstration itself."

33. According to Ehud Benor, "Meaning and Reference in Maimonides' Negative Theology," *Harvard Theological Review* 88 (1995): 351–52, Maimonides assumes a sharp distinction between meaning and reference. Thus p. 350: "Negative predication identifies the entity God by determining the ref-

erence of the word 'God' but leaves the word devoid of meaning." And again, p. 351: "Negative theology uniquely identifies absolute or necessary being, and determines the reference of the name 'God.'" In this way we can talk *about* God even if God remains a total mystery. Although ingenious, Benor's interpretation faces a major obstacle: Even negative predicates fail, because they particularize God. With the possible exception of the Tetragrammaton, any word or phrase that seeks to identify God is suspect. To Benor's question "Can Maimonides have wanted people to think of God as an intellect and to be aware that the wholly other nature of God renders that absurd?" I think the answer is yes *if* we treat intellect in the same way we treat essence. It is helpful, even necessary, up to a point; but we must still insist that God falls under no description.

34. *GP* 1.61, pp. 147–49; 1.63, p. 156. In view of Exodus 3:14, the Tetragrammaton is associated with the name "I Am that I Am." Maimonides interprets the name as a tautology that means "the existent that is existent." This, in turn, is taken as another way of saying that God exists but not *through* existence. Cf. *ST* 1.13.11. On the popularity of identifying God's name with necessary existence, see Etienne Gilson, *The Spirit of Medieval Philosophy*, p. 51. On the difficulty of beginning with a conception of God as "The One who is" and ending up with positive knowledge of the divine essence, see Joseph Owens, "Aquinas—'Darkness of Ignorance' in the Most Refined Notion of God," in *Southwestern Journal of Philosophy* 5 (1974): 110: "The being that is luminous to human cognition remains accordingly multiple and variable, while the nature of being in its unicity and unchangeableness is eminently respected. But the condition is a 'darkness of ignorance' in which the nature of being is attained only by way of a conclusion to something beyond the human intellect's power to intuit or conceive. The privation of both intuitional and conceptual light requires that the most refined notion of the primary efficient cause be enshrouded in his darkness in order to permit, on the metaphysical level, the successive predication of its infinite richness without the hindrance of finite restrictions."

35. Anton C. Pegis, "*Penitus Manet Ignotum*," *Medieval Studies* 27 (1965): 219.

36. Ludwig Wittgenstein, *Tractatus Logico-Philosophicus*, p. 151. Cf. Mark Jordan, "The Names of God and the Being of Names," in A. Freddoso, ed., *The Existence and Nature of God*, p. 182: "Long before Heidegger began using terms 'under erasure' before Derrida borrowed the practice, the divine names were names which were always used 'under erasure.' They were names which crossed themselves out. They were, in short, names which silenced themselves." It is regrettable that Jordan does not see how close Maimonides is to his position. For an account of Maimonides' view, see Oliver Leaman, *Moses Maimonides*, p. 36: "To understand what a religious sentence really means is a considerable intellectual achievement which cannot be expected of most believers. Yet they can still grasp a version of that sentence and, through its ability to move them in certain directions, they can participate in its real meaning."

37. Cf. Plotinus' remark (*EN* 5.5.6) that sometimes there is more truth in silence. Isaac Franck, "Maimonides and Aquinas on Man's Knowledge of God," in *M*, pp. 301–2, argues that negative theology does not lead to silence, because one still has to specify what God is not. True enough, but saying what God is not can hardly be the ultimate goal; as we saw, even negative predicates particularize God to a certain extent.

38. *DF*, p. 15.

39. Maimonides' proofs for the existence of God can be found at the beginning of book 2 of the *Guide*. Note, however, that the conclusions of these proofs are almost entirely negative. At *GP* 2.1, p. 246, he tells us that God is separate from the outermost sphere, immobile, atemporal, indivisible, and unchangeable. In short, motion in the sublunary realm presupposes a being who is unlike anything the sublunary realm contains. Later, p. 248, he tells us that God is uncaused and neither a body nor a force in a body. In effect, what we know is that God is not the subject of motion and rest, act and potency, matter and form, generation and corruption, or any of the other categories that apply to creatures. It is true that we know that creatures depend on God in some way or exist by the grace of God; but I will argue below that the dependence involved is not causal. In other words, God's relation to creatures does not resemble the relation of one creature to another. So once again our inquiry culminates in negation. Cf. Davidson, "Maimonides on Metaphysical Knowledge," pp. 91–92, who points out that a philosopher could use concepts like *one, first, cause, necessary*, and *existence* to frame demonstrations of a single, first, incorporeal cause of the motion of the universe. But Davidson goes on to say that even if we had such demonstrations, we would still not have an adequate conception of God. What, then, would our demonstrations be about? Davidson answers, "The First Cause of the universe," yet clearly this begs the question. It would be better to say that while we can demonstrate the *need* for a first cause, we cannot demonstrate anything positive about it—even that it *is* a cause in the normal sense. Causality, after all, is a relation, and Maimonides is quite clear that God does not enter into relation with anything else. So once again, our "knowledge" calls attention to its own inadequacy.

40. Davidson, "Maimonides on Metaphysical Knowledge," pp. 70–72, argues that while we cannot know incorporeal beings "as they truly are," we can know them in other senses, e.g., we can know that God exists. True enough, but all this means is that we can have negative theology; it does not establish positive knowledge of the sort obtained in mathematics.

41. Burrell, *Knowing the Unknowable God*, p. 17.

42. Steven Katz, "Utterance and Ineffability," p. 281.

43. Clearly "apprehension" must be taken negatively, as apprehending why we cannot apprehend in the normal sense.

44. *LPR*, 2, pp. 170 ff. According to Hegel (pp. 208–19), the infinite distance between God and us cannot help but express itself as tyranny. For the development of Hegel's view of Judaism vis-à-vis other religions, see Louis Dupre, "Transitions and Tensions in Determinate Religion," in D. Kolb, ed.,

New Perspectives on Hegel's Philosophy of Religion, pp. 81–92. Note that Hegel's criticism of Judaism parallels his criticism of Kant: If the former makes us a slave to an abstract God, the latter makes us a slave to an abstract principle.

45. See *LPR* 2, pp. 347–49. For comment, see Charles Taylor, *Hegel*, pp. 480–82.

46. Hegel, *Encyclopedia*, section 564.

47. On the anti-Jewish sentiment in the romantic age, see Karl Löwith, *From Hegel to Nietzsche*, pp. 19–24, 167–70.

48. Note the importance of joy or bliss at *LPR* 3, pp. 122–23. On the ability of Christianity to overcome the estrangement between the divine and human, see Emil Fackenheim, *The Religious Dimension in Hegel's Thought*, p. 144: "The Hegelian help consists, not of constructing a philosophical bridge between the eternal and the historical which would otherwise remain unbridged, but it consists of showing *that the bridge already exists* apart from all philosophic activity. It exists in the cult which is the life of the Christian church."

49. Fackenheim, "Moses and the Hegelians," *Encounters Between Judaism and Modern Philosophy*, pp. 81–169.

50. Fackenheim, "Martin Buber's Concept of Revelation," in P. Schilpp, ed., *The Philosophy of Martin Buber*, p. 294.

51. See, for example, Fackenheim, "Moses and the Hegelians," pp. 118–19, and *God's Presence in History*, pp. 28 ff.

52. Schwarzschild, "The Lure of Immanence," *Pursuit*, pp. 61–81.

53. Cf. Fackenheim, "Moses and the Hegelians," p. 124.

54. *DF*, p. 236.

3. Speaking of and to God

1. *Berakhot* 12b.

2. Cf. *Pirkei Avot* 1.17: "Whoever speaks at length brings on sin."

3. *MT* 2. Laws of Prayer 1.2.

4. For discussion of these issues, see Alvin Reines, "Maimonides' True Belief Concerning God," in *MP*, pp. 24–35. Surely Reines goes too far when he says (p. 25), "Thus denying that God is in any way an object of human knowledge means that there is no being called God that the human person can understand or believe in." (1) There is a being called God, and the purpose of religion is to enable us to recognize that this being is not a bigger, better version of ourselves; (2) although we cannot know the "essence" of God, we can know God's attributes of action. For criticism of Reines and Fox (n. 5 below), see Ehud Benor, *Worship of the Heart*, pp. 63–128.

5. *MT* 1. Laws of Repentance 10.1–2, 4–9. Cf. Benor, *Worship of the Heart*, p. 77: "It is important to notice that unlike many writers on prayers and its laws, Maimonides says absolutely nothing about conditions under which a prayer will be answered." By accepting the Mosaic theory of creation

(*GP* 2.25, pp. 328–29), Maimonides does admit the *possibility* of miracles. But after making this admission, he has very little to say about them and generally ignores them. In fact, his normal view is that serious disruptions of nature are unnecessary and would render the Torah useless. Note, for example, that according to Maimonides, the messiah will not be a miracle worker.

6. Marvin Fox, *Interpreting Maimonides*, p. 306. Ultimately Fox (p. 319) argues that conventional and philosophical ideas of prayer "live together in severe dialectical tension." I hope to show that he has overstated the case by a good bit. For more on Fox's view of dialectical tension, see the appendix.

7. Cf. *ST* 1.1.10.

8. Also see *SCG* 3.39.1 and 3.49.9.

9. Actually Aquinas lumps Maimonides' position together with a causal view according to which "God is good" means "God is the cause of goodness." But causality is a relation that implies similarity between the terms, and Maimonides firmly denies that any such similarity exists. For more on this point, see Seymour Feldman, "A Scholastic Misinterpretation of Maimonides' Doctrine of Divine Attributes," in *M*, pp. 267–83.

10. *WL* 3.3. It is well to remember that Gersonides' discussion is part of a larger treatment of the nature of divine omniscience. It is certainly true that the *via negativa* leaves us with very little to say on this subject except that God's knowledge does not resemble ours and lacks nothing.

11. Cf. Feldman's synopsis of *WL* 3.3, pp. 78–80.

12. David Burrell, "Aquinas and Islamic and Jewish Thinkers," in Kretzmann and Stump, eds., *The Cambridge Companion to Aquinas*, pp. 76–77. Cf. Kathryn Tanner, *God and Creation in Christian Theology*, p. 12: "Theologians simply assume that what they say about God is meaningful and true: They have no way of actually specifying what they are talking about (the *res significata* of their statements) apart from the meanings of the terms they use and it is just those meanings whose applicability to God they admit to failing to understand."

13. *Ḥagigah*, 11b, 13a. The two things that cannot be discussed are "the account of the beginning" and "the account of the [Ezekiel's] chariot." At *GP* 1. Introduction, pp. 6–9, Maimonides identifies these subjects with physics and metaphysics, the subject matter of the *Guide*. For more on Maimonides' esotericism, see the appendix.

14. It is true, of course, that Maimonides tried to introduce formal articles of faith, but his attempt was and still is controversial. For further discussion, see Menachem Kellner, *Dogma in Medieval Jewish Thought*, and chapter 6 of this book.

15. For further comment, see *MT* 1. Laws of Moral Conduct, 2.4.

16. Cf. Tanner, *God and Creation*, p. 14.

17. On this point, see James F. Ross, "Analogy as a Rule of Meaning for Religious Language," in Anthony Kenny, ed., *Aquinas*, pp. 93–94. Ross's position is itself derived from A. N. Prior, "Can Religion Be Discussed?" in Anthony Flew and Alasdair MacIntyre, eds., *New Essays in Philosophical Theology*, p. 3.

18. Burrell, "Aquinas and Islamic and Jewish Thinkers," p. 79. But note Burrell's claim that Maimonides' position is "self-defeating." For more on this issue, see Idit Dobbs-Weinstein, *Maimonides and St. Thomas Aquinas on the Limits of Reason*, pp. 185–97. I take exception to Dobbs-Weinstein's claim that both Maimonides and Aquinas regard biblical language as the highest form of discourse about God. For Maimonides, the Torah is the product of Mosaic prophecy, and Moses is the greatest prophet who ever lived. But the Torah is *also* Moses' attempt to communicate with "the sons of man." So while everything in it is true, it does follow that everything in it is expressed in the most rigorous or precise way.

19. Cf. *SCG* 3.49.9.

20. *ST* 1.13.5: "God is not a measure proportioned to the things measured."

21. Again Aquinas' position is similar to that of Gersonides in *The Wars of the Lord*, 3.3. According to Gersonides, it is not true that positive attributes always imply plurality in their subjects. For example, the proposition "this redness is a red color" does not imply that the redness is a composite of red and color. In Gersonides' view, color is not a separately existing thing that serves as a real subject for red but, as Feldman translates it, "a linguistic subject." Gersonides appears to be relying on Aristotle's distinction between real and nominal definition. For further discussion, see Gersonides, *Wars of the Lord*, translated with appendix and notes by Seymour Feldman, pp. 112–13.

22. *Categories*, 7b15.

23. *ST* 1a.13.7; cf. *De Potentia Dei* 3. 3c.

24. Although the primary attributes of action are the qualities (*middot*) revealed to Moses at Exodus 34:6–7, in the previous chapter (*GP* 1.53, pp. 120–22), Maimonides indicates that there are reasons for putting life, power, knowledge, and will in this group as well. This is confusing because life, power, and knowledge are treated as negative attributes at *GP* 1.58. I take this to mean that neither attributes of action nor negative attributes give us knowledge of God's essence. In that respect, it is possible to look at knowledge, life, or power as either one. But for reasons discussed in chapter 2, negative attributes are preferable.

25. Feldman, "A Scholastic Misinterpretation," pp. 271–73.

26. Again, it cannot be taken as "God *causes* Q" because causality is a relation.

27. Benor, *Worship of the Heart*, p. 98.

28. Note that the *Seventh Letter* (342a) claims that the doctrine it contains is not new but "has been expounded many times before." Although the authenticity of the *Seventh Letter* has been challenged, the dominant view is now that it is genuine and contains an important statement of Plato's view of language and the search for knowledge. For a classic study, see Glenn R. Morrow, *Plato's Epistles*, pp. 44–80. For a more recent study, see Kenneth M.

Sayre, *Plato's Literary Garden*. For further reflection on Sayre's interpretation, see my "Of Dialogues and Seeds," *Philosophy and Literature* 21 (1997): 167–78.

29. *MT* 1. Laws Concerning Idolatry, 1.2. Cf. Joshua 24:14. For the seemingly intractable nature of idolatry, see Deuteronomy 31:16–21.

30. *MT* 2. Laws of Prayer, 1.3–5, 2.1. For the decline in intelligence and linguistic prowess, see Isadore Twersky, *Introduction to the Code of Maimonides*, pp. 223–26, and Benor, *Worship of the Heart*, pp. 99–106.

31. Twersky, *Introduction*, ibid.

32. For the democratizing effects of prayer, see *RR*, p. 388.

33. Fox, *Interpreting Maimonides*, pp. 320–21.

34. It could be objected that while this language is not offensive in itself, it becomes so when viewed as part of a system that denies women full participation. See, for example, Rita M. Gross, "Steps Toward Feminine Imagery of Deity in Jewish Theology," in S. Heschel, ed., *On Being a Jewish Feminist*, pp. 237–38. I have no hesitation in calling for full participation. My point is that, properly interpreted, the language does not glorify power or domination as we understand them.

35. On the general issue of God's concessions to humanity and its importance for Maimonides, see Stephen D. Benin, *The Footprints of God*, pp. 147–62. Note how important the concession view is to the practice of justifying the commandments, in particular those commandments (*hukkim*) whose purpose may not be apparent.

36. Benor, *Worship of the Heart*, p. 128.

37. According to Maimonides (*GP* 3.54, p. 635), the acquisition of rational virtue and true opinion is the only end in itself. But since intellectual apprehension is equivalent to the love of God (*GP* 3.51, 621), it could be said that everything takes a second seat to this end.

38. Maimonides, *Perek Ḥelek*.

39. Note that unlike in his discussion of prophecy in book 2, Maimonides plays down the role of imagination in book 3, claiming that the exhortation to seek God "always refers to intellectual apprehension, not to imagination; for thought concerning imaginings is not called *knowledge* but *that which cometh into your mind*." But it is unclear whether he is using *prophet* in a different sense or merely shifting the focus of his discussion. According to Menachem Kellner, *Maimonides on Human Perfection*, pp. 13–40, we should understand Maimonides' categories as concentric circles. Thus philosophers are a subset of talmudists, and prophets are a subset of philosophers.

40. *GP* 3.51, p. 624: "This [Moses' prophecy] is not a rank that, with a view to the attainment of which, a person like myself may aspire for guidance. But one may aspire to attain that rank which was mentioned before this one through the training that we described." This sentence is ambiguous because, as Pines points out, the Arabic can mean either (1) someone like myself cannot aspire to be guided with a view to achieving this rank, or (2)

someone like myself cannot aspire to guide others with a view to their achieving this rank. Samuel ibn Tibbon took it to mean 2. From things Maimonides says elsewhere, no one can achieve the rank of Moses. If 2 is right, and I suspect it is, it would be possible to achieve the rank of prophet as exemplified by the patriarchs. But one cannot get to the rank of prophet by following a method outlined by one's teacher: One has to draw one's own conclusions and make one's own decision to turn wholly to God. Since prophecy cannot come to one during moments of sadness or languor, Maimonides argues at *GP* 2.36, p. 373, that Israel will not have any prophets until the coming of the messiah, when political persecution will stop.

41. David Shatz argues that since worship comes after apprehension, it is a higher form of perfection; "Worship, Corporeality, and Human Perfection: A Reading of *Guide of the Perplexed*, 3:51–54," in *TMM*, pp. 77–129. It is true that Maimonides' characterization of human perfection in 3.51 is not the same as it is in 3.54; whereas the former emphasizes concentration on God alone, the latter emphasizes apprehension in more general terms. But it does not follow that the worship described in 3.51 represents a stage above and beyond pure apprehension of God. That it represents a stage beyond apprehension of physical reality and the heavenly intelligences is clear; but apprehension of God is an end in itself and there is nothing in Maimonides' system that surpasses it. In short, apprehension of this sort is worship of the highest order and enhances worship of a more traditional form.

42. See *Republic* 516a–c.

43. Cf., *DH* 2, pp. 343–45.

44. On humility, see *MT* 1. Laws of Moral Conduct, 1.5 and 2.3. Note that this is one area where Maimonides rejects the idea of the mean and favors the extreme. For further discussion, see Daniel H. Frank, "Humility as a Virtue: A Maimonidean Critique of Aristotle's Ethics," in *MT*, pp. 89–99, as well as "Anger as a Vice: A Maimonidean Critique of Aristotle's Ethics," *History of Philosophy Quarterly* 7 (1990): 269–81.

45. I take it that Maimonides' claim (*GP* 1.54, p. 126) that "all passions are evil" applies to passions connected to the body and earthly affairs.

46. Benor makes the same point in *Worship of the Heart*, p. 126.

47. On the importance of courage for prophecy, see *GP* 2.38, pp. 376–77.

4. The Problem of Creation

1. Cf. Etienne Gilson, *The Spirit of Medieval Philosophy*, p. 86.

2. Cf. *SCG* 1.29 and Spinoza, *Ethics*, 1.3.

3. Maimonides describes God as the efficient cause of the world at *GP* 1.69, pp. 176–79, but clearly this is a loose or imprecise way of speaking. What he says in this passage is that he does not *disagree* with those philosophers who hold that God is an efficient, formal, and final cause. But sensing that this admission might lead to a misunderstanding, he goes on to reaffirm that there is no analogy between God's causality and the causality of things

endowed with matter. In fact, the whole discussion of 1.69 is described as provisional, with the full discussion to come at 2.12.

4. *CPR* B637.

5. *SCG* 2.37.

6. For the similarity of cause and effect in Plotinus, see *EN* 5.1.7: "The Intellectual-Principle stands as the Image of The One, firstly because there is a certain necessity that the first should have its offspring, carrying on much of its quality, in other words that there be something in its likeness as the sun's rays tell of the sun"; as well as 5.2.1: "This second outflow is an image or representation of the Divine Intellect as the Divine Intellect represented its own prior, The One." But Plotinus too faces the question of how The One, which is simple, can give rise to a multiplicity of forms. See, for example, *EN* 5.2.1. His answer is that The One can produce all things because it is not all things. In the words of Cristina D'Ancona Costa, "Plotinus and Later Platonic Philosophers on the Causality of the First Principle," in Lloyd P. Gerson, ed., *The Cambridge Companion to Plotinus*, p. 370, The One "produces what it does not possess." This causes D'Ancona Costa to argue that The One has two different kinds of causality: one in which similarity between cause and effect is preserved, one in which it is not. For the likeness of effect to cause in the ancient world, see A. C. Lloyd, "The Principle that the Cause Is Greater than the Effect," *Phronesis* 21 (1976): 146–56.

7. At *GP* 2.12 Maimonides praises the theory of emanation on the grounds that it does not involve physical contact. At 2.36 he uses it to explain prophecy. But we will see below that he is critical of it as an explanation of the origin of the world. For Maimonides' misgivings about the term emanation (*fayḍ*), see *GP* 2.12, pp. 279–80. For further discussion of the problem, see Josef Stern, "The Fall and Rise of Myth in Ritual: Maimonides versus Nachmanides on the *Huqqim*, Astrology, and the War Against Idolatry," *The Journal of Jewish Thought and Philosophy* 6 (1997): 216–25.

8. See, for example, *PJ*, 165–69; Harry Wolfson, "The Meaning of *Ex Nihilo* in the Church Fathers, Arabic and Hebrew Philosophy, and St. Thomas," in Isadore Twersky, ed., *Studies in Medieval Jewish History and Literature*, pp. 207–21; Arthur Hyman, "Maimonides on Creation and Emanation," in J. F. Whipple, ed., *Studies in Medieval Philosophy*, pp. 45–61; Marvin Fox, *Interpreting Maimonides*, chap. 10; Lenn Goodman, *God of Abraham*, pp. 239–42.

9. See Shlomo Pines, "Translator's Introduction," *Guide of the Perplexed*, pp. cxxv–cxxxi; Warren Zev Harvey, "A Third Approach to Maimonides' Cosmology-Prophetology Puzzle," in *M*, pp. 71–88. Harvey's position owes much to Lawrence Kaplan, "Maimonides on the Miraculous Element in Prophecy," *Harvard Theological Review* 70 (1977): 233–56. Kaplan and Harvey make a great deal out of the fact that Maimonides claims (*GP* 2.32, p. 360) that people's opinions about prophecy resemble their opinions about creation. But this claim is short and highly ambiguous. Certainly there is nothing in the claim itself to imply that the resemblance must be a one-to-one correspondence.

10. See Herbert Davidson, "Maimonides' Secret Position on Creation," in Twersky, *Studies*, pp. 16–40; Alfred Ivry, "Maimonides on Creation," in Norbert Samuelson and David Novak, eds., *Creation and the End of Days*, pp. 185–213; Norbert Samuelson, "Maimonides' Doctrine of Creation," *Harvard Theological Review*, 84:3 (1991): 249–71. Actually Davidson does not say conclusively that Maimonides accepted the Platonic position; rather Davidson's claim is that *if* we read Maimonides as an esotericist, then there is much more evidence for the Platonic position than for the Aristotelian. Samuelson's article contains a good review of the recent literature.

11. Sarah Klein-Braslavy, "Maimonides' Interpretation of the Verb *Bara* and the Problem of the Creation of the World," [Hebrew], *Da'at* 16 (1986): 39–55, "The Creation of the World and Maimonides' Interpretation of Gen. I–V," in *MP*, pp. 65–71.

12. Cf. Ivry, "Providence, Divine Omniscience, and Possibility: The Case of Maimonides," in Tamar Rudavsky, ed., *Divine Omniscience and Omnipotence in Medieval Philosophy*, pp. 148: "He [Maimonides] is very eager to establish the possibility of creation from nothing, but completely opposed to speculating about its nature"; as well as Goodman, *God of Abraham*, p. 29: "Genesis is silent as to the mechanics of creation and its motives." Also see Barry Kogan, "The Problem of Creation in Late Medieval Jewish Philosophy," in R. Link-Salinger, ed., *A Straight Path*, pp. 172–73. But it is not true, as Kogan argues, that if an account tells us nothing about how the world was created then it is without content. The content is that categories derived from human experience are insufficient to explain the origin of the world and therefore the Aristotelian objections to creation are invalid.

13. Davidson, "Maimonides' Secret Position," p. 19. Note, however, that Davidson is thinking about creation ex nihilo, not creation de novo. It would seem, however, that the latter is what implies spontaneity. For criticism of Davidson, see William Dunphy, "Maimonides' Not-So-Secret Position on Creation," in *MM*, pp. 151–72. For more on the connection between newness and contingency, see Lenn Goodman, "Three Meanings of the Idea of Creation," in David Burrell and Bernard McGinn, eds., *God and Creation*, pp. 89–106.

14. This view is reiterated at *GP* 2.30, pp. 349–50; 3.32, p. 531; 3.50, p. 613.

15. At *EN* 5.4.2, Plotinus argues that the process of emanation is both eternal and necessary (*anagke*). According to A. H. Armstrong, *Plotinus: A Volume of Selections*, p. 33: "*Nous* proceeds from the One (and soul from *Nous*) without in any way affecting its Source. There is no activity on the part of the One, still less any willing or planning or choice (planning and choice are excluded by Plotinus even on a much lower level when he comes to consider the forming and ruling of the material universe by Soul)." Armstrong's interpretation is challenged by J. M. Rist, *Plotinus: The Road to Reality*, pp. 66–83. Not, however, that much of Rist's evidence comes from *EN* 6.8, where Plotinus uses terms "not strictly applicable" (6.8.13). Although

the One is not the effect of a prior cause, and in that sense manifests a kind of freedom, strictly speaking, it is higher than will (6.8.9). For a recent discussion of this issue, see Georges Leroux, "Human Freedom in the Thought of Plotinus," in L. P. Gerson, ed., *The Cambridge Companion to Plotinus*, p. 294: "Plotinus in effect adheres to necessity as the superior form of all existence and all essence, rather than to freedom conceived, for example, in Aristotle's moral philosophy, as the power to chose and to act, since this latter concept is immediately marked by hesitation and contingency and for this reason is irreconcilable with the Neoplatonic worldview."

16. As indicated on p. 195, n.31, Maimonides could have been exposed to several Arabic paraphrases of Plotinus. As for Plotinus himself, the usual view is that he believed matter is ungenerated. But some passages, e.g., *EN* 2.9.3 and 4.8.6, suggest otherwise. Here I am indebted to Cristina D'Ancona Costa.

17. Also see *FMM*, 459.

18. More recently this line of argument has been used in a scientific context by Stephen Weinberg, *Dreams of a Final Theory*, p. 174: "I am not trying here to argue that the universe undoubtedly has some finite age, only that it is not possible to say on the basis of pure thought that it does not." Note the explicit reference to Maimonides' view of the creation of time in the previous paragraph of Weinberg.

19. *ST* 1.46.2. At *GP* 2.16, p. 294, Maimonides does say that creation should be accepted "without proof because of prophecy which explains things to which it is not in the power of speculation to accede." But it is difficult to know whether this means that the average worshipper should accept creation because of prophecy or whether it means that creation must be taken as an article of faith as it is for Aquinas. We saw that Maimonides allows for the possibility that the prophet may be superior to the philosopher in some cases (*GP* 2.38, p. 377). Note too that at *GP* 2.25, Maimonides says that one reason for accepting creation is that it upholds the foundation of the Law. But we must still keep in mind that prophecy consists of the ability to provide visual images for abstract truths and that prophetic utterances like the opening lines of Genesis are notoriously ambiguous. At *GP* 2.25, pp. 327–29, he argues that the opening lines of Genesis could be taken to support any of the three views of creation he discusses. At *GP* 2.29, p. 347, he warns the reader not to rely on the imagination alone in trying to make sense of creation. And at *GP* 3.51, p. 619, he insists that those who believe true opinions on the basis of traditional authority are inferior to those who believe them on the basis of rational argument. Most important, after saying that creation should be accepted without proof because of prophecy, Maimonides says immediately that he will offer speculative proofs to make creation prevail over eternity.

20. At *GP* 2.30, p. 358, Maimonides interprets it as "bringing into existence out of nonexistence."

21. For the Neoplatonic reading, see *GP* 2.26, pp. 330–31; for the Aristotelian, 2.30, p. 349. For a recent discussion of rabbinic commentary on the opening lines of Genesis, see Samuelson, *Judaism and the Doctrine of Creation*, chap. 4.

22. Fox, *Interpreting Maimonides*, p. 269. For the range of opinion after Maimonides, see Seymour Feldman, "'In the Beginning God Created': A Philosophical Midrash," in Burrell and McGinn, eds., *God and Creation*, pp. 3–26.

23. In keeping with *GP* 1.57, p. 133, *eternal* does not mean "exists throughout all time" but "exists outside of time completely."

24. *ST* 1.46.1.

25. H. Wolfson, "The Meaning of *Ex Nihilo*." Cf. Klein-Braslavy, "The Creation of the World," p. 67: "It would appear that he [Maimonides] was afraid that the expression 'out of nonexistence' (or 'from nonexistence') might be taken to mean that the world was created from 'nonexistence,' that is, 'something,' i.e., from 'matter.'"

26. Cf. *ST* 1.44.2. For a similar interpretation of the problem of creation ex nihilo, see Goodman, *God of Abraham*, p. 264: "But creationists do not argue that the world came from nothingness but from God. What they mean by ex nihilo is that God's ultimate creative act was conditioned by no prior limitation but only by limitations inherent in finitude itself and in the determinate character of the things to be created."

27. For creation "out of nothing," see *GP* 2.30, p. 358, and 3.10, p. 438.

28. See n. 11.

29. Plato, *Sophist* 257b–259c; cf. *EN* 2.4.6.

30. See Aristotle, *Physics* 192a6–7; *On Generation and Corruption*, 318a15.

31. Cf. *ST* 1.46.1: "Before the world existed, it was possible for the world to be, not, indeed, according to the passive power which is matter, but according to the active power of God."

32. Cf. Aristotle, *Physics* 251a15: "[S]o there must be something capable of being burned before there can be a process of being burned, and something capable of burning before there can be a process of burning."

33. For the creation of prime matter, also see *GP* 1.28, p. 61. Note that in a way Maimonides agrees with Aristotle: Prime matter is not created *if* what is meant is creation in the normal sense, i.e., the way in which a person is created from a seed. But it *is* created if what is meant is creation ex nihilo.

34. Cf. *ST*. 1.46.1.

35. For example, *GP* 2.213, p. 281: "For time is consequent on motion, and motion is an accident in what is moved. Furthermore, what is moved— that is, that upon which the motion of which time is consequent—is itself created in time and came to be after not having been." Or *GP* 2.30, p. 349: "Now the world has not been created in a temporal beginning, as we have explained, for time belongs to the created things. For this reason it says: *In the*

beginning [*bereishit*]. For the 'be' has the meaning of 'in.' The true translation of this verse is: In the origin God created what is high and what is low. This is the translation that fits in with creation in time."

36. Richard Sorabji, *Time, Creation, and the Continuum*, pp. 280–81; cf. *CPR*, A430/B458 ff. One commentator who gets this point right is Jonathan Malino, "Aristotle on Eternity: Does Maimonides Have a Reply?" in *MP*, pp. 54–55.

37. See *WL* 6.1.21.

38. Philoponus, *Against Aristotle on the Eternity of the World*, trans. by Christian Wildberg, p. 139.

39. *Metaphysics* 1049b17 ff., as well as *Physics* 251a23 ff.

40. See Harvey, "Maimonides' Puzzle," p. 77, and Tamar Rudavsky, "Creation and Time in Maimonides and Gersonides," in Burrell and McGinn, eds., *God and Creation*, pp. 131–32. Also see Klein-Braslavy, *Maimonides' Interpretation*, pp. 81–87. For a view closer to mine, see Barry Kogan's response to Rudavsky, p. 150, and William Dunphy, "Maimonides and Aquinas on Creation: A Critique of Their Historians," in L. Gerson, ed., *Graceful Reason*, pp. 361–79.

41. Again this implies that the phrase "after nonexistence" does not refer to a time before creation. For a contrary view, see Harvey, "Maimonides' Puzzle," p. 81, n. 9, who thinks that creation after nonexistence implies "that *before* creation there had been nonexistence."

42. On the distinction between creation de novo and creation ex nihilo, and the failure of some of Maimonides' commentators to recognize it, see Dunphy, "Maimonides and Aquinas on Creation"; "Maimonides Not-So-Secret Position on Creation," in *MM*, 151–72; and Alexander Broadie, "Maimonides and Aquinas," in *HJP*, pp. 285–87. Where I disagree with Dunphy is over the claim that Maimonides proves creation ex nihilo prior to 2.13, when he proves the existence of God. For Aquinas, creation ex nihilo can be demonstrated (*ST* 1.45) even though creation de novo cannot (*ST* 1.46.2). But there are two problems with ascribing Aquinas' position to Maimonides: (1) creation ex nihilo is still very much at issue at 2.13 and one of the things Maimonides says he intends to prove, and (2) if creation ex nihilo had been demonstrated, why would Maimonides at *GP* 2.25 allow someone to hold the Platonic view?

43. Failure to see this point damages the argument of Alfred Ivry in "Maimonides on Creation," in D. Novak and N. Samuelson, eds., *Creation and the End of Days*, pp. 185–213. That Maimonides' terminology is ambiguous no one denies. But Ivry thinks that because creation ex nihilo is absurd, Maimonides must have taken "nothing" in a privative rather than an absolute sense. Thus the Mosaic position, in Ivry's opinion, is committed to "pure and absolute privation." Since Maimonides clearly holds that prime matter was created, Ivry concludes that there must be a special privation that underlies prime matter so that even prime matter has a material cause. What is it? Here Ivry runs into trouble, saying that it possesses something

analogous to existence ("subsistence") and that "it *is* a state of non-existent being." In response to Ivry: (1) creation ex nihilo is not absurd if we understand it properly; (2) Maimonides never says, in fact he denies, that we can imagine what creation ex nihilo is like; and (3) if creation ex nihilo presents problems, it is hard to see how Ivry's subsistent, nonexistent being helps us solve them. The obvious solution is to say that like everything else, prime matter is created ex nihilo. For further criticism of Ivry, see Idit Dobbs-Weinstein, *Maimonides and St. Thomas*, pp. 73–74.

44. For the historical background, see H. Wolfson, "The Meaning of *Ex Nihilo*," and Sorabji, *Time*, pp. 313–15. According to Sorabji, the idea of creation without matter is as old as Porphyry.

45. Curiously enough, Harvey, "Maimonides' Puzzle," p. 76, cites the fact that Aristotle's theory conforms to our observation of nature as grounds for saying that Maimonides accepts it.

46. On this point, see Alfred Ivry, "Maimonides on Possibility," in Y. Reinharz and D. Swetschinski, eds., *Mystics, Philosophers, and Politicians*, pp. 67–84, and Malino, "Aristotle on Eternity," pp. 57–59.

47. Cf. Descartes, *Meditation* IV: "The faculty of will consists alone in our having the power of choosing to do a thing or choosing not to do it."

48. See Philoponus, *De Aeternitate Mundi contra Proclum*, edited by H. Rabe, pp. 78, 568, 613; Al-Ghazali, *The Incoherence of the Philosophers*, trans. by Michael E. Marmura, pp. 15–17; Aquinas *ST* 1.46.1. For the history of the problem, see Sorabji, *Time*, pp. 240–42.

49. *SCG*, 35.

50. For a discussion of the logic of this distinction, see Tanney, *God and Creation*, pp. 72–79.

51. According to Harvey, "Maimonides' Puzzle," p. 77, Maimonides "effectively strips the concept of God's will of any cognitive meaning." This is true if Harvey means that we cannot know or infer what God's will is like; but it is false if it means, as Harvey seems to think, that we have no reason to think that God's will might be very different from what the Aristotelians take it to be. Put otherwise, it is the Aristotelians who violate negative theology if they claim to know that God cannot will change.

52. Another difference is that unlike many of the *Kalam* thinkers, Maimonides does not think God's will is arbitrary. He tries to show that God had a purpose in creating the world; the problem is that given the limited knowledge at our disposal, we cannot know what it is. On this point, see Josef Stern, "Maimonides on the Growth of Knowledge," p. 9.

53. The argument considered here deals with the speed and direction of heavenly bodies and is linked with one dealing with their identity and diversity. Because the issues raised are similar, I am disregarding the second.

54. *GP* 2.19, p. 307.

55. Isaac Husik, *A History of Medieval Jewish Philosophy*, p. 275. For discussion of the medieval reaction to this argument, see Feldman, "Abravanel on Maimonides' Critique of the Kalam Arguments for Creation," in

Maimonidean Studies 1 (1990): 15–25; for the antecedents, see Davidson, *Proofs for Eternity, Creation, and the Existence of God in Medieval Islamic and Jewish Philosophy*, pp. 194–212.

56. For more on Maimonides' astronomy, see Menachem Kellner, "On the Status of Astronomy and Physics in Maimonides' *Mishneh Torah* and *Guide of the Perplexed*," *British Journal for the History of Science* 24 (1991): 453–63. Note Kellner's claim that Maimonides is so skeptical of astronomy that he opts for an instrumental view according to which the goal is not to say what is really happening but only to offer a theory that can "save the phenomena." In addition to the question of how to explain planetary orbits, medieval astronomy also faced the question of how to explain the action of heavenly bodies like the sun and moon on the earth. This issue was particularly difficult given the view that action at a distance is impossible and that the sun is *not* a fire. For the view that emanation does not apply to heavenly bodies like stars and intelligences, see, again, *GP* 2.12, p. 280. Also see Tzvi Langermann, "Maimonides' Repudiation of Astrology," *Maimonides Studies* 2 (1991): 149–51.

57. Harvey, "Maimonides' Puzzle," p. 77.

58. For further discussion of this principle, see Arthur Hyman, "From What is One and Simple Only What Is One and Simple Can Come to Be," in Goodman, ed., *Neoplatonism and Jewish Thought*, pp. 111–35.

59. Davidson, "Maimonides' Secret Position," pp. 34–35.

60. For a readable though somewhat personal discussion of these issues, see Gerald L. Schroeder, *Genesis and the Big Bang*, pp. 50–52.

61. On this point, see Josef Stern's reply to Lenn Goodman in *God and Creation*, pp. 115–16.

62. Alan Guth, *The Inflationary Universe*, pp. 86–87.

63. In "Maimonides' Doctrine," Samuelson takes Maimonides' recommendation to mean that he was really committed to the Platonic view. Samuelson makes this interpretation because he himself thinks that the external sense of Genesis implies the existence of uncreated matter. But at *GP* 2.25, pp. 328–29, Maimonides offers the external sense as an alternative to the Platonic position. Cf. *GP* 2.17, p. 298, where in a different context, Maimonides says he will not take the text in its external sense. I agree with Pines that this refers to temporal terms discussed at 2.30.

64. In taking this view, I follow Lenn Goodman, "Three Meanings," pp. 101–2.

65. Both Harvey and Klein-Braslavy think that this passage rules out "a temporal beginning of the world." It is true that Maimonides says that *bereishit* refers to a principle rather than a historical process. But note: (1) Maimonides also says his interpretation of *bereishit* is compatible with creation de novo; (2) contrary to what Harvey (p. 77) implies, Maimonides *distances* himself from the rabbinic sages who read Genesis in an Aristotelian fashion; and (3) Maimonides reminds the reader that time is created, a fact that is perfectly compatible with creation de novo.

66. Aquinas asserts the same thing at *ST* 1.46.3.

67. *BBO*, 1.1. Cf. Goodman, "Three Meanings," p. 89: "The notions of creation that we accept, reject, or entertain when we envision creation in the cosmogonic vignettes of a Cecil B. DeMille movie or a *Nova* broadcast are curiously devoid of the values which the idea of creation once bore rather proudly and explicitly."

68. Cf. David Hartman, *A Living Covenant*, p. 259: "Creation involves an irreducible separation between the world and God. It encourages us to take God and the world with extreme seriousness in the radical separateness."

69. See *GP* 1.57, p. 132: "It is known that existence is an accident attaching to what exists. For this reason it is something that is superadded to the quiddity of what exists."

70. *GP* 2.31, pp. 359–60.

71. *MT* 3, Laws of the Sabbath, 30.15.

72. *Pirkei Avot*, 2.2.

73. *MT* 3, Laws of the Sabbath, 30.15.

74. *GP* 3.50, p. 613.

5. *Imitatio Dei*

1. For recent discussions of the principle of *imitatio Dei* in Judaism, see Lawrence Berman, "The Political Interpretation of the Maxim: The Purpose of Philosophy Is the Imitation of God," *Studia Islamica* 15 (1061): 53–61; David Shapiro, "The Doctrine of the Image of God and *Imitatio Dei*," *Judaism* 12 (1963): 57–77; Warren Harvey, "Holiness: A Command to *Imitatio Dei*," *Tradition 16* (1976–77): 7–28. For *imitatio Dei* in Maimonides, see Menachem Kellner, *Maimonides on Human Perfection*, chaps. 4, 6, 7; Jacqueline Genot-Bismuth, "Perfection Humaine et 'Imitatio Dei' chez Maïmonide," in *TTM*, pp. 42–68; and Howard Kreisel, "*Imitatio Dei* in Maimonides' *Guide of the Perplexed*," *AJS Review* 19 (1994): 169–211.

2. The verse Maimonides is quoting is the *Siphre* to Deuteronomy 10:12 and continues, "They said: He is gracious, so be you also gracious; He is merciful, so be you also merciful."

3. See *GP* 3.47, p. 595. For this point, I am indebted to Josef Stern.

4. Steven S. Schwarzschild, *The Pursuit of the Ideal: The Jewish Writings of Steven Schwarzschild*, p. 20.

5. Cf. William James, *The Varieties of Religious Experience*, p. 321: "In Mystic States, we both become one with the Absolute and we become aware of our oneness."

6. *EN* 3.8.9; 6.9.8. According to Steven Katz, "Utterance and Ineffability in Jewish Neoplatonism," in Lenn Goodman, ed., *Neoplatonism and Jewish Thought*, p. 292: the accessibility of the One is "predicated on the assumption that ultimately there is a commonality, a shared ontic nature, that will become apparent and dominant."

7. Gershom Scholem, *Major Trends in Jewish Mysticism*, pp. 122–23, as well as his "Devekut or Communion with God," in *The Messianic Idea in Judaism*, pp. 203–4. It is important to recognize that one of Scholem's goals was to draw a sharp distinction between the mystical tradition and the philosophic and to argue that the former came much closer to capturing the spirit of Jewish piety. For a more nuanced view, see Elliot Wolfson, "Jewish Mysticism," in *HJP*, pp. 450–98. That mystics and philosophers often used the same vocabulary is clear; what is not clear is whether they invested this vocabulary with the same meaning. For example, both mystics and philosophers use Neoplatonic terms like *union* or *emanation*; but given Maimonides' skepticism about use of the imagination, it is questionable whether they meant the same thing.

8. Salo Baron, *A Social and Religious History of the Jews*, vol. 8, pp. 112–13.

9. See, for example, *RR*, p. 212.

10. See, for example, Moshe Idel, *Kabbalah: New Perspectives*, chaps. 3–4, as well as *The Mystical Experience in Abraham Abulafia*, pp. 124–25.

11. At *GP* 1.68, p. 165, Maimonides accepts the view that the intellect in action, the intellectually cognizing subject, and the intellectually cognized object are one not only in God but in us. In other words, the intellect unites with the object of its apprehension. This passage is controversial and is discussed in the appendix. Like that of his predecessors Baḥya and Halevi, Maimonides' epistemology is expressed in the language Sufi mysticism. For a recent study, see Diana Lobel, *Between Mysticism and Philosophy: Arabic Terms for Religious Experience in R. Yehudah Ha-Levi's Kuzari*, chap. 2.

12. For historical precedents, see Alfarabi, *The Letter Concerning the Intellect*, and Aristotle, *De Anima* 430a20, 431a1.

13. Cf. *GP* 3.8, p. 432.

14. For similar interpretations of Maimonides, see Alexander Altmann, "Maimonides on the Intellect and the Scope of Metaphysics," in *Von der Mittelalterlichen zur Modernen Aufklärung*, pp. 83–85; Shlomo Pines, "The Limitations of Human Knowledge According to Alfarabi, ibn Bajja, and Maimonides," in *M*, pp. 101–3; and Howard Kreisel, "*Imitatio Dei* in Maimonides *Guide to the Perplexed*," pp. 193–201.

15. The issue of divine reward and punishment will be taken up in greater detail in chapter 7.

16. For passages that imply greater knowledge, see *MT* 1, Basic Principles of the Torah, 7.1, and Laws of Repentance, 8.2.

17. On this point, Maimonides' position stands in sharp contrast to that of Aquinas. According to Aquinas (*ST* 1.12; *SCG* 3.51), it is possible to see the essence of God in the next life for two reasons. First it is promised in Scripture. Thus Matthew 5:8: "Blessed are the pure in heart: for they shall see God." And 1 Corinthians 13:12: "For now we see through a glass, darkly; but then face to face." Second, it is contrary to reason for God to give us the desire to know but have this desire thwarted. It should be understood, however,

that according to Aquinas we cannot see the essence of God by natural reason but require the gift of grace.

18. For further discussion of the difference between Maimonides' position and the classical rabbinic one, see Kellner, *Maimonides on Human Perfection*, pp. 41–45.

19. *DH* 2, p. 343.

20. Plato, *Seventh Letter* 344a–b; cf. *Republic* 486d–487a; *Phaedo* 67b–c, 80d, 81a–82c.

21. *Seventh Letter* 341c–d.

22. See, for example, *Phaedo* 69b–d, *Phaedrus* 250b–c.

23. Grube translation. For *imitatio Dei* in Plato, also see *Theaetetus* 176.

24. *Seventh Letter* 340d–341e.

25. See, for example, *GP* 1.39, p. 89; 3.51, p. 627; 3.52, p. 630.

26. *GP* 3.14; cf. *MT* 1, Basic Principles of the Torah, 2.2: "And when he ponders these matters, he will recoil frightened, and realize that he is a small creature, lowly and obscure, endowed with slight and slender intelligence, standing in the presence of Him who is perfect in knowledge."

27. For further discussion of this point, see Genot-Bismuth, "Perfection Humaine," pp. 43–50.

28. Recall that while Maimonides does not accept emanation as an explanation of the existence of the world, he does accept it as an explanation of prophetic activity. Put otherwise, both the Agent Intellect and the mind of the prophet are part of the created order, and to the degree that the prophet achieves perfection, his or her mind establishes some form of union with the heavenly intelligence. But neither of these conditions applies to God's relation to the world.

29. The qualification "in a manner unknown to us" is important. Throughout the *Guide* Maimonides continues to warn us not to think we can extrapolate from our governance of a city to God's governance of the world. See, for example, *GP* 3.23, p. 496.

30. On the comparison between prophets and philosopher-kings, see Leo Strauss, *Philosophy and Law*, pp. 53–55, 103–110, and "How to Begin to Study Medieval Philosophy," in Thomas L. Pangle, ed., *The Rebirth of Classical Political Rationalism*, pp. 207–26. The idea behind Strauss's argument is that in Judaism and Islam, civil law is given by God through the prophet, whereas in Christianity there is a distinction between king and pope, or the city of humans and the city of God. Thus the key text for Judaism and Islam is the *Republic*, where philosophy and politics are merged in the person of the philosopher-king, while the key text for Christianity is Aristotle's *Politics*, where in Strauss's opinion they are not. Note, however, that Strauss plays down the importance of the theory of forms in order to stress the political aspect of Plato's philosophy. On the relation between philosophy and politics in Maimonides, Strauss argues that because the philosopher must live in a political community, he or she must answer to the prophet, who, in addition to

being a philosopher, is also a statesman, seer, miracle worker, and so on. The prophet, after all, is the source of religious law, and the philosopher must obey the law. But this still leaves open the question of whether philosophy and the contemplation of God's transcendence is a higher activity than founding or running a state. For another defense of the political interpretation of Maimonides, see Lawrence Berman, "The Political Interpretation of the Maxim: The Purpose of Philosophy Is the Imitation of God," *Studia Islamica* 15 (1961): 53–61. For criticism, see Kellner, *Maimonides on Human Perfection*, pp. 49–53, as well as "Politics and Perfection: Gersonides and Maimonides," *Jewish Political Studies Review* 6:1–2 (1994): 49–82.

31. *GP* 3.51, p. 620–21; 3.52, p. 629.

32. The qualification "for the most part" is necessary; as we saw, Maimonides admits the possibility of exceptional cases at *GP* 2.38, p. 377.

33. See, for example, *GP* 1.64, p. 157; 3.32, p. 330.

34. See, for example, *GP* 1.2, pp. 24–25.

35. Pines, "Limitations," p. 111.

36. Lawrence Berman, "Maimonides on Political Leadership," in Daniel Elazar, ed., *Kinship and Consent*, p. 118. For Berman's view of the relation between Maimonides and Alfarabi, see "Maimonides, the Disciple of Alfarabi," in *M*, pp. 195–214. For criticism of Berman, see Steven Harvey, "Maimonides in the Sultan's Palace," in *PM*, pp. 70–72, and Kellner, *Maimonides on Human Perfection*, pp. 49–53. Kellner is right to point out that Berman's emphasis on *founding* a perfect society raises the question of what to say about prophets other than Moses.

37. Schwarzschild, *Pursuit*, p. 144.

38. It is not clear that knowledge of God's governance is identical with practical knowledge in our sense. It might also include theoretical subjects like cosmology or various aspects of earthly physics.

39. Cf. *DF*, p. 17: "The knowledge of God which we can have and which is expressed, according to Maimonides, in the form of negative attributes, receives a positive meaning from the moral 'God is merciful,' which means: 'Be merciful like him.' The attributes of God are given not in the indicative, but in the imperative. The knowledge of God comes to us in a commandment, like a *Mitzvah*. To know God is to know what must be done."

40. *RR*, p. 51.

41. *PJ*, p. 200. For a similar claim, see Lawrence Berman, "Maimonides on Political Leadership," p. 116: "Action in imitation of God after intellectual perfection is on a higher plane than practical activity before achieving theoretical perfection." Also see Daniel Frank, "Reason in Action: The 'Practicality' of Maimonides' *Guide*," in Daniel Frank, ed., *Commandment and Community*, pp. 69–84.

42. For others who defend a unified or integrated approach to human perfection, see Lawrence Kaplan, "'I Sleep, But My Heart Waketh': Maimonides' Conception of Human Perfection," in *TMM*, p. 148; Warren Harvey, "Maimonides on Human Perfection, Awe, and Politics," in *TMM*, pp. 1–15;

Barry Kogan, "What Can We Know and When Can We Know It?" pp. 135–37;
Ehud Benor, *Worship of the Heart*, pp. 54–58.

43. Hegel, *Faith and Knowledge*, p. 62.

44. Alfred Ivry, "The Problematics of the Ideal of Human Perfection for Maimonides," in *TMM*, p. 22.

45. Note that in the passage from *MT* cited above, Maimonides goes on to say that in the days of the messiah the sages will have knowledge of concealed things, but he adds *according to human capacity.*

46. Kant, *The Metaphysics of Morals*, p. 446. For further discussion, see Henry Allison, *Kant's Theory of Freedom*, pp. 171–72.

47. Some might object that Kant does have separate ontological realms, namely noumenon and phenomenon or freedom and nature. Certainly there are passages where Kant appears to talk this way, but I follow those who take the distinction between noumenon and phenomenon in a practical rather than a theoretical sense. In other words, the noumenal realm is not a collection of entities but a system of values or targets for behavior. According to Schwarzschild, "The Tenability of H. Cohen's Construction of the Self," *Journal of the History of Philosophy* 13 (1975): 378–79: "Indeed, ontological noumena do not make sense, but then Kant never proposed them. Noumena are, however, normative constructs; they are the reasons for, not the causes of, their phenomena; and so the noumenal self is the definition of the self as an ethical task." For a similar interpretation, see Allison, *Kant's Theory*, pp. 141–43.

48. See, for example, Hegel, *Die Vernunf in der Geschichte*, p. 77 (also Walter Kaufmann, *Hegel: Reinterpretation, Texts, and Commentary*, pp. 260–61): "Thus the insight to which philosophy should help us is that the actual world is as it ought to be. . . . God rules the world; the content of his government, the execution of his plan, is world history; to grasp this is the task of the philosophy of world history, and its presupposition is that the ideal accomplishes itself, that only what accords with the idea has actuality. . . . Thus philosophy is not a comfort; it is more, it reconciles, it transfigures the actual, which seems unjust, into the rational." For comment, see Walter Kaufmann, *Hegel*, pp. 261 ff. Note how Kaufmann tries to take the sting out of the identification of *is* and *ought.*

49. Cf. Schwarzschild, "An Agenda for Jewish Philosophy in the 1980's," in Norbert Samuelson, ed., *Studies in Jewish Philosophy*, p. 108.

50. *CPrR*, pp. 122–23.

51. *RR*, pp. 103, 204–5.

52. Also see *CPrR*, p. 122; Kant, *Metaphysics of Morals*, p. 446.

53. Note that Kant (*RWL*, p. 24) distinguishes a propensity [*Hang*] from a predisposition on the grounds that the former does not have to be viewed as innate.

54. Although evil can be predicated of man as a species, Kant (*RWL*, p. 270) still insists that it cannot be inferred from the concept of the species.

55. *RWL*, pp. 27–28. Allen Wood, *Kant's Moral Religion*, pp. 224–25, ar-

gues that the fact that evil is rooted in human nature explains the universality of evil but not the cause of evil. As Kant insists several times, the cause of why the will chooses evil maxims is unknown to us. The problem is that universality usually indicates necessity. But we saw in the previous note that Kant's voluntarism prohibits him from saying that evil can be inferred from the concept of humanity.

56. Wood, *Kant's Moral Religion*, p. 179.

57. For criticism of Kant on this point, see Lewis White Beck, *A Commentary on Kant's Critique of Practical Reason*, p. 270. Note that Kant's view of immortality as quasi-temporal was revised after *RWL*. For discussion, see Anthony N. Perovich, "'For Reason . . . Also Has Its Mysteries': Immortality, *Religion*, and 'The End of All Things,'" in Philip J. Rossi and Michael Wreen, eds., *Kant's Philosophy of Religion Reconsidered*, pp. 165–80.

58. Wood, *Kant's Moral Religion*, pp. 122–24.

59. Beck, *Commentary*, p. 269. Also see Allison, *Kant's Theory*, pp. 172–73, and Roger Sullivan, *Immanuel Kant's Moral Theory*, pp. 139–41.

60. On the inadvertent nature of sin, see Cohen's discussion of *shegagah* (*RR*, pp. 200–201).

61. At *RR*, p. 207, Cohen says, "The solution is infinite, for it is only a moment in the infinite task; but the solution signifies [*bedeuten*] infinite success, the infinite result." I am not sure what he means by "signifies." If repentance implies complete success, the need for infinite time vanishes; if all it can furnish is a taste of success, then self-sanctification would amount to a labor of Sisyphus.

62. Allison, *Kant's Theory*, pp. 173–75.

63. For an excellent discussion of the problem, and Kant's apparent departure from Christian doctrine, see Nicholas P. Wolterstorff, "Conundrums in Kant's Rational Religion," in P. Rossi and M. Wreen, eds., *Kant's Philosophy of Religion Reconsidered*, pp. 40–53. Note Wolterstorff's solution: that according to Christianity, even the unworthy are saved.

64. Again it should be emphasized that strictly speaking, God does not have an essence.

65. *Leviticus Rabbah* 24.9.

66. Cf. Benor, *Worship of the Heart*, p. 41: "Furthermore, I think it would be a mistake to attribute to him [Maimonides] the belief that great effort and dedication in pursuit of an ultimately impossible goal is more noble than the desired achievement. This is a Romantic idea that conflicts with Maimonides' Aristotelian normative standards that assign value to achievements that exhibit excellence."

67. *RWL*, p. 66.

68. For Cohen's rejection of original sin, see *RR*, pp. 181–83. Cf. *Berakhot* 60b: "The soul which You placed within me is pure. You have created it; You have formed it; You have breathed it into me." Following Ibn Ezra, Cohen argues that *yetzer* does not refer to an instinct or natural inclination

but refers to the product or outcome of desire. Thus the desire of the heart is not evil, only the product in which desire manifests itself. In Cohen's words: "In no way does the passage [Genesis 8:21] assert an inborn predisposition to evil in the human heart. It is, however, acknowledged that the effects of the musings and aspirations of the human heart are bad." Cf. *RWL*, pp. 23–24, where Kant distinguishes between a propensity and a predisposition.

69. For further discussion of Cohen's view, see Andrea Poma, *The Critical Philosophy of Hermann Cohen*, pp. 216–18. Note, however, that if we accept Cohen's view, sin is still inevitable; all he has done is insist that we, rather than Adam or an inherited disposition, are responsible for it.

70. Ephraim E. Urbach, *The Sages*, pp. 421–29.

71. *Genesis Rabbah* 9:7.

72. *Yoma* 69b.

73. Note Saadia's interpretation of Ecclesiastes 7:20: It applies to the *capacity* for evil. Thus: "What was meant by it was that there is not a single pious person possessing the faculty of doing what is good who does not also have the power to do evil."

74. See, for example, *Eruvin* 13b, where the rabbis debate for two and a half years whether it would have been better for the human race to have been created or not to have been created and decide that the latter is the case. But note, as Urbach (*The Sages*, pp. 252–54) does, that the fact that the debate lasted so long should warn us that we are not dealing with a fixed doctrine. In fact, the real meaning of the passage seems to be in the conclusion: Given that humanity was created, let them examine their deeds. Also see *Sanhedrin* 101a and *Ta'anit* 68c. At *Shabbat* 55b we are told that four people died because of the serpent: Benjamin the son of Jacob, Amram the father of Moses, Jesse the father of David, and Chileab the son of David. In other words, all people die as a consequence of having sinned except these four (insignificant) people. Therefore sin is something everyone, including Jacob, Moses, and David, has. Maimonides, too, sounds pessimistic at *GP* 3.36, p. 540: "For an individual cannot help but sin and err." But this remark is ambiguous. Does he mean that an individual cannot help but sin over the course of a lifetime or that sin is inevitable all the time? The context suggests that all Maimonides means is that belief in the power of repentance has a positive effect on people because it implies that they can return to a better and more perfect life. This is a long way from saying that sin puts us in a metaphysical category from which we cannot liberate ourselves. If anything, the thrust of Maimonides' remarks is that liberation from sin is a real possibility.

75. *Berakhot* 4d, *Shabbat* 152b.

76. *MT* 1, Laws of Repentance, 7.4.

77. *MT* 1, Laws of Repentance, 10.2

78. *MT* 1, Laws of Repentance, 2.6; 7.7.

79. *GP* 1.54, p. 125.

80. *GP* 3.53, p. 631.

81. On the problems of distraction, see *GP* 3.51, pp. 622–25.

82. Though Kant claims that the guilt is infinite, he also suggests in this passage that the problem has to do with the place from which we start. Even if I decide to change my ways and renounce sin, I cannot pay back the debt for past transgressions, because they have already taken place. But earlier, e.g., *RWL* 60, Kant says quite clearly that the holiness of the law "is impossible of execution at any given time" and that the act is *"always"* defective. Moreover, we saw that the propensity to evil cannot be eradicated (*RWL*, p. 27). This implies that the problem goes much deeper than a guilty conscience for past wrongs. Though a person can undergo a change of heart, or what Kant terms a "revolution," all that will happen is that she will manifest the disposition to *pursue* holiness. As Kant points out (*RWL*, p. 42), there will still be "a great gap between the maxim and the deed." For further comment, see Wood, *Kant's Moral Religion*, pp. 226–31.

83. Kant, *The Metaphysics of Morals*, p. 409. Cf. *RR*, p. 204: "It [the moment at which we repent] should never grow old, and it must and can constantly rejuvenate and renew itself."

84. Kant, *The Metaphysics of Morals*, p. 409.

85. Gerhard von Rad, *Old Testament Theology*, p. 205.

86. On this point, see *MT* 7, Sabbatical Year and Jubilee, 13.13, and the discussion by David Hartman in *Maimonides: Torah and Philosophic Quest*, pp. 51–53.

87. See Maimonides' "Epistle to the Jews of Yemen," in A. S. Halkin, ed., *Crisis and Leadership: Epistles of Maimonides*, pp. 111 and 113. For further discussion of gentile prophecy as well as the place of gentiles in the messianic age, see Menachem Kellner, *Maimonides on Judaism and the Jewish People*, chaps. 4–5. Though it may be true, as Kellner remarks (p. 121, n. 11), that Maimonides' position on gentile prophecy is mainly agreement in principle, it is important to note how different his view was from that of Judah Halevi.

88. Leviticus 19:33–34; Deuteronomy 10:19.

89. *DH* 1, pp. 194–95.

90. For the type of reason that devises the best means for realizing a given end, whether good or evil, see *GP* 3.54, pp. 632–33.

91. On the "erotic" nature of Kant's conception of reason, see Y. Yovel, *Kant and the Philosophy of History*, pp. 15–16. But where is the evidence for Yovel's claim (p. 15) that "Plato drew a fundamental distinction between the rational and the motivational aspect of the mind"?

92. *CPR*, A318/B375; cf. Plato, *Theaetetus* 176a–b.

93. As was noted in chapter 3, n. 40, this passage is ambiguous.

94. For Maimonides' praise of solitude, see *GP* 3.51, p. 621. For further discussion of the issue, see Ralph Lerner, "Maimonides' Governance of the Solitary," in *PM*, p. 33: "The pursuit of perfection is necessarily the pursuit of the few—so few perhaps as to be numbered on one's fingers." But it is not true, as Lerner says in the next sentence, that the relation between the few and the rest of mankind is problematic at best. Maimonides leaves no doubt that

a community founded on divine law must not only keep the majority of mankind from destroying each other but educate them about speculative matters, including God. So there is no possibility of devoting oneself to contemplation alone. On Maimonides' life and problems in achieving solitude, see Steven Harvey, "Maimonides in the Sultan's Palace," in *PM*, pp. 47–48.

95. In this connection, Maimonides (*GP* 3.53, p. 631) cites Psalm 89:3.

6. *Monotheism and Freedom*

1. It should be kept in mind that unity implies immateriality.

2. Cf. *ST* 1.1.1; 1.1.8; 1.2.2; 1.12.13.

3. For the classic statement of the anti-dogmatist position, see Moses Mendelssohn, *Jerusalem*, p. 100: "Among all the prescriptions and ordinances in the Mosaic law, there is not a single one which says: *You shall believe or not believe*. They all say: *You shall do or not do*. Faith is not commanded, for it accepts no other commands than those that come to it by way of conviction." As well as p. 100: "Hence, ancient Judaism has no symbolic books, no *articles of faith*." Cf. Spinoza, *A Theologico-Political Treatise*, introduction: "I draw the conclusion that Revelation has obedience for its sole object, and therefore, in purpose no less than in foundation and method, stands entirely aloof from ordinary knowledge." For modern theologians sympathetic to this view, see Solomon Schechter, "The Dogmas of Judaism," *Studies in Judaism*, First Series, p. 151; Martin Buber, *Two Types of Faith*, p. 7 ff.; A. J. Heschel, *Man is Not Alone*, p. 166.

4. David Bleich, "General Introduction," *With Perfect Faith*, p. 2.

5. According to Rosenzweig (*SR*, pp. 176–79), the problem can be resolved by pointing out that love cannot be commanded by a third party; but it can be commanded by the lover, because "in his mouth the commandment to love is not a strange commandment; it is none other than the voice of love itself." But this seems to beg the question. How can we be *commanded* to see God's voice as "none other than the voice of love itself"? Does this not imply that we have already accepted and come to love God? Behind Rosenzweig's position is the claim that God's love for us is prior to our love for God; thus it is only because God loves us that we can love other things. This point will be taken up in the next chapter.

6. Cf. Exodus 35:5 and 22.

7. See, for example, Numbers 15:39; Deuteronomy 30:14; I Kings 9:3; Psalms 28:3, 55:22, 73:13–18; Isaiah 1:5, 29:13; Jeremiah 22:17.

8. See MT 1, Laws Concerning the Study of the Torah, 1.12, as well as 1, Laws of Repentance, 10.6.

9. For a recent discussion of the problem, see Moshe Halbertal and Avishai Margalit, *Idolatry*, pp. 173–76. Note, as they do, that if beliefs are voluntary, the "*ought* implies *can*" principle would have to apply to beliefs as well. In other words, if a belief is commanded, it must be within my power to believe it.

10. Cf. *MT* 1, Basic Principles of the Torah, 2.1–2.

11. Maimonides, *Eight Chapters*, 2.

12. For an extended discussion of Maimonides' conception of freedom, in particular the idea of moral efficacy or *reshut*, see Josef Stern, "Maimonides' Conceptions of Freedom and the Sense of Shame," in C. Manekin and M. Kellner, eds., *Human Freedom and Moral Responsibility*, pp. 217–66. This article is also valuable for attacking the deterministic interpretations of Pines and Altmann. The latter interpretations are based on *GP* 2.48, where Maimonides says, in opposition to the Mutakallimun, that everything that is produced in time must have a proximate cause. But as Stern argues, this doctrine is still a long way from determinism. For the deterministic reading, see Shlomo Pines, "Translator's Introduction," *GP*, p. xcv, n. 63, and Alexander Altmann, "Free Will and Predestination in Saadia, Baḥya, and Maimonides," in S. D. Goitein, ed., *Religion in a Religious Age*, pp. 25–52. The price one pays for reading the *Guide* as a statement of determinism is, as Pines notes, that it becomes completely incompatible with the view taken in the *Mishneh Torah* and *Eight Chapters*.

13. Harry Wolfson, "The Terms *Tasawwur* and *Tasdiq* in Arabic Philosophy and Their Greek, Latin, and Hebrew Equivalents," in *Studies in the History of Philosophy and Religion*, pp. 468–92. For additional comment on Maimonides' use of these terms, see Charles H. Manekin, "Belief, Certainty, and Divine Attributes in the *Guide of the Perplexed*," *Maimonidean Studies* I (1990): 117–41.

14. *The Philosophical Works of Descartes*, vol. I, p. 174.

15. Crescas, *Light of the Lord*, preface. For a translation and commentary, see Kellner, *Dogma*, pp. 108–39.

16. Hume, *Treatise*, p. 624.

17. Halbertal and Margalit, *Idolatry*, p. 174. Cf. Anthony Kenney, *What Is Faith? Essays in the Philosophy of Religion*, p. 32: "So if we are to assess a person's noetic structure we must not only inquire whether the beliefs he has pass a test of rationality, but whether he has beliefs on topics where it is important that he should have them."

18. Abravanel, *Rosh Amanah*, chap. 11. For an English translation and commentary, see Kellner, *Principles of Faith*, pp. 106–10. Also see Blaise Pascal, *Pensées*, 233: "But at least learn your inability to believe, since reason brings you to this, and yet you cannot believe. Endeavor then to convince yourself, not by increase in proofs of God, but by the abatement of your passions." For modern proponents of the indirect alternative, see Bleich, *With Perfect Faith*, p. 10, and L. Jonathan Cohen, "Belief and Acceptance," *Mind*, 48 (1989): 367–89.

19. Aristotle, *Nicomachean Ethics* 1103a26–1103b2.

20. *MT* 1, Moral Dispositions, 1.7.

21. Cf. Kellner, *Dogma*, pp. 38–48.

22. Cf. *GP* 1.34, pp. 76–77: "It being impossible to achieve true, rational acts—I mean perfect rationality—unless it be by a man thoroughly trained with respect to his morals and endowed with the qualities of tranquility and quiet."

23. On the issue of interpretation, see *GP* 2.25, pp. 327–28.

24. David Hartman, *A Living Covenant*, p. 263.

25. Hartman, *Living Covenant*, p. 257.

26. As I see it, Aquinas would have no difficulty accepting principles 1–6. In regard to principle 2, Maimonides would say that belief in the trinity is incompatible with divine unity, but Aquinas would disagree. Aquinas also would have no trouble with principles 8, 10, 11, and 13. The difficulties would concern principles 7, that Moses is the greatest prophet; 9, that the Torah is valid for all time; and 12, the coming of the messiah.

27. MT 14, Laws of Kings and Wars, 8.10–11, 9.1. This passage is a commentary on the doctrine that the righteous of every nation will have a share in the world to come. The laws include prohibitions on idolatry, blasphemy, murder, sexual immorality, theft, and eating the flesh of a living animal, as well as one that requires the establishment of courts of justice. For the history of the controversy over this passage, see Steven Schwarzschild, *The Pursuit of the Ideal: The Jewish Writings of Steven Schwarzschild*, pp. 29–59. According to Schwarzschild, Maimonides was trying to call attention to the limits of natural law. But the issue is complicated because Maimonides regarded Moses' prophecy not as a miracle but as the supreme act of human intellectual perfection. For further discussion on the seven Noachide commandments, see David Novak, *The Image of the Non-Jew in Judaism*.

28. Although Isadore Twersky, *Introduction to the Code of Maimonides*, pp. 455–56, cites the requirement that gentiles accept Mosaic prophecy as evidence that Maimonides rejected natural law and wanted to introduce some aspect of "imperatival awareness and submission," according to Novak, *The Image*, pp. 275–80, all Maimonides wanted to say was that a gentile who does not accept the commandments on the basis of Mosaic prophecy cannot understand the philosophic principles without which a justification for the commandments cannot be given. More recently Novak has suggested that Maimonides may be reaching out to Christians, since their religion accepts Mosaic prophecy anyway.

29. Hartman, *Maimonides: Torah and Philosophic Quest*, p. 226, n. 92.

30. Hilary Putnam, *The Many Faces of Realism*, pp. 49–50.

31. Putnam, *Faces*, p. 49.

32. Again, Maimonides' concession to the Platonic theory of creation is an exception.

33. Josef Stern, "Maimonides on the Growth of Knowledge," unpublished manuscript.

34. *GP* 2.22, pp. 319–20; 2.24, pp. 326–27. For further discussion, see Kellner, "Maimonides on the Science of the *Mishneh Torah*: Provisional or Permanent?" *AJS Review* 18 (1993): 169–94.

35. Hartman, *Living Covenant*, p. 259.

36. Putnam, *Faces*, p. 51: "A moral image in the sense in which I am using the term is not a declaration that this or that is a virtue, or that this or that is what one ought to do; it is a picture of how our virtues or ideals hang together with one another and of what they have to do with the position we

are in." For the tentative way in which such frameworks are accepted and the difficulty of arriving at a definitive formulation, see Charles Taylor, *Sources of the Self*, pp. 17–18. Note how the issue of conceptual pluralism affects Kellner's assessment of Schwarzschild in *Pursuit*, p. 3. According to Kellner, Schwarzschild is the last of the major medieval Jewish thinkers, not because Schwarzschild was outdated or old-fashioned but because he was "absolutely convinced that Judaism is a consistent, rational system, possessed of authoritative, normative character, and susceptible to clear-cut exposition."

7. *Popular Religion and a Personal God*

1. Yirmiahu Yovel, "God's Transcendence and Its Schematization," in *MP*, p. 273.

2. *Eight Chapters*, 8.

3. One consequence of the distinction between willing change and changing the will is that miracles would have to be preordained during creation so that what looked like a change in God's will was really something that had been planned since the beginning. Again, see *Eight Chapters*, 8, as well as *GP* 2.29, p. 345.

4. On the basis of *GP* 3.13 it is hard to tell whether the problem is (1) we do not know what things were intended for their own sakes and what things for the sake of something else, or (2) everything was intended for its own sake because existence is valuable just in itself. The first argument is epistemological, the second metaphysical. According to *GP* 3.10, discussed later, it appears that Maimonides believes the latter. Perhaps his argument is that even if he were wrong about metaphysics, the epistemological argument would still be true. In any case, his main point is that the world was not created for the sake of human beings.

5. Maimonides' intention to strike a middle course, though noble enough, creates a host of problems. In humans, rational decisions are made when a person contemplates a range of alternatives and chooses the one that reason identifies as the best course of action. Unfortunately, it is impossible to apply this model to God without creating a duality between cognitive and conative faculties. At *GP* 3.25, p. 505, Maimonides writes: "He . . . wills only what is possible, and not everything that is possible, but only what is required by His wisdom as such. . . . For while we believe that the world has been produced in time, none of our scholars and none of our men of knowledge believe that this came about through the will and nothing else." How can this be if will and wisdom are the same in God? It is interesting to note that the same problem arose in early modern philosophy. Descartes took the identity of will and wisdom as an argument for arbitrariness, Spinoza took it as an argument for necessity, whereas Leibniz, like Maimonides, tried to argue for a God who selects the best of a range of alternatives. In his own way, Kant tries to show a way in which we might make sense of the unity of wisdom and will and still preserve divine volition. Ultimately Maimonides'

point would have to be that statements like the one taken from *GP* 3.25 are speculative at best and only our (highly imperfect) way of making sense of divinity. From his perspective, a God ruled by necessity cannot issue commandments, while a capricious God does not issue commandments that we can understand. For fuller discussion of the problem in early modern philosophy, see Kenneth Seeskin, *Jewish Philosophy in a Secular Age*, pp. 78–92. For a "Spinozistic" reading of Maimonides, see Warren Z. Harvey, "Maimonides and Spinoza on Knowledge of Good and Evil [Heb.]," *Iyyun* 28 (1978): 165–85, and "Maimonides' Commentary on Genesis 3:22 [Heb.]," *Da'at* 12 (1984): 15–21. For a critique of Harvey and extended discussion of Maimonides' understanding of goodness, see Howard Kreisel, *Maimonides' Political Philosophy: Studies in Ethics, Law, and the Human Ideal*, forthcoming, chap. 3

6. On the purpose of the commandments, see *GP* 3.27. Note that when it comes to commandments, we can recognize that some exist for the sake of others: Those that promote the welfare of the body are subordinate to those that promote the welfare on the soul.

7. *MT* 1, Laws of Moral Dispositions and Ethical Conduct, 2.3. Cf. *Eight Chapters*, 7.

8. *Shabbat* 105b.

9. On this point, see *GP* 3.30, where people are told that worship of the stars will lead to natural disasters.

10. See Kreisel, *Maimonides' Political Philosophy*, p. 363, and "The Suffering of the Righteous in Medieval Jewish Philosophy [Heb.]," *Da'at* 19 (1987): 17–29.

11. Note that like his views on creation, Maimonides' position on providence is provisional (*GP* 3.18, p. 475) and that his argument is dialectical rather than demonstrative.

12. *Apology* 41c–d.

13. In view of the Socratic Paradox that virtue is knowledge, *evil* would either be identical with or imply ignorance. For Maimonides' acceptance of this view, and the claim that knowledge is to human form what sight is to the eye, see *GP* 3.11, pp. 440–41.

14. Menachem Kellner, "Rambam on Reward and Punishment," in "Must a Jew Believe Anything?" pp. 132–33.

15. In regard to the next life, Maimonides quotes *Berakhot* 17a: "In the world to come there is no eating, drinking, washing, anointing, or sexual intercourse; but the righteous sit with their crowns on their head enjoying the radiance of the Divine Presence."

16. Strictly speaking, prophecy is an intellectual phenomenon: an overflow from God to the mind of the prophet (*GP* 2.36, p. 369). According to *GP* 1. 65, pp. 158–59, "God spoke" really means "the prophet apprehended what God willed." It is true, of course, that Maimonides considers the Torah divine; but as elsewhere, he tries to play down the miraculous nature of the phenomenon. *GP* 3.51 and *Perek Ḥelek* both describe prophecy in purely in-

tellectual terms. Even *Perek Ḥelek* (8) claims that to say the Torah is the word of God is to speak metaphorically. Maimonides does leave room for miracles at *GP* 2.32, when he claims that while God cannot bestow prophecy on someone unsuited for it, it is possible for God to withhold prophecy from someone who is suited. Since the idea of withholding prophecy is never mentioned again, I take it that all Maimonides wants to say is that God's free choice is involved *in principle* in the sense that God could prevent a gifted person from being a prophet. But except for a few insignificant cases, *could* does not imply *will*. On this issue, see Kreisel, "Moses Maimonides," in *HJP*, p. 267: "Maimonides thereby hints that even in reference to the prophetic experience God never operates in a direct manner. His 'command' simply refers to his role as the remote cause of the experience and its contents."

17. Hannah Kasher, "'Torah for Its Own Sake,' 'Torah Not for Its Own Sake,' and the Third Way," *Jewish Quarterly Review* 79 (1988/89): 157.

18. *MT* 1, Laws of Repentance, 9.1.

19. Martin Buber, *Eclipse of God*, p. 60.

20. See, for example, *Berakhot* 54a, 61b.

21. Cf. *Apology* 28b: "You are wrong if you think a person who is worth anything should consider the prospects of life or death. Rather such a person should consider one thing when taking action: whether the action is right or wrong, the act of a good person or a bad one."

22. Buber, *Eclipse of God*, p. 49.

23. Cf. Robert Gibbs, *Correlations in Rosenzweig and Buber*, p. 98: "A human loves because God loves her or him first (and not because God has a relation somehow similar to lovers)."

24. See Ezekiel 18:19–20 and Cohen's discussion of it at *RR*, p. 192.

25. On this point, see, Nathan Rotenstreich, *Jewish Philosophy in Modern Times*, pp. 98–100; Andrea Poma, *The Critical Philosophy of Hermann Cohen*, pp. 232–33; as well as Gibbs, *Correlations*.

26. *RR*, pp. 100–101.

27. *RR*, p. 98.

28. Yovel, *Kant and the Philosophy of History*, p. 116.

29. Cf. *SR*, p. 202: "All true statements about love must be words from its own mouth, borne by the I. The only exception is this one sentence, that it is as strong as death."

30. I say "according to the view put forward in the *Guide*," because at *MT* 1, Basic Principles of the Torah, 1.2, Maimonides talks as if love and fear go hand in hand. For a view similar to that put forward in the *Guide*, see *DH* 2, pp. 339–41.

31. For a passage where Maimonides uses *fear* in both senses, see *GP* 3.24, p. 501. Note that according to Maimonides, Abraham agreed to sacrifice Isaac not because he was afraid of reprisals if he did not, but because he feared God in the proper way.

32. *GP* 3.52, pp. 629–30.

33. *MT* 1, Basic Principles of the Torah, 2.2.

34. *MT* 1, Laws of Repentance, 10.6.

35. *DF*, p. 20.

36. Buber, *Eclipse of God*, p. 62.

37. *MT* 1, Laws of Repentance, 10:3, and *GP* 3.51, p. 625. Also see Maimonides' distinction between *one who loves* and *one who loves passionately* at *GP* 3.51, p. 627.

38. *SR*, p. 177.

39. Cf. Emmanuel Levinas, *Totality and Infinity*, p. 34: "Desire is desire for the absolutely other. Besides the hunger one satisfies, the thirst one quenches, and the senses one allays, metaphysics desires the other beyond satisfactions, where no gesture by the body to diminish the aspiration is possible, where it is not possible to sketch out any known caress nor invent any new caress. A desire without satisfaction which, precisely, *understands* [*entend*] the remoteness, the alterity, and the exteriority of the other. For Desire this alterity, non-adequate to the idea, has a meaning. It is understood as the alterity of the Other and of the Most-High." The difference between Maimonides and Levinas is, of course, that the former understands this desire in terms of negation, while the latter (p. 23) does not.

40. *GP* 3.53, p. 631; cf. *ST* 1.20.2.

41. See *Pirkei Avot* 3.18 for a classic statement of this view.

42. On this point see David Hartman, *Maimonides: Torah and Philosophic Quest*, pp. 151–53. Cf. *DF*, p. 20: "Judaism believes in this regeneration of man without the intervention of extrahuman factors other than the consciousness of God, and the Law."

43. *MT* 1, Laws of Repentance, 2.3.

44. *MT* 1, Laws of Repentance, 2.6, 7.6.

45. *GP* 3.29–30. For an excellent treatment of Maimonides' view of Sabianism, see Josef Stern, "The Fall and Rise of Myth in Ritual: Maimonides versus Nachmanides on the *Huqqim*, Astrology, and the War Against Idolatry," *The Journal of Jewish Thought and Philosophy* 6 (1977): 185–263, esp. p. 211: "Therefore, it is not enough for the philosopher simply to point out the fallacies and false premises from which the conclusions of Sabianism follow. The task of the philosopher is to free those caught in the grip of the Sabian myth. A crucial step in this process is exposing the Sabian origins of present day 'popular religion.'"

46. Kellner, *Maimonides on Human Perfection*, p. 21.

47. *MT* 1, Laws Concerning Idolatry and Ordinances of the Heathens, 11.16.

48. For a similar reading of Maimonides and critique of Strauss, see Joel Kraemer, "Maimonides on the Philosophic Sciences in his *Treatise on the Art of Logic*," in *PM*, pp. 98–101.

49. *LPR*, 2, p. 211. The concept of servitude is complicated. In Hebrew the same root (*avad*) is used to describe slavery, idolatry (strange service), and worship or service to God. Thus Israel is asked to love and *serve* God with all

its heart and soul (Deuteronomy 11:13). But etymology alone will not support Hegel, because the same idea is used to describe Paul's relation to Jesus at Romans 1:1 and Philippians 1:1. In the Bible a master does not have life-and-death authority over slaves; in fact, the Bible often points out that slaves have rights (e.g., Exodus 21:1 ff.) and should not be treated in a cruel or haughty manner. We saw that slaves participate in Sabbath observance with their masters. Hebrew slaves were not held for life but had to be released after seven years.

50. *LPR* 2, p. 206.

51. *LPR* 2, p. 189.

52. *LPR*, 2, p. 204.

53. See Genesis 18:22–26, Exodus 32:7–14, and Numbers 14:13–19 and 16:20–22, as well as the continuation of this theme in Job, Jeremiah, and Habakkuk.

54. *Bava Metzia* 59b.

55. Emil Fackenheim, "Moses and the Hegelians," in *Encounters Between Judaism and Modern Philosophy*, p. 99.

56. *Genesis Rabbah*, 44.1; cf. *Berakhot* 63a, where "The Lord was pleased for His righteousness' sake" is taken to mean "The Lord was pleased for your righteousness' sake." Also see Yehezkel Kaufmann, *The Religion of Ancient Israel*, pp. 125–26. According to Kaufmann, the prophets never warned the people that God does not need the flesh of sacrificial animals in order to exist, because no one was foolish enough to believe it.

57. Cf. Goodman, *God of Abraham*, p. 88: "Human goodness begins with human nature; and the call to emulate God's holiness, then, contains no paradox, so long as we recall that what we seek is our perfection, not God's."

58. Isadore Twersky, *Introduction to the Code of Maimonides*, p. 386. For Maimonides' view of statutory commandments, see *GP* 3.26, pp. 506–07, as well as Josef Stern, "The Idea of a *Hoq* in Maimonides' Explanation of the Law," in *MP*, pp. 92–138. Note that the process of finding reasons for commandments cannot go on indefinitely. According to Maimonides, there is a justification for the sacrificial cult but not for why a lamb is needed in one case but a ram in another.

59. The exceptions are the prohibitions against idolatry, murder, and illicit sexual unions. For further discussion, see *MT* 3, Laws of the Sabbath, 2.1.

60. See, for example, Amos 5:21–24, Hosea 6:6, and Jeremiah 6:20.

61. Cf. Fackenheim, "Moses and the Hegelians," p. 118: "We have seen that Hegel surpasses Kant in his recognition that the law of Moses is a bridge between the Divine and the Human, rather than a bar. It now emerges that he fails to pass beyond Kant when he, too, fails to recognize the Grace that is in that 'law.'"

62. Sifra to Leviticus 19:1.

Appendix

1. The question of how to read the Guide is as old as the book itself. Maimonides' Hebrew translator, Samuel Ibn Tibbon, argued that the book contained a doctrine so esoteric that it eluded many of those who sought to defend Maimonides against allegations of heresy. We should keep in mind, however, that ibn Tibbon was himself an Aristotelian. For this history of the problem of interpretation, see Aviezer Ravitzky, "Samuel Ibn Tibbon and the Esoteric Character of the *Guide of the Perplexed*," *AJS Review* 6 (1981): 87–123. Note, as Ravitzky does, that there is no clear evidence that Maimonides either approved or disapproved of ibn Tibbon's reading of him. For the extent to which recent attempts to argue for esotericism parallel those of the Middle Ages, see Ravitzky, "The Secrets of the Guide to the Perplexed: Between the Thirteenth and Twentieth Centuries," in I. Twersky, ed., *Studies in Maimonides*, pp. 159–207. For the history of the esoteric/exoteric distinction, see Miriam Galston, *Politics and Excellence: The Political Philosophy of Alfarabi*, pp. 27–35.

2. Leo Strauss, "The Literary Character of the *Guide of the Perplexed*," in *Persecution and the Art of Writing* p. 55.

3. Strauss, "The Literary Character," p. 59.

4. Cf. Alfred Ivry, "Leo Strauss on Maimonides," in A. Udoff, ed., *Leo Strauss's Thought*, p. 83. According to Ivry, the choice is between an esotericism in which Maimonides knows that his beliefs are founded on opinion rather than demonstration and an esotericism in which Maimonides does not believe what he seems to assert.

5. Strauss, "The Literary Character," p. 73, and "How to Begin to Study *The Guide of the Perplexed*," in *GP*, p. xv.

6. Strauss, "The Literary Character," p. 73.

7. Strauss, "The Literary Character," pp. 73–74.

8. For more on the subject of contradictions in Maimonides, see Marvin Fox, *Interpreting Maimonides*, pp. 67–90. Fox points out that Maimonides introduces this subject by talking about contraries and contradictories; but when Maimonides discusses the works of philosophers, or his own work, he introduces another term: divergences. According to Fox, a contradiction has to do with the truth or falsity of propositions while a divergence has to do with actions. Thus Maimonides' procedure is not to make contradictory statements but to make one statement and *do* the opposite. As an example Fox cites *GP* 2.35, where Maimonides says he will not discuss the prophecy of Moses; the fact is, however, that he says a great deal about it in the rest of the book. But it is difficult to know whether the distinction between contradiction and divergence is significant. In the passage from *GP* 1. Introduction, quoted above, Maimonides talks explicitly about contradictory statements. Moreover, even if we follow Fox, the same question arises: Does Maimonides have a well-formulated doctrine he is trying to conceal? Fox responds by saying that given contradictory statements, we have to affirm one and deny the

other; but when presented with a divergence, we experience "a dialectical tension" or balancing act. I agree that Maimonides presents the reader with dialectical tensions, but contrary to Fox's suggestion, he does not leave the reader with tensions that are unresolved. Recall that the dialectical method typically begins with views on either side of an important question. Rather than pointing out that Maimonides presents both sides and letting the matter drop, Fox should have said more about how the puzzle is solved. Is the resolution systematically concealed or could it be discovered by a reader with adequate training? If the former, Fox sides with Strauss. If the latter, then Maimonides' procedure is no different from that of dozens of philosophers who used the dialectical method. In short, the distinction between contradiction and divergence does not get us very far.

9. Aristotle, *Prior Analytics* 24a24–25.

10. See *Republic* 498, 538–39.

11. Joel Kraemer, "Maimonides on the Philosophic Sciences, in His *Treatise on the Art of Logic,*" in *PM*, p. 102.

12. Strauss, "The Literary Character," pp. 59–60.

13. Strauss, "The Literary Character," p. 74.

14. Strauss, "How to Begin to Study *The Guide of the Perplexed,*" pp. xxxvi–xxxv2.

15. Strauss, "How to Begin to Study *The Guide of the Perplexed,*" pp. xvi–xv2.

16. *MT* 14, Laws of Kings and Wars, 12.1–2.

17. Fox, *Interpreting Maimonides*, p. 82.

18. On the basis of *GP* 2.48, where God is described as a cause, Shlomo Pines, "Notes on Maimonides' Views Concerning Free Will," *Studies in Philosophy, Scripta Hierosolymitana* 6 (1960): 195–198, and Alexander Altmann, "Free Will and Predestination in Saadia, Baḥya, and Maimonides," in S. D. Goitein, ed., *Religion in a Religious Age*, pp. 25–52, argue that Maimonides adopts a determinist position in the Guide. Since there is considerable evidence that he adopts a libertarian position in his legal writings (e.g., *MT* 1, Laws of Repentance, 5.1), the Pines-Altmann interpretation, if true, would mean that there is a sharp disparity between Maimonides' exoteric and esoteric view. But the Pines-Altmann interpretation has been effectively challenged by Josef Stern, in "Maimonides' Conceptions of Freedom and the Sense of Shame," in C. Manekin and M. Kellner, eds., *Freedom and Moral Responsibility*, pp. 217–266.

19. Ravitzky, "The Days of the Messiah," in *PM*, p. 251.

20. *MT* I, Basic Principles of the Torah, 1.10

21. See, for example, Pines, "The Limitations of Human Knowledge According to Alfarabi, ibn Bujja, and Maimonides," in *M*, pp. 104–5. Pines refers to the fact that the theory is first presented as a generally accepted (*shuhra*) dictum. True enough, but later in the same chapter Maimonides says more than once that it has been demonstrated.

22. Steven Harvey, "Maimonides in the Sultan's Palace," in *PM*, pp. 53–54.

23. For a sustained criticism of Strauss's attempt to separate Maimonides the philosopher from Maimonides the talmudic expositor, see David Hartman, *Maimonides: Torah and Philosophic Quest*, especially pp. 20–26, 241–42. Also see Joseph Buijs, "The Philosophical Character of Maimonides' *Guide*: A Critique of Strauss's Interpretation," *M*, pp. 59–70. For the compatibility of philosophy and Talmud study in the Parable of the Palace, see Menachem Kellner, *Maimonides on Human Perfection*, chapter 6. For recent scholars sympathetic with the Athens–Jerusalem split or with Strauss's approach to the *Guide*, see Raymond L. Weiss, *Maimonides' Ethics*; Kenneth Green, *Jew and Philosopher: The Return to Maimonides in the Jewish Thought of Leo Strauss*, especially chapter 3; and Hillel Fradkin, "A Word Fitly Spoken: The Interpretation of Maimonides and the Legacy of Leo Strauss," in David Novak, ed., *Leo Strauss and Judaism*, pp. 55–86.

Bibliography

Abelson, Joshua, *The Immanence of God in Rabbinical Literature*. London: Macmillan, 1912.

Al-Ghazali, *The Incoherence of the Philosophers*. Translated by Michael E. Marmura. Provo, Utah: Brigham Young University Press, 1997.

Allison, Henry E., *Kant's Theory of Freedom*. Cambridge: Cambridge University Press, 1990.

Altmann, Alexander, "The Divine Attributes: An Historical Survey of the Jewish Discussion," *Judaism* (1966): 40–60.

———, "Essence and Existence in Maimonides." In *M*, pp. 148–65.

———, "Free Will and Predestination in Saadia, Baḥya, and Maimonides." In *Religion in a Religious Age*, edited by S. D. Goitein. New York: KTAV, 1974, pp. 25–52.

———, *Von der Mittelalterlichen zur Modernen Aufklärung*. Tubingen: Mohr, 1987.

Aquinas, Thomas, *Summa Contra Gentiles*. Translated by Anton C. Pegis. Garden City, N. Y., Random House.

———, *Summa Theologiae*. Translated by Anton C. Pegis. New York: Random House, 1945.

Armstrong, A. H., *Plotinus: A Volume of Selections*. London: Allen & Unwin, 1953.

Averroes, *Tahafut Al-Tahafut: The Incoherence of the Incoherence*. Translated by S. Van den Bergh. 1954. Reprinted, London: Aris & Phillips, 1978.

Baḥya ibn Pakudah, *Duties of the Heart*. Translated by Moses Hyamson. 1962. Reprinted, Jerusalem: Feldheim, 1970.

Baron, Salo, *A Social and Religious History of the Jews*, vol. 8. New York: Columbia University Press, 1958.

Beck, Lewis White, *A Commentary on Kant's Critique of Practical Reason*. Chicago: University of Chicago Press, 1960.

Benin, Stephen D., *The Footprints of God*. Albany, N.Y.: SUNY Press, 1993.

Benor, Ehud, "Meaning and Reference in Maimonides' Negative Theology," *Harvard Theological Review* 88 (1995): 339–60.

——, *Worship of the Heart*. Albany, N.Y.: SUNY Press, 1995.

Berman, Lawrence, "Maimonides, The Disciple of Alfarabi." In *M*, pp. 195–214.

——, "Maimonides on Political Leadership." In *Kinship and Consent*, edited by Daniel J. Elazar. Ramat Gan: Turtedove, 1981, pp. 13–25.

——, "The Political Interpretation of the Maxim: The Purpose of Philosophy Is the Imitation of God," *Studia Islamica* 15 (1961): 53–61.

Birnbaum, Philip, *Daily Prayer Book*. New York: Hebrew Publishing, 1949.

Bleich, David, *With Perfect Faith*. New York: KTAV, 1983.

Blumenthal, David R., "Maimonides' Intellectual Mysticism and the Superiority of the Prophecy of Moses," *Studies in Medieval Culture* 10 (1977): 51–67.

Broadie, Alexander, "Maimonides and Aquinas." In *HJP*, pp. 281–93.

——, "Maimonides and Aquinas on the Names of God," *Religious Studies* 23 (1987): 157–70.

Buber, Martin, "Dialogue Between Heaven and Earth." In *Four Existentialist Theologians*, edited by W. Herberg. Garden City, N. Y.: Doubleday, 1958, pp. 215–25.

——, *Eclipse of God*. 1952. Reprinted, Atlantic Highlands, N. J.: Humanities Press International, 1988.

——, *Two Types of Faith*. Translated by Norman P. Goldhawk. New York: Collier, 1986.

Buijs, Joseph A., ed. *Maimonides*. Notre Dame, Ind.: University of Notre Dame Press, 1988.

——, "The Philosophical Character of Maimonides' *Guide*: A Critique of Strauss's Interpretation." In *M*, pp. 59–70.

Burrell, David, "Aquinas and Islamic and Jewish Thinkers." In *The Cambridge Companion to Aquinas*, edited by N. Kretzman and E. Stump. Cambridge: Cambridge University Press, 1993, pp. 60–84.

——, *Aquinas: God and Action*. Notre Dame, Ind.: University of Notre Dame Press, 1985.

——, "Aquinas's Debt to Maimonides." In *A Straight Path: Studies in Medieval Philosophy and Culture*, edited by Ruth Link-Salinger. Washington, D.C.: Catholic University of America Press, 1987, pp. 37–48.

——, *Knowing the Unknowable God: Ibn Sina, Maimonides, and Aquinas*. Notre Dame, Ind.: University of Notre Dame Press, 1986.

Burrell, David, and Bernard McGinn, eds., *God and Creation*. Notre Dame, Ind.: University of Notre Dame Press, 1990.

Cohen, Hermann, "Charakteristic der Ethik Maimunis," *Jüdische Schriften,* vol. 3., 1924. Reprinted, New York: Arno Press, 1980, pp. 221–89.

——, *Religion of Reason out of the Sources of Judaism.* Translated by S. Kaplan. 1972. Reprinted, Atlanta: Scholars Press, 1995.

Cohen, L. Jonathan, "Belief and Acceptance," *Mind* 48 (1989): 367–89.

Cohen, Richard, *Elevations: The Height of the Good in Rosenzweig and Levinas.* Chicago: University of Chicago Press, 1994.

Craig, William L., "Maimonides' Proofs for the Existence of God." In *M,* pp. 122–47.

D'Ancona Costa, Cristina, "Plotinus and Later Platonic Philosophers on the Causality of the First Principle." In *The Cambridge Companion to Plotinus,* edited by Lloyd P. Gerson. Cambridge: Cambridge University Press, 1996, pp. 356–85.

Dannhauser, Werner, "Athens and Jerusalem or Jerusalem and Athens?" In *Leo Strauss and Judaism,* edited by David Novak, pp. 155–71.

Davidson, Herbert, "Maimonides on Metaphysical Knowledge," *Maimonidean Studies* 3 (1992–93): 49–103.

——, "Maimonides' Secret Position on Creation." In *Studies in Medieval Jewish History and Literature,* edited by Isadore Twersky. Cambridge, Mass.: Harvard University Press, 1979, pp. 16–40.

——, *Proofs for Eternity, Creation, and the Existence of God in Medieval Islamic and Jewish Philosophy.* New York: Oxford University Press, 1987.

——, "The Study of Philosophy as a Religious Obligation." In *Religion in a Religious Age,* edited by S. D. Goitein. New York: KTAV, 1974, pp. 53–68.

Davies, Brian, *The Thought of Thomas Aquinas.* Oxford: Oxford University Press, 1992.

Descartes, René, *The Philosophical Works of Descartes,* vol. 1. Translated by E. S. Haldane and G. R. T. Ross. 1911. Reprinted, Cambridge: Cambridge University Press, 1968.

Dobbs-Weinstein, Idit, "The Maimonidean Controversy." In *HJP,* pp. 331–49.

——, *Maimonides and St. Thomas on the Limits of Reason.* Albany, N.Y.: SUNY Press, 1995.

Dunphy, William, "Maimonides and Aquinas on Creation: A Critique of Their Historians." In *Graceful Reason,* edited by Lloyd P. Gerson. Toronto: Pontifical Institute of Medieval Studies, 1983, pp. 361–79.

——, "Maimonides' Not-So-Secret Position on Creation." In *MM,* pp. 151–72.

Dupre, Louis, "Transitions and Tensions in Determinate Religion." In *New Perspectives on Hegel's Philosophy of Religion,* edited by David Kolb. Albany, N.Y.: SUNY Press, 1992.

Efros, Israel, *Philosophical Terms in the Moreh Nevukim.* 1924. Reprinted, New York: Arno, 1966.

Evans, J. D. G., *Aristotle's Concept of Dialectic.* Cambridge: Cambridge University Press, 1977.

Fackenheim, Emil, *Encounters Between Judaism and Modern Philosophy.* New York: Basic Books, 1973.

——, *God's Presence in History*. New York: New York University Press, 1970.

——, "Martin Buber's Concept of Revelation." In *The Philosophy of Martin Buber*, edited by Paul A. Schilpp. LaSalle, Ill.: Open Court, 1967, pp. 273–96.

——, *Quest for Past and Future*. Bloomington: Indiana University Press, 1968.

——, *The Religious Dimension in Hegel's Thought*. Bloomington: Indiana University Press, 1968.

Fakhry, Majid, *A History of Islamic Philosophy*, second edition. New York: Columbia University Press, 1983.

Falk, Marcia, "Toward a Feminist Jewish Reconstruction of Monotheism," *Tikkun* 4 (1990): 53–56.

Feldman, Seymour, "Abravanel on Maimonides' Critique of the Kalam Arguments for Creation," *Maimonidean Studies* 1 (1990): 15–25.

——, "'In the Beginning God Created': A Philosophical Midrash." In *God and Creation*, edited by David Burrell and Bernard McGinn, pp. 3–26.

——, "A Scholastic Misinterpretation of Maimonides' Doctrine of Divine Attributes." In *M*, pp. 267–83.

——, Translation of and commentary on Gersonides, *Wars of the Lord*, vols. 1–3. Philadelphia: Jewish Publication Society, 1984–87.

Fox, Marvin, *Interpreting Maimonides*. Chicago: University of Chicago Press, 1990.

Fradkin, Hillel, "A Word Fitly Spoken: The Interpretation of Maimonides and the Legacy of Leo Strauss." In *Leo Strauss and Judaism*, edited by David Novak, pp. 55–85.

Franck, Isaac, "Maimonides and Aquinas on Man's Knowledge of God: A Twentieth Century Perspective." In *M*, pp. 284–306.

Frank, Daniel H., "Anger as a Vice: A Maimonidean Critique of Aristotle's Ethics," *History of Philosophy Quarterly* 7 (1990): 269–81.

——, "The End of the Guide: Maimonides on the Best Life for Man," *Judaism* 34 (1985): 485–95.

——, "Humility as a Virtue: A Maimonidean Critique of Aristotle's Ethics." In *MM*, pp. 89–99.

——, "Reason in Action: The 'Practicality' of Maimonides' *Guide*." In *Commandment and Community*, edited by Daniel Frank. Albany, N.Y.: SUNY Press, 1995, pp. 69–84.

Frank, Daniel H., and Oliver Leaman, eds., *History of Jewish Philosophy*. London: Routledge, 1997.

Galston, Miriam, "Philosopher-King vs. Prophet," *Israel Oriental Studies* 7 (1978): 204–18.

——, *Politics and Excellence: The Political Philosophy of Alfarabi*. Princeton, N.J.: Princeton University Press, 1990.

——, "The Purpose of the Law According to Maimonides." In *M*, pp. 215–33.

Genot-Bismuth, Jacqueline, "Perfection Humaine et '*Imitatio Dei*' chez Maïmonide." In *TM*, pp. 42–68.

Gerson, Lloyd P., ed., *The Cambridge Companion to Plotinus*. Cambridge: Cambridge University Press, 1996.

Gibbs, Robert, *Correlations in Rosenzweig and Levinas*. Princeton, N.J.: Princeton University Press, 1992.

Gilson, Etienne, *The Spirit of Medieval Philosophy*. Translated by A. H. C. Downes. 1936. Reprinted, New York: Charles Scribner's Sons, 1940.

Goodman, Lenn, *God of Abraham*. New York: Oxford University Press, 1996.

———, "Maimonidean Naturalism." In *Neoplatonism and Jewish Thought*, edited by Lenn Goodman, pp. 157–67.

———, *Monotheism*. Totowa, N.J.: Littlefield, Adams, 1981.

———, ed., *Neoplatonism and Jewish Thought*. Albany, N.Y.: SUNY Press, 1992.

———, "Three Meanings of the Idea of Creation." In *God and Creation*, edited by David Burrell and Bernard McGinn, pp. 89–106.

Green, Kenneth Hart, *Jew and Philosopher: The Return to Maimonides in the Jewish Thought of Leo Strauss*. Albany, N.Y.: SUNY Press, 1993.

Gross, Rita M., "Steps Toward Feminine Imagery of Deity in Jewish Theology." In *On Being a Jewish Feminist*, edited by S. Heschel. 1983. Reprinted, New York: Schocken, 1995, pp. 234–47.

Guth, Alan H. *The Inflationary Universe*. Reading, Mass.: Addison-Wesley, 1997.

Guttmann, Julius, *The Philosophy of Judaism*. Translated by D. W. Silverman. 1964. Reprinted, Northvale, N. J.: Jason Aronson, 1988.

Halbertal, Moshe, and Avishai Margalit, *Idolatry*. Translated by N. Goldblum. Cambridge, Mass.: Harvard University Press, 1992.

Halkin, Abraham, ed., *Crisis and Leadership: Epistles of Maimonides*. Philadelphia: Jewish Publication Society, 1985.

Hartman, David, *A Living Covenant*. New York: Macmillan, 1985.

———, *Maimonides: Torah and Philosophic Quest*. Philadelphia: Jewish Publication Society, 1976.

Harvey, Steven, "Maimonides in the Sultan's Palace." In *PM*, pp. 47–76.

Harvey, Warren Z., "Holiness: A Command to *Imitatio Dei*," *Tradition* 16 (1976–77): 7–28.

———, "Maimonides and Spinoza on Knowledge of Good and Evil [Heb.]," *Iyyun* 28 (1978): 165–85.

———, "Maimonides' Commentary on Genesis 3:22 [Heb.]," *Da'at* 12 (1984): 15–21.

———, "Maimonides on Human Perfection, Awe, and Politics." In *TMM*, pp.1–15.

———, "A Third Approach to Maimonides' Cosmogony-Prophetology Puzzle." In *M*, pp. 71–90.

Hegel, G. W. F., *Faith and Knowledge*. Translated by H. S. Harris. Albany, N.Y.: SUNY Press, 1977.

———, *Lectures on the Philosophy of Religion*. Translated by E. B. Spears and J. B. Sanderson. New York: Humanities Press, 1962.

Heschel, A. J., *Man Is Not Alone: A Philosophy of Religion*. New York: Farrar, Straus, and Young, 1951.

Hume, David, *A Treatise of Human Nature*. 1888. Reprinted, Oxford: Oxford University Press, 1967.

Husik, Isaac, *A History of Medieval Jewish Philosophy*. 1916. Reprinted, New York: Atheneum, 1976.

Hyman, Arthur, "Demonstrative, Dialectical, and Sophistic Arguments in the Philosophy of Moses Maimonides." In *MM*, pp. 35–51.

———, "From What Is One and Simple Only What Is One and Simple Can Come to Be," *Neoplatonism and Jewish Thought*, edited by Lenn Goodman, pp. 111–35.

———, "Maimonides on Causality." In *MP*, pp. 157–72.

———, "Maimonides on Creation and Emanation," *Studies in Medieval Philosophy*, edited by J. F. Whippel. Washington, D.C.: Catholic University of America Press, 1988, pp. 45–61.

Idel, Moshe, *Kabbalah: New Perspectives*. New Haven, Conn.: Yale University Press, 1988.

———, *The Mystical Experience in Abraham Abulafia*. Translated by J. Chipman. Albany, N.Y.: SUNY Press, 1988.

Irwin, Terence, *Aristotle's First Principles*. Oxford: Oxford University Press, 1988.

Ivry, Alfred, "Leo Strauss on Maimonides." In *Leo Strauss's Thought*, edited by A. Udoff. Boulder, Co.: Rienner, 1991, pp. 75–91.

———, "Maimonides and Neoplatonism: Challenge and Response." In *Neoplatonism and Jewish Thought*, edited by Lenn Goodman, pp. 137–56.

———, "Maimonides on Creation." In *Creation and the End of Days*, edited by David Novak and Norbert Samuelson, pp. 185–213.

———, "Maimonides on Possibility." In *Mystics, Philosophers, and Politicians*, edited by Y. Reinharz and D. Swetschinski. Durham, N.C.: Duke University Press, 1982, pp. 67–84.

———, "Neoplatonic Currents in Maimonides." In *PM*, pp. 115–40.

———, "The Problematics of the Ideal of Human Perfection." In *TMM*, pp. 16–25.

———, "Providence, Divine Omniscience, and Possibility: The Case of Maimonides." In *Divine Omniscience and Omnipotence in Medieval Philosophy*, edited by Tamar Rudavsky. Dordrecht: D. Reidel, 1985, pp. 143–59.

Jacobs, Louis, *A Jewish Theology*. New York: Behrman House, 1973.

James, William, *The Varieties of Religious Experience*. New York: Mentor, 1958.

Jordan, Mark D., "The Names of God and the Being of Names." In *The Existence and Nature of God*, edited by A. Freddoso. Notre Dame, Ind.: University of Notre Dame Press, 1984, pp. 161–90.

———, *Ordering Wisdom: The Hierarchy of Philosophical Discourses in Aquinas*. Notre Dame, Ind.: University of Notre Dame Press, 1986.

Kant, Immanuel, *Critique of Practical Reason.* Translated by Lewis White Beck. Indianapolis: Bobbs-Merrill, 1956.

———, *Critique of Pure Reason.* Translated by Norman Kemp Smith. 1929. Reprinted, New York: Saint Martin's Press, 1965.

———, *Foundations of the Metaphysics of Morals.* Translated by Lewis White Beck. Indianapolis: Bobbs-Merrill, 1959.

———, *The Metaphysics of Morals.* Translated by M. Gregor. Cambridge: Cambridge University Press, 1991.

———, *Religion within the Limits of Reason Alone.* Translated by T. M. Greene and H. H. Hudson. 1934. Reprinted, New York: Harper and Row, 1960.

Kaplan, Lawrence, "'I Sleep, But My Heart Waketh': Maimonides' Conception of Human Perfection." In *TMM,* pp. 130–66.

———, "Maimonides on the Miraculous Element in Prophecy," *Harvard Theological Review* 70 (1977): 233–56.

Kasher, Hannah, "'Torah for Its Own Sake,' 'Torah Not for Its Own Sake,' and the Third Way," *Jewish Quarterly Review* 79 (1988/89): 157.

Katz, Steven T., "Utterance and Ineffability in Jewish Neoplatonism." In *Neoplatonism and Jewish Thought,* edited by Lenn Goodman, pp. 279–98.

Kaufmann, Walter, *Hegel: Reinterpretation, Texts, and Commentary.* Garden City, N.Y.: Doubleday, 1965.

Kaufmann, Yehezkel. *The Religion of Ancient Israel.* Translated by M. Greenberg. 1937. Reprinted, New York: Schocken, 1972.

Kellner, Menachem, *Dogma in Medieval Jewish Thought.* New York: Oxford University Press, 1986.

———, *Maimonides on Human Perfection.* Atlanta: Scholars Press, 1990.

———, *Maimonides on Judaism and the Jewish People.* Albany, N.Y.: SUNY Press, 1991.

———, "Maimonides on the Science of the *Mishneh Torah*: Provisional or Permanent?" *AJS Review* 18 (1993): 169–94.

———, *Must a Jew Believe Anything?* London: Littman Library of Jewish Civilization, 1999.

———, "On the Status of Astronomy and Physics in Maimonides' *Mishneh Torah* and *Guide of the Perplexed,*" *British Journal for the History of Science* 24 (1991): 453–63.

———, "Politics and Perfection: Gersonides and Maimonides," *Jewish Political Studies Review* 6: (1994): 49–82.

———, *Principles of Faith.* Rutherford, N. J.: Fairleigh Dickenson University Press, 1982.

Kenny, Anthony, *What Is Faith? Essays in the Philosophy of Religion.* Oxford: Oxford University Press, 1992.

Klein-Braslavy, Sarah, "The Creation of the World and Maimonides' Interpretation of Gen. I–V." In *MP,* pp. 65–71.

———, *Maimonides' Interpretation of the Adam Stories in Genesis* [Heb.]. Jerusalem: Reuben Mass, 1986.

——, "Maimonides' Interpretation of the Verb *Bara* and the Problem of the Creation of the World [Heb.]," *Da'at* 16 (1986): 39–55.

Kogan, Barry S., "The Problem of Creation in Late Medieval Jewish Philosophy." In *A Straight Path*, edited by R. Link-Salinger, pp. 172–73.

——, "'What Can We Know and When Can We Know It?' Maimonides on the Active Intelligence and Human Cognition." In *MT*, pp. 121–37.

Kraemer, Joel L., "Maimonides on the Philosophic Sciences in His *Treatise on the Art of Logic*." In *PM*, pp. 77–104.

——, ed., *Perspectives on Maimonides*. Oxford: Oxford University Press, 1991.

Kreisel, Howard, "*Imitatio Dei* in Maimonides' *Guide of the Perplexed*," *AJS Review* 19 (1994): 169–211.

——, *Maimonides' Political Philosophy: Studies in Ethics, Law, and the Human Ideal*. Albany, N.Y.: SUNY Press, forthcoming.

——, "Moses Maimonides." In *HJP*, pp. 245–80.

——, "The Suffering of the Righteous in Medieval Jewish Philosophy [Heb.]," *Da'at* 19 (1987): 17–29.

Kretzmann, Norman, and Eleonore Stump, eds., *The Cambridge Companion to Aquinas*. Cambridge: Cambridge University Press, 1993.

Langermann, Tzvi, "Maimonides' Repudiation of Astrology," *Maimonidean Studies* 2 (1991): 149–51.

——, "The 'True Perplexity': The *Guide of the Perplexed*, Part II, Chapter 24." In *PM*, pp. 159–74.

Leaman, Oliver, *Moses Maimonides*. London: Routledge, 1990.

Le Blond, J. M., *Logique et Methode chez Aristotle*. Paris: Vrin, 1939.

Lerner, Ralph, "Maimonides' Governance of the Solitary." In *PM*, pp. 33–46.

Leroux, Georges, "Human Freedom in the Thought of Plotinus." In *The Cambridge Companion to Plotinus*, edited by L. P. Gerson, pp. 292–314.

Levinas, Emmanuel, *Difficult Freedom*. Translated by S. Hand. Baltimore: Johns Hopkins Press, 1990.

——, *Totality and Infinity*. Translated by A. Lingis. Pittsburgh: Duquesne University Press, 1969.

Link-Salinger, Ruth, ed., *A Straight Path: Studies in Medieval Philosophy and Culture*. Washington, D.C.: Catholic University of America Press, 1987.

Lloyd, A. C., "The Principle that the Cause is Greater than the Effect," *Phronesis* 21 (1976): 146–56.

Lobel, Diana N., *Between Mysticism and Philosophy: Arabic Terms for Religious Experience in R. Yehudah Ha-Levi's Kuzari*. Albany, N.Y.: SUNY Press, forthcoming.

Löwith, Karl, *From Hegel to Nietzsche*. Translated by D. E. Green. 1964. Reprinted, Garden City, N.Y.: Doubleday, 1967.

Maimonides, *Dalālat al-Ha'irīn*, edited by I. Joel. Jerusalem: Junovitch, 1929.

——, *Ethical Writings of Maimonides*, edited by Raymond L. Weiss and Charles Butterworth. New York: Dover, 1975.

———, *Guide of the Perplexed*. Translated by Shlomo Pines. Chicago: University of Chicago Press, 1963.

———, *A Maimonides Reader*, edited by Isadore Twersky. New York: Behrman House, 1972.

———, *Mishneh Torah*, edited by S. T. Rubenstein et al. Jerusalem: Mossad Harav Kook, 1967–73.

———, *Moreh Nevukhim*, edited by Y. E. Shmuel. Jerusalem: Mossad Harav Kook, 1987.

Malino, Jonathan W., "Aristotle on Eternity: Does Maimonides Have a Reply." In *MP*, pp. 52–64.

Manekin, Charles H., "Belief, Certainty, and Divine Attributes in the *Guide of the Perplexed*," *Maimonidean Studies* 1 (1990): 117–41.

Mendelssohn, Moses, *Jerusalem*. Translated by Allan Arkush. Hanover: University Press of New England, 1983.

Morgan, Michael, *Dilemmas in Modern Jewish Thought*. Bloomington: Indiana University Press, 1992.

Morrow, Glen R., *Plato's Epistles*, second edition. Indianapolis: Bobbs-Merrill, 1962.

Novak, David, *The Election of Israel*. Cambridge: Cambridge University Press, 1995.

———, *The Image of the Non-Jew in Judaism*. Toronto: Edwin Mellon, 1983.

———, "Maimonides and the Science of the Law," *Jewish Law Association Studies* IV (1990): 99–134.

———, "Philosophy and the Possibility of Revelation: A Theological Response to the Challenge of Leo Strauss." In *Leo Strauss and Judaism*, edited by David Novak, pp. 173–92.

———, "The Talmud as a Source for Philosophical Reflection." In *HJP*, pp. 62–80.

———, ed., *Leo Strauss and Judaism*. Lanham, Md.: Rowman & Littlefield, 1996.

Novak, David, and Norbert Samuelson, eds., *Creation and the End of Days*. Lanham, Md.: University Press of America.

Ormsby, Eric, ed., *Moses Maimonides and His Time*. Washington, D.C.: Catholic University of America Press, 1989.

Otto, Rudolph, *The Idea of the Holy*. Translated by John W. Harvey. New York: Oxford University Press, 1923.

Owens, Joseph, "Aquinas—'Darkness of Ignorance' in the Most Refined Notion of God," *Southwestern Journal of Philosophy* 5 (1974): 93–110.

———, *The Doctrine of Being in the Aristotelian Metaphysics*. 1951. Reprinted, Toronto: Pontifical Institute for Medieval Studies, 1963.

Pascal, Blaise, *Pensées*. Translated by W. F. Trotter. New York: E. P. Dutton, 1958.

Pegis, Anton C., "*Penitus Manet Ignotum*," *Medieval Studies* 27 (1965): 212–26.

Perovich, Anthony N., " 'For Reason . . . Also Has Its Mysteries': Immortality, *Religion*, and 'The End of All Things.'" In *Kant's Philosophy of Religion Reconsidered*, edited by P. J. Rossi and M. Wreen, pp. 165–80.

Peskowitz, Miriam, and Laura Levitt, eds., *Judaism since Gender*. London: Routledge, 1997.

Philoponus, *Against Aristotle on the Eternity of the World*. Translated by Christian Wildberg. Ithaca, N.Y.: Cornell University Press, 1987.

Pines, Shlomo, "The Limitations of Human Knowledge According to Al-farabi, ibn Bajja, and Maimonides." In *M*, pp. 91–121.

———, "Notes on Maimonides' Views Concerning Free Will," *Studies in Philosophy, Scripta Hierosolymitana* 6 (1960): 195–98.

———, "The Philosophic Sources of *The Guide of the Perplexed*." In *GP*, pp. lvii–cxxxiv.

Pines, Shlomo, and Yirmiyahu Yovel, eds., *Maimonides and Philosophy*. Dordrecht: Martinus Nijoff, 1986.

Plaskow, Judith, "Jewish Feminist Thought." In *HJP*, pp. 885–94.

———, *Standing Again at Sinai: Judaism from a Feminist Perspective*. San Francisco: Harper & Row, 1990.

Plotinus, *The Enneads*. Translated by Stephen MacKenna. 1917–30. Reprinted, London: Faber and Faber, 1969.

Poma, Andrea, *The Critical Philosophy of Hermann Cohen*. Translated by John Denton. Albany, N.Y.: SUNY Press, 1997.

Prior, A. N., "Can Religion Be Discussed?" In *New Essays in Philosophical Theology*, edited by Anthony Flew and Alasdair MacIntyre. London: SCM Press, 1955, pp. 1–11.

Putnam, Hilary, *The Many Faces of Realism*. LaSalle, Ill.: Open Court, 1987.

Ravitzky, Aviezer, "The Days of the Messiah." In *PM*, pp. 221–56.

———, "Samuel Ibn Tibbon and the Esoteric Character of the *Guide of the Perplexed*," *AJS Review* 6 (1981): 87–123.

———, "The Secrets of the *Guide to the Perplexed*: Between the Thirteenth and Twentieth Centuries." In *Studies in Maimonides*, edited by Isadore Twersky. Cambridge: Harvard University Press, 1990, pp. 159–207.

Reines, Alvin, "Maimonides' True Belief Concerning God." In *MP*, pp. 24–35.

Rist, J. M., *Plotinus: The Road to Reality*. Cambridge: Cambridge University Press, 1967.

Rosenzweig, Franz, *The Star of Redemption*. Translated by William W. Hallo. 1970. Reprinted, Notre Dame, Ind.: University of Notre Dame Press, 1985.

Ross, James F., "Analogy as a Rule of Meaning for Religious Language." In *Aquinas*, edited by Anthony Kenny, pp. 93–138.

Rossi, Philip J., and Michael Wreen, eds., *Kant's Philosophy of Religion Reconsidered*. Bloomington: Indiana University Press, 1991.

Rotenstreich, Nathan, *Jewish Philosophy in Modern Times*. New York: Holt, Rinehart, & Winston, 1968.

Rudavsky, Tamar, "Creation and Time in Maimonides and Gersonides." In

God and Creation, edited by David Burrell and Bernard McGinn, pp. 122–47.

Saadia Gaon, *The Book of Beliefs and Opinions*. Translated by Samuel Rosenblatt. 1948. Reprinted, New Haven, Conn.: Yale University Press, 1976.

Samuelson, Norbert, *Judaism and the Doctrine of Creation*. Cambridge: Cambridge University Press, 1994.

———, "Maimonides' Doctrine of Creation," *Harvard Theological Review* 84:3 (1991): 249–71.

Savage, Denis, "Kant's Rejection of Divine Revelation and His Theory of Radical Evil." In *Kant's Philosophy of Religion*, edited by P. J. Rossi and M. Wreen. Bloomington: Indiana University Press, 1991, pp. 64–74.

Sayre, Kenneth M., *Plato's Literary Garden*. Notre Dame, Ind.: University of Notre Dame Press, 1995.

Schechter, Solomon, *Aspects of Rabbinic Theology*. 1909. Reprinted, New York: Schocken, 1961.

———, "The Dogmas of Judaism." In *Studies in Judaism*, first series. Philadelphia: Jewish Publication Society of America, 1911.

Scholem, Gershom G., *Major Trends in Jewish Mysticism*. 1941. Reprinted, New York: Schocken, 1961.

———, *The Messianic Idea in Judaism and Other Essays*. New York: Schocken, 1971.

Schroeder, Gerald L., *Genesis and the Big Bang: The Discovery of Harmony Between Modern Science and the Bible*. New York: Bantam, 1990.

Schwarzschild, Steven S., "An Agenda for Jewish Philosophy in the 1980's." In *Studies in Jewish Philosophy*, edited by Norbert Samuelson. Lanham, Md.: University Press of America, 19, pp. 101–25.

———, *The Pursuit of the Ideal: The Jewish Writings of Steven Schwarzschild*, edited by Menachem Kellner. Albany, N.Y.: SUNY Press, 1990.

———, "The Tenability of H. Cohen's Construction of the Self," *Journal of the History of Philosophy* 13 (1975): 361–84.

Schweid, Eliezer, *Maimonidean Studies* 1 (1990): 163–95.

Seeskin, Kenneth, *Jewish Philosophy in a Secular Age*. Albany, N.Y.: SUNY Press, 1990.

———, "Of Dialogues and Seeds," *Philosophy and Literature* 21 (1997): 167–78.

Shapiro, David, "The Doctrine of the Image of God and *Imitatio Dei*," *Judaism* 12 (1963): 57–77.

Shapiro, Susan E., "A Matter of Discipline: Reading for Gender in Jewish Studies." In *Judaism Since Gender*, edited by M. Peskowitz and L. Levitt. London: Routledge, 1997, pp. 158–73.

Shatz, David, "Worship, Corporeality, and Human Perfection." In *TMM*, pp. 77–129.

Sirat, Colette, *A History of Jewish Philosophy in the Middle Ages*. Cambridge: Cambridge University Press, 1985.

Sokol, Moshe, "Personal Autonomy and Religious Authority." In *Rabbinic*

Authority and Personal Autonomy, edited by M. Sokol. Northvale, N. J.: Jason Aronson, 1992, pp. 169–216.

Sorabji, Richard, *Time, Creation, and the Continuum.* Ithaca, N.Y.: Cornell University Press, 1983.

Spinoza, Baruch, *A Theologico-Political Treatise.* Translated by R. H. M. Elwes. New York: Dover, 1951.

Stern, Josef, "The Fall and Rise of Myth in Ritual: Maimonides versus Nachmanides on the *Huqqim,* Astrology, and the War Against Idolatry," *Journal of Jewish Thought and Philosophy* 6 (1977): 185–263.

———, "The Idea of a *Hoq* in Maimonides' Explanation of the Law." In *MP,* pp. 92–139.

———, "Logical Syntax as a Key to a Secret of the *Guide of the Perplexed* [Heb.]," *Iyyun* 38 (1989): 137–66.

———, "Maimonides in the Skeptical Tradition," unpublished manuscript.

———, "Maimonides on the Growth of Knowledge and the Limitations of the Intellect," unpublished manuscript.

———, "Maimonides' Conceptions of Freedom and the Sense of Shame." In *Freedom and Moral Responsibility,* edited by C. Manekin and M. Kellner. College Park, Md.: University Press of Maryland, 1997.

———, *Problems and Parables of Law: Maimonides and Nachmanides on the Reasons for the Commandments.* Albany, N.Y.: SUNY Press, 1998.

———, "Skeptical Themes in the *Guide of the Perplexed,*" unpublished manuscript.

Strauss, Leo, "How to Begin to Study Medieval Philosophy." In *The Rebirth of Classical Political Rationalism,* edited by Thomas L. Pangle. Chicago: University of Chicago Press, 1989, pp. 207–26.

———, "How to Begin to Study *The Guide of the Perplexed.*" In *GP,* pp. xi–lvi.

———, "The Mutual Influence of Theology and Philosophy." In *Faith and Political Philosophy,* translated and edited by Peter Emberly and Barry Cooper. University Park, Penn.: Pennsylvania State University Press, 1993, pp. 217–33.

———, *Persecution and the Art of Writing.* Glencoe, Ill.: Free Press, 1952.

———, *Philosophy and Law.* Translated by F. Baumann. Philadelphia: Jewish Publication Society of America, 1987.

Sullivan, Roger, J., *Immanuel Kant's Moral Theory.* Cambridge: Cambridge University Press, 1989.

Tanner, Kathryn, *God and Creation in Christian Theology.* Oxford: Basil Blackwell, 1988.

Taylor, Charles, *Hegel.* Cambridge: Cambridge University Press, 1975.

———, *Sources of the Self.* Cambridge, Mass.: Harvard University Press, 1989.

Twersky, Isadore, *Introduction to the Code of Maimonides* (Mishneh Torah). New Haven, Conn.: Yale University Press, 1980.

———, ed., *Studies in Medieval Jewish History and Literature.* Cambridge, Mass.: Harvard University Press, 1979.

Urbach, Ephraim E., *The Sages*. Translated by I. Abrahams. Jerusalem: Magnes Press, 1979.

von Rad, Gerhard, *Old Testament Theology*, vol. 1. New York: Harper, 1962.

Weinberg, Steven, *Dreams of a Final Theory*. New York: Random House, 1992.

Weiss, Raymond L., *Maimonides' Ethics*. Chicago: University of Chicago Press, 1991.

Wittgenstein, Ludwig, *Tractatus Logico-Philosophicus*. Translated by D. F. Pears and B. F. McGuinness. London: Routledge & Kegan Paul, 1961.

Wolfson, Elliot, "Jewish Mysticism." In *HJP*, pp. 450–98.

———, *Through a Speculum that Shines*. Princeton, N.J.: Princeton University Press, 1994.

Wolfson, Harry A., *Studies in the History of Philosophy and Religion*, vols. 1 and 2. Edited by I. Twersky and G. H. Williams. Cambridge, Mass.: Harvard University Press, 1973–77.

Wolterstorff, Nicholas P., "Conundrums in Kant's Rational Religion." In *Kant's Philosophy of Religion Reconsidered*, edited by P. Rossi and M. Wren. Bloomington: Indiana University Press, 1991, pp. 40–53.

Wood, Allen, *Kant's Moral Religion*. Ithaca, N.Y.: Cornell University Press, 1970.

Yovel, Yirmiahu, "God's Transcendence and Its Schematization." In *MP*, pp. 269–82.

———, *Kant and the Philosophy of History*. Princeton, N.J.: Princeton University Press, 1980.

General Index

Abelson, Joshua, 28
Abraham, 4, 56, 118, 120, 147, 151, 163, 172
Abravanel, 70, 132
absolute spirit (*Geist*), 40
accidents, 49, 51
action, 50–53, 62, 100, 103, 128, 144, 148
affirmation, 127–30
afterlife, 95–96, 99, 110–12, 115–16, 152
Alfarabi, 5, 18, 69, 120
Algazali, 78, 79
Altmann, Alexander, 25
analolgy, 47–50
angels, 26–28, 193n.4
anger, 147–48, 153, 154
animal sacrifice, 146–47
anthropomorphism, 4, 7–10, 19
apprehension, 98, 99, 101, 103, 150, 181, 202n.41
Aquinas, Thomas, 20, 45–49, 51, 53, 66–67, 72, 79, 136, 139, 200n.18, 200n.21, 211n.17

Aristotle, 12–14, 16, 17, 20, 33, 49, 51, 66, 69–72, 74–77, 80, 82, 120, 134, 140, 143, 174, 175, 180, 182, 185, 188, 191n.31, 212n.30
astrology, 28, 166
astronomy, 80–81, 137, 140, 209n.56
atheism, 36
Athens/Jerusalem controversy. *See* Jerusalem/Athens controversy
atonement, 115, 118
attributes of action, 50–53, 62, 100, 103, 144, 148
Avicenna, 5, 18, 24, 33, 69, 120
awe, 18, 97, 108, 141, 146, 158

Baḥya ibn Pakudah, 30, 31, 44, 98, 121, 125–27, 141
Baron, Salo, 94
Beck, Lewis White, 113
belief, 125, 127–29, 131–36, 218n.3
Benor, Ehud, 53, 59, 195–96n.33
Berman, Lawrence, 102

243

Big Bang, 84–85
Bleich, David, 125
bodily functions, 97–98
Book of Beliefs and Opinions, The
(Saadia), 3
Buber, Martin, 155–57, 160–61
Burrell, David, 37, 46, 48

causality, 66–67, 87–88, 182,
199n.9
change, 72–73
Christianity, 7, 41, 170, 175,
198n.48, 212n.30
cognition, 16
Cohen, Hermann, 25, 57, 60, 92, 94,
103, 105, 107–9, 111, 113–15,
117, 121, 124, 155–57, 160
comfort, 38–39
commandments, 68, 92, 97, 101,
109, 116, 124–28, 133, 134,
145–46, 149–52, 158, 159,
162, 172.
See also Law; Torah
contemplation, 57, 61–65, 98–99,
105, 145
contradiction, 179–85, 226–27n.8
conviction, 135–41
creation, 15, 17, 52, 66–90, 136,
137, 142, 182–83, 205n.19,
207–8nn.42–43
Crescas, 130–31
Critique of Practical Reason (Kant),
108, 109, 112
Critique of Pure Reason (Kant), 179

Davidson, Herbert, 68, 83
Descartes, René, 129–30, 171
desire, 224n.39
determinism, 219n.12
devotion, 103, 105
dialectical argument, 12–13,
191n.35
divine retribution, 146–47
doctrine of analogy, 47–50
Duties of the Heart (Baḥya), 125, 126

Eliezer, Rabbi, 17, 86, 87, 151
emanation, 67, 69, 81, 88, 93, 183,
203n.7, 204n.15, 212n.28
error, 129

esotericism, 177–88
essence, 33, 34, 195n.30
eternity, 68, 75, 136
Euclid, 185
evidence, 135–41
evil, 110, 116–17, 145, 151,
215n.55, 216n.68, 216n.73,
217n.82
Ezekiel, 28, 108, 156

Fackenheim, Emil, 41, 171
faith. *See* belief
fanaticism, 139, 141
fear, 158
Feldman, Seymour, 51
forgiveness, 117, 118, 156
*Foundations of the Metaphysics of
Morals* (Kant), 69, 107, 113
Fourth Meditation (Descartes),
129
Fox, Marvin, 44, 57, 64, 71, 182,
183, 226–27n.8
Frank, Daniel, 202n.44, 213n.41
freedom, 124–41, 170, 171
free will. *See* will

gender, 8–10
gentiles, 139, 220n.28
Gersonides, 70, 74, 200n.21
God
attributes of action, 50–53, 62,
100, 103, 144, 148
and creation, 66–90, 142
definition of, 33, 34, 161
essence of, 33, 34, 45, 47
experience of, 21–22
Goodman on, 18, 140–41
hierarchical conceptions of,
24–25
in human form, 4, 6–10
imitation of, 91–123, 183
as infinite, 24
love of, 154–65
as one, 14–15, 23–24, 152
personal, 143–47, 153–54, 155,
161, 163
and reward and punishment,
146–54
separation from created order,
25–31, 42, 142, 182

speaking of and to, 43–65
uniqueness, 25, 30–31, 35, 91
will, 143–44, 183, 208nn.51–52,
   221n.5
wisdom, 48, 183, 221n.5
See also monotheism
good, 144, 145, 199n.9
Goodman, Lenn, 6, 18, 140
grace, 163, 166
graciousness, 118, 134, 148
Greek religion, 41, 170
Gross, Rita, 8, 9, 37
Guide of the Perplexed, The
   (Maimonides), 5, 11, 12, 14–18,
   33, 36, 38, 46, 97, 103, 105,
   128, 133, 136–37, 161, 177–81,
   183–84, 186–88, 197n.39,
   226n.1
Guth, Alan, 84
Guttmann, Julius, 3, 6, 104

Haggadah, 27
Halbertal, Moshe, 7, 132
Hartman, David, 21, 138, 139, 140
Harvey, Steven, 187
Harvey, Warren, 82
heart, 126
heavenly intelligences, 27–28, 29,
   106, 122
Hebrew language, 8, 126
Hegel, G.W.F., 20, 39–42, 92, 105,
   107, 120, 168–71, 173–74, 175
holiness, 93, 94, 97, 101, 103, 108,
   109, 134, 151
  and human capacity, 115–20
  as rationality, 120–23
human nature, 163–64
Hume, David, 131–32
humility, 18, 97, 108, 141, 146, 174
Husik, Isaac, 81
Hyman, Arthur, 191n.35

ibn Gabirol, 70
ibn Tibbon, Samuel, 188
Idel, Moshe, 94
idolatry, 4, 7, 53–55, 118
imagination, 201n.39
immortality, 95, 110
intellectual freedom, 137
intellectual perfection, 101

intelligibility, 30–31
intention, 143, 144
intermediaries, 26–30, 88, 106
involuntariness, 130–32
isolation, 62, 120
Ivry, Alfred, 106, 207–8n.43

Jacobs, Louis, 9
Jerusalem/Athens controversy,
   11–14, 37, 40, 188, 190n.22
Job, 39, 105, 150
joy, 106
Judaism
  angelology, 26
  and anthropomorphism, 9
  Baḥya on, 125–27
  and belief, 134, 135
  bifurcations in, 25–26
  commandment to walk in God's
    ways, 96
  and enslavement, 168–74
  Hegel's critique of, 39–42,
    169–71
  hellenizing of, 167–68
  lack of articles of faith, 47, 71, 124
  and monotheism, 7, 37–39, 168
  mystical tradition, 93, 211n.7
  as orthopraxy, 124
  and philosophy, 3–22, 175
  and reward and punishment,
    148–49

Kant, Immanuel, 20, 67, 69–70,
   102, 104–17, 119–21, 138–39,
   164, 175, 214n.47, 217n.82
Kasher, Hannah, 153
Katz, Steven, 37, 194n.27
Kellner, Menachem, 152, 166,
   209n.56
Klein-Braslavy, Sarah, 68, 72
knowledge, 32, 49, 51, 54, 94, 95,
   98, 103, 125, 127, 135, 140–41,
   184–86, 195n.32
Kogan, Barry, 185
Kraemer, Joel, 180
Kreisel, Howard, 150

language, 183–84
  figures of speech, 28–29, 60,
    64, 181

as form of idolatry, 53–55
Hebrew, 8, 126
of prayer, 52, 58, 64
religious, 33–35, 45, 47–48,
   200n.18

Law, 92, 137, 165–67, 171–74, 180.
   See also commandments; Torah
lev, 126
Levinas, Emmanuel, 6, 9, 36, 42,
   159, 168
love, 154–65, 218n.5

Maimonides
   and attributes of action, 50–53,
      100, 144, 148
   on commandments and Law,
      132–33, 134, 172–74
   and/on contemplation, 61–65,
      105
   as contemporary, 19–22
   contradictions in, 179–85,
      226–27n.8
   and/on creation, 67–90, 142,
      182–83, 205n.19,
      207–8nn.42–43
   on definition of God, 33
   esotericism, 177–88
   on evidence and conviction,
      135–41
   on figures of speech, 28–29
   and God as person, 143–46, 147
   on God's essence, 34
   on God's heavenly court, 26
   on God's oneness, 23–24, 31
   on God's separation from all
      things, 25, 42, 66, 182
   and imitation of God, 91–92,
      95–106
   intellectualism, 100, 119
   interpretation of Bible, 38
   and Jerusalem/Athens contro-
      versy, 14–19
   on language, 33–35, 48, 54–55,
      57–58, 72
   and love of God, 154, 155,
      158–65
   and mystical union, 94
   negative predicates/theology, 25,

      32, 44–47, 76, 102, 142, 182
   objection to astrology, 28
   on perfection, 97, 98
   and/on philosophy, 3–6, 8,
      10–12, 14–22, 37, 175, 181–82
   and popular religion, 165–68
   and/on prayer, 43–44, 49–50,
      55–60, 142
   proofs for existence of God,
      197n.39
   on prophets and prophecy, 16–18,
      101, 104, 122, 152, 182,
      212n.28
   on representation and affirma-
      tion, 127–30
   and reward and punishment,
      146–54
   similarity to Plato, 53–55
   skepticism, 36, 49, 72
   on wisdom, 124
Margalit, Avishai, 7, 132
matter, 96–97
meaning, 129
mediation, 26–30
Mendelssohn, Moses, 124, 139
mercy, 118, 134, 148, 153, 166
messiah, 182
metaphors, 60, 64, 181
metaphysics, 97, 101, 105, 106, 120,
   127, 137, 159–60, 166, 195n.32
Metaphysics (Aristotle), 13–14,
   180, 191n.31
miracles, 183, 199n.5
Miriam, 10
Mishneh Torah (Maimonides), 5,
   43, 56, 63, 118, 134, 136–37,
   149, 158, 161, 184, 187
moments, 74–75
monotheism, 6–7, 118, 142, 158,
   171, 174
   of Abraham, 4, 56, 147, 163, 172
   challenge of, 23–42
   and enslavement, 39–42, 168
   and fanaticism, 141
   and freedom, 124–41
   and religion, 37–39
   and skepticism, 30–36, 60
morality, 69, 103, 107
moral perfection, 108, 113

moral purity, 112
moral radicalism, 111
moral virtue, 104
Moses, 4, 5, 16, 17, 21, 27, 56, 71,
    86, 92, 94, 97, 98, 101, 103,
    125, 139, 144, 166, 181, 182,
    200n.18, 201–2n.40
Moses of Narbonne, 71
motion, 71, 74, 75, 206n.35
mystical union, 92–95, 211n.7

nature, 144–45
necessity, 80, 88
negative predicates, 32, 45–47, 62,
    194n.27, 195–96n.33
negative theology, 25, 76, 102–5,
    142, 182, 185, 196n.33
Novak, David, 21

obedience, 133
Owens, Joseph, 13

paganism, 30, 55–56, 60, 171, 174
pain, 150–51
Parable of the Palace (Maimonides),
    10, 61, 103, 128, 165–66
Pascal, Blaise, 6, 132, 155, 157
Paul, 173, 225n.49
Pegis, Anton, 35
Perek Ḥelek (Maimonides), 133,
    148, 151, 178, 182, 187,
    222–23n.16
perfection, 97–98, 100–106, 108,
    113, 117, 118, 121, 122, 145,
    151, 157, 172, 202n.41
Philoponus, 74, 79
philosopher–kings, 55, 101, 175,
    212n.30
philosophy, 3–22, 37, 137–38, 188
    and creation, 66–67
    Plato on, 53
    and politics, 212–13n.30
    and religion, 147
    and thirteen principles, 181–82
physics, 97, 101, 106, 120, 127, 140,
    159–60, 166
Pines, Shlomo, 102, 178
planets, 80–81
Plaskow, Judith, 8, 9

Plato, 17, 20, 53–55, 71, 72, 76–77,
    98–99, 111, 120, 137, 175, 180,
    184, 185, 200n.28
Plotinus, 34, 40, 69, 93, 98, 175,
    184, 203n.6, 204–5n.15
politics, 212–13n.30
Politics (Aristotle), 212n.30
Posterior Analytics (Aristotle), 185
power, 32
praise, 44, 63–64
prayer, 43–44, 49–50, 52–64, 142,
    162
prophets and prophecy, 16–18, 101,
    104, 122, 152, 166, 175, 182,
    201–2n.40, 212n.28, 212n.30,
    222–23n.16
Ptolemy, 80, 120
punishment, 146–54, 182
purity, 109, 112
purpose, 143, 144, 145
Putnam, Hilary, 139, 140
puzzlement, 12, 14

radical empiricism, 154
rationality, holiness as, 120–23.
    See also reason
Ravitzky, Aviezer, 183
reason, 12–13, 87, 104, 107,
    137–38, 175
reconciliation, 174
reconstruction, 20
redemption, 164
relations, 31, 49, 51
religion, 137–38
    contemplation as ideal, 61–65
    and monotheism, 37–39
    perplexity on, 135
    and philosophy, 11–22
    popular, 142–76, 178
    principles of, 133
    See also prayer; *specific religions*
Religion within the Limits
    (Kant), 110
religious language, 33–35, 45,
    47–48, 200n.18
repentance, 114, 115, 118, 156,
    157, 164
representation, 127–30
Republic (Plato), 99, 180, 212n.30

revelation, 36, 40, 68, 188
reward, 146–54, 182
ritual, 134, 171, 172–73
Rorty, Richard, 20
Rosenzweig, Franz, 21, 154–57, 161–62, 218n.5

Saadia Gaon, 3, 70, 87, 117
Sabbath, 89–90
sacrifice, 59, 146–47
salvation, 139, 152–53
Samuelson, Norbert, 204n.10, 206n.21, 209n.63
Schechter, Solomon, 27
Scholem, Gershom, 93–94, 211n.7
Schwarzschild, Steven, 29, 41–42, 92, 102, 103
science, 166
self–doubt, 63
self–sanctification, 109–15, 121
separation, 25, 26–30, 42, 66, 120
Seventh Letter (Plato), 53, 55, 98, 200n.28
shame, 97
Shekhinah, 28–29, 41
similies, 181
sin, 114, 116–18, 119, 151, 156, 173, 216n.74, 217n.82
skepticism, 30–36, 49, 60, 72, 137
Socrates, 54, 151, 171, 180
solitude, 62
Song of Songs, 161
Sorabji, Richard, 74
soul, 95–96, 98–101, 110, 152–53
space, 84
speculative knowledge, 16–17
statutory prayer, 58–59, 61, 64
steadfastness, 137
Stern, Josef, 140, 194n.27
Strauss, Leo, 11–12, 14, 16, 19, 37, 177–81, 186–88, 190n.22, 212n.30
Summa Theologiae (Aquinas), 11, 12, 46, 49
superstition, 166

Tabernacle, 28
Talmud, 180, 185
Taylor, Charles, 158

Ten Commandments. *See* commandments
Tetragrammaton, 33, 35
theology, 14
time, 74, 75, 84
tolerance, 140–41
Topics (Aristotle), 12–13
Torah, 5, 14, 44, 58, 124, 149, 177–83, 200n.18, 222–23n.16
Tractatus (Wittgenstein), 35
tradition, 38, 58
truth, 18, 39, 127, 129, 137–38, 186–87
Twersky, Isadore, 5, 20, 172

Urbach, Ephraim, 28, 117

virtue, 104, 119–20
volition. *See* will
von Rad, Gerhard, 120

will, 32, 68, 69, 78–83, 129, 130, 132–35, 143–44, 183, 208nn.51–52, 221n.5
wisdom, 12, 18, 35, 48, 124, 134, 183, 221n.5
Wittgenstein, Ludwig, 35, 175
Wolfson, Harry, 71–72, 129
wonder, 12
Wood, Allen, 111
worship, 44, 61–62, 64, 139, 202n.41

Xenophanes, 7

Yovel, Yirmiahu, 143, 157

Index of Principal Sources

THE HEBREW BIBLE

Genesis
1   70
1:14–19   26
1:31   144, 145
2:15   89
8:21   117
22:12   151
3:6   97
4:6   124, 176
4:39   126
6:5   125, 155, 156
6:13   158
7:1–16   141
20:8–11   89
20:16   141
24:10–11   97–98
29   7
29:45   28
33   7
33:20–23   16
40:34–35   28

Exodus
3:6   97

20:8–11   89
24:10–11   97
29   7
33   7, 33
33:19   144
33:20–23   16

Leviticus
11:4   116
19:2   91, 120, 123
19:17   126
19:18   126
25:4   89
26   170

Deuteronomy
4:6   124, 176
4:12   4
4:39   126
6:5   38, 125, 155, 156
6:13   158
7:1–16   141
10:12   96
13:5   96
20:16   141
30:11–14   92, 116

Isaiah
40:15–17   169
40:25   23
55:8   30

Jeremiah
3:15   126
7:22–23   59

Ezekiel
1:27–28   28
18:31   108
43:2–5   28

Psalms
145:9   165

Proverbs
16:23   126

Job
42:6   105

Ecclesiastes
1:9   143

Daniel
8:16   26
9:21   26

THE CHRISTIAN
BIBLE

Romans
3:9   111
5:12   116

RABBINIC SOURCES

Berakhot
4b   118
12b   43
13a   27
60b   116

Shabbat
7.4   118

Eruvin
13b   118

Megillah
13a   4

Hagigah
11b   46–47
13a   46–47

Sotah
14a   96

Sanhedrin
91b   182

Pirke Avot
3.9   134
3.17   47
4.7   149

Genesis Rabbah
44.1   171

Leviticus Rabbah
24.9   215

Sifre Deuteronomy
28   4

PLATO

Apology
41   151

Seventh Letter
341   53, 55
343   54, 98
344   54, 98

Phaedrus
250   98

Phaedo
69   98

Republic
500   99

ARISTOTLE

Topics
101   12–13
104   13

Nicomachean Ethics
1098   13

Physics
8.1   73, 74

Metaphysics
1026   12–13
1029   33
1064   14
12.6   74

PLOTINUS

Enneads
3.8.9   93
5.2.1   93
6.8.13   34
6.9.0   93
6.9.9   93

SAADIA

Book of Beliefs and
Opinions
4   3
217–18   117

BAHYA

Duties of the Heart
1. Introduction
  125–27

1.105   43
1.19   126
1.117   30
1.194–95   121
2.343   98

MAIMONIDES

Mishneh Torah
1, Basic Principles, 1.6
  5
1, Basic Principles,
  2.1–2   128
1, Basic Principles,
  4.12   63
1, Moral Dispositions,
  1.7   134
1, Moral Dispositions,
  2.3   147
1, Laws of Idolatry, 1.2
  56, 163
1, Laws of Repentance,
  2.6   118
1, Laws of Repentance,
  7.4   118
1, Laws of Repentance,
  7.7   118
1, Laws of Repentance,
  9.1   153
1, Laws of repentance,
  10.1   149
1, Laws of Repentance,
  10.2   118
1, Laws of Repentance,
  10.6   158
2, Laws of Prayer, 1.2
  43
2, Laws of Prayer, 1.4
  56

Eight Chapters   130

Perek Ḥelek   94, 95,
  133, 148, 153

Guide of the Perplexed
1. Epistle   133
1. Introduction   18,
  36, 38, 55, 179, 186

1.2 123
1.16 182
1.18 29, 99
1.25 28
1.26 45
1.31 14, 56
1.32 15, 19, 135–36
1.33 133
1.35 24, 36, 143
1.36 14
1.50 128
1.51 24
1.52 31, 33, 49
1.53 45, 50, 51, 54
1.54 50, 91, 102, 144, 148
1.56 32
1.57 8, 23, 24, 32, 33, 47, 55
1.58 32, 34–35, 52
1.59 3, 35, 43, 45, 58, 94
1.60 32
1.61 33
1.68 184
1.69 182
1.71 15, 70
1.73 85
2.2 15
2.5 54
2.6 26
2.7 27
2.12 17, 87
2.13 71, 75, 82, 85
2.14 73
2.16 77
2.17 70, 73, 77, 78
2.18 78, 79
2.19 80
2.20 82
2.22 66, 82, 83, 183
2.24 80, 81
2.25 69, 76, 85, 86
2.26 17, 86
2.29 17
2.30 72, 86
2.31 134
2.33 68

2.35 152
2.36 100
2.38 16–17
2.40 167
3. Introduction 18, 36
3.8 10, 97
3.9 36
3.10 145
3.11 100
3.12 145, 165
3.13 144, 183
3.18 151
3.20 184
3.23 105
3.24 151
3.25 145, 183
3.27 101–102, 128
3.28 38, 128, 146, 158
3.31 172
3.32 38, 56, 59, 146, 150, 163–64
3.36 146, 164
3.51 10, 16, 17, 61, 62, 94, 95, 96, 99, 101, 103, 106, 122, 138, 179
3.52 19, 94
3.53 128, 136
3.54 97, 101

AQUINAS

Summa Theolgiae
1.1.8 136
1.2.2 136
1.3. Introduction 45
1.12.11–12 43
1.13.2 45, 48
1.13.5 45, 48
1.46.2 136

DESCARTES

Meditations 4
129–30

KANT

Critique of Pure Reason
B ix 104
B xxix 69
A 318 121
A 818 107

Critique of Practical Reason
32–33 112–13
120–21 108
122 109
123 108

Religion within the Limits of Reason Alone
17 110
36 110
40 115
43 121
60–61 109
66 119
68 113
70 113
149 112
152 138
179 115

The Metaphysics of Morals
446 113

HEGEL

Lectures on the Philosophy of Religion
2.172 169
2.206 169
2.207 169
2.211 173
2.328 40
2.347 41
2.257–58 40–41
2.346–47 170
3.73 41
3.303–304 40

COHEN

Religion of Reason
35–58   25
94   103
96   103
98   103
161   156
164   94
168   156
193   156
204–205   113
206   114
207   92, 114, 115
209   117
305   111
357   57
371   57

ROSENZWEIG

*The Star of Redemp-
tion*
164   21, 154, 157
169   156
202   162
215   156
381   21–22, 161–62

BUBER

Eclipse of God
49   155
62   160

DATE DUE